Firestorm of the Lord

*The History of and Prospects for Revival
in the Church and the World*

Firestorm of the Lord

*The History of and Prospects for Revival
in the Church and the World*

Stuart Piggin

paternoster
press

First published in 2000 by Paternoster Press

06 05 04 03 02 01 00   7 6 5 4 3 2 1

Paternoster Press is an imprint of Paternoster Publishing,
P.O. Box 300, Carlisle, Cumbria, CA3 0QS, UK
and
P.O. Box 1047, Waynesboro, GA 30830–2047, USA

Website: www.paternoster-publishing.com

British Library Cataloguing in Publication Data
A catalogue record for this book is available from the British Library

ISBN 1–84227–031–1

Cover Design by Campsie, Glasgow
Typeset by WestKey Ltd, Falmouth, Cornwall
Printed in Great Britain by Omnia Books Ltd, Glasgow

For
Mum & Dad,
Gran,
Cath & Grey,
the sweet, humble and loving human
parameters of my life

Contents

Acknowledgements

This book originated, I trust, deep in the heart of God. Humanly speaking, it probably originated in two coincidental invitations to speak on the subject of revival – one from a group of university students, and the other from David Woodbridge, an Anglican Rector in the Diocese of Sydney, Australia. These two groups represent those who have chiefly encouraged me in this study. Students in the University of Wollongong, including my able research assistant, Margaret Lamb, heard the first rudimentary draft of this book in ten lunch hour gatherings in the late 1980s. Don Lewis invited me to speak on the same subject at the 1995 Regent College, Vancouver, Summer School. Many of the insights in this book come from those two (to me unforgettable) teaching experiences. Michael and Valerie Griffiths also shared that Summer School with me, as well as their thoughts on revival, for Valerie was then in the thick of her doctoral studies on revival in China. Jim Houston also contributed to making my time at Regent a special one, as did Kristin Dunnan, my Teacher's Assistant. In the 1990s, students of Robert Menzies College, Macquarie University and members of the chapel congregation attached to the college also helped me to develop these thoughts. To one of them, John Lillyman, I owe a special debt as will be evident later in these pages.

David Woodbridge, who had been a missionary on Groote Eylandt immediately before the beginning of the Aboriginal Revival in 1979, was the first of numerous clergy in the Diocese of Sydney who have influenced this book in countless ways. That so many come readily to mind testifies to the commitment of this evangelical diocese to seek again the great experience of God in which the evangelical movement originated: Richard Andrew,

Stuart Barton Babbage, Greg Blaxland, Max Boys, Neil Brain, Roger Chilton, Ken Churchward, Hugh Cox, Mark Eaton, Trevor Edwards, Stephen Fifer, Neil Flower, Robert Forsyth, Harry Goodhew, John Gray, David Hewetson, Don Howard, Rod Irvine, David Irwin, David Jones, Peter Jones, Tony Lamb, Marcus Loane, Robert Luscombe, Trevor Middleton, Jason Page, Ross Poulton, Ian Powell, Andrew Reid, Brian Roberts, Peter Robinson, Barry Schofield, David Short, Lindsay Stoddart, Greg Thompson, Tony Tress and Paul Watson.

One group of Sydney Anglican clergy had a special link with the development of this book. In the late 1980s and early 1990s the Prayer Task Force for Spiritual Awakening and the Spread of the Gospel convened a large number of prayer gatherings in Sydney. They were organized mainly by Bishop Dudley Foord and his wife Elizabeth, their sons Nick and Martin, their son-in-law Bruce Clarke, and Barry George, and throughout the 1990s they produced a revival magazine, *The Cry for a Spiritual Awakening*, with the able administrative assistance of Keith Young. It was a privilege to meet with this group as we planned these gatherings.

Among the theologians who have given me more help than I deserved, although I fear less than I needed, have been the late Broughton Knox, principal of Moore Theological College, and four college lecturers: Paul Barnett, Bill Dumbrell, Bill Lawton and Peter O'Brien. A far larger team of historians has also come to my aid: David Bebbington, Brian Dickey, Robert Evans, Stewart Gill, Bruce Harris, John Harris, David Hilliard, Mark Hutchinson, Bob Linder, Ken Manley, Iain Murray, Mark Noll, Darrell Paproth, Walter Phillips, Dick Pierard, Stuart Johnson, Richard Owen Roberts, Geoff Treloar, Geoff Waugh and John Wolffe. At Yale University, Wilson Kimnach and John Edwards introduced me to the thought of the church's greatest theologian of revival, Jonathan Edwards. Among my own doctoral students are some who have studied aspects of revival and shared their discoveries with me: Barry Chant, Michael Chavura, Colin Reed and Jeff Stacey.

Then there are those from every walk of life and religious denomination who have stoked the fires of my passion for revival, for they have themselves burnt brightly: Robert and Linda Banks, John Blacket, Janette Boyd, Clive Cook, John Cox, Arthur Deane, Colin Dyer, Joan Eatch, Gordon Griffiths, Tony Golsby-Smith,

Graeme and Bronwyn Hughes, Neil Holme, Ian Jagelman, the late George Piper ('Praying George'), Adrian and Chris McComb, Barry McMurtrie, Barry Newman, Allan Norling, Bill Price, Richard Quadrio, Arthur Ransom, Sir Alan Walker and Rowland Ward. Finally, let me thank God for the little communities who have invited me into their fellowships where the revival fires are always fanned with prayer and hope: Laurie McIntosh and Les Follent and the saints in the Cornerstone communities in Australia; the remarkably influential New Creation Ministry of Geoff Bingham and his able lieutenants, including John Dunn, John Helm, Rod Denton and the Baptist pastors of South Australia; Len Buck, Will Renshaw and the members of the Revival Fellowship of Victoria; Robert Emory, Peter Bentley and the Evangelicals within the Uniting Church of Australia; Don Hardgrave and Neville Cave of the Wesleyan Methodist Church of Australia; Tom Slater and Gil Cann of the Australian Evangelical Alliance; Rex Dale of the Evangelical LIbrary, Melbourne; Joe Mullins of the Evangelical Fellowship in the Anglican Communion (Canberra); and the Christian and Missionary Alliance Church at Lindfield, Sydney, where, beginning with the leadership of Canadian pastor Jim Peetoom and his wife, Janet, and ably assisted by Glenda Weldon, Steve Clarke, Rob Trevor, John and Anne Harding and others, the sacred fire has been wont to fall.

Introduction

One of the most conspicuous features of contemporary Christianity is the eager longing for religious revival among many Christians in many parts of the world. The longing itself is an exciting phenomenon. In the history of the church, heightened expectation has frequently preceded genuine spiritual awakening.

The danger is, of course, that longing easily translates into over-eagerness, even desperation. These tendencies have produced the worst aspects of 'revivalism', a human technology for producing 're-vival'. This book has been written partly to encourage zealous souls most at risk not to yield to the temptation to take revival production out of the hands of the sovereign God. But my principal purpose in writing this book is to foster legitimate longing and heartfelt prayer for spiritual awakening. This is not an impartial study of revival. It is written out of the conviction that a powerful outpouring of God's Holy Spirit to re-establish reality – which is the way God views the world – is what churches and nations most need today.

So, I am more interested in removing prejudices against the ardent pursuit of revival than in addressing the excesses of those engaged in the pursuit. I would like to see a lot more fire before crying out for water. Accordingly, my desire to address systematically the objections of those who disapprove of the church's interest in religious revival shapes this book. The most important such objections to revival are:

- Revival is a late and temporary experience of the church that is not to be found in the Bible.
- Revival is the product of unbalanced delusion, is productive of much division and error, and is not compatible with a healthy, mature, evangelizing church.

- Revivals are merely human-induced, manipulated responses to human stress, and it is wrong to attribute any spiritual value to them.
- Revival is the manifestation of a false spirituality based on aberrant teaching on the role of the Holy Spirit in the Christian life normally associated with Pentecostalism.
- Revival is not a characteristic of mainstream Catholicism, Anglicanism or Orthodoxy – the denominations to which most Christians belong – and can therefore hardly be necessary.
- Revival is a sovereign work of God, who will send it independently of any interest we might have in it.

If the treatment of such objections comprises the body of this book, two other factors shape the treatment itself: the theology of Jonathan Edwards and the definition of revival proposed in Chapter 1.

Jonathan Edwards (1703–58) is the church's greatest theologian of revival. He wrote his influential and definitive studies on revival at a time not so dissimilar to our own, in that a powerful spiritual movement was creating widespread interest among the populace and deep division among church leaders. In our day both the spokespersons and the opponents of 'the Toronto Blessing' and subsequent analogous movements are appealing for support to Jonathan Edwards. I dare say that not the least of the blessings of the Toronto Blessing has been the recovery of a deep interest in Edwards' understanding of revival.

In this book I not only follow Edwards' direction in analyzing revival phenomena, but I also share his basic aim. His motivation was a desire to win over the opponents of the Great Awakening of the 1740s. Likewise, my aim is to address the deepest objections found among church leaders today, so that they will feel able with heartfelt enthusiasm to enlist in the growing army of those who long and pray for heaven-sent revival. I also hope that this book might encourage those same leaders to look for the divine anointing on their own preaching, and to study the experiences of God's people in times of revival and the commentaries on Scripture written by those who have experienced revival. If they are able to do this, the circumscribed experience of those who have not experienced revival will not limit the church's understanding of the possibilities for blessing. Such study will bring knowledge and passion to preaching.[1] The definition of revival with which this study commences (Chapter 1) has been carefully crafted to facilitate both theological and historical analysis. The definition is explicit about the nature of the outpouring of the Holy Spirit, which constitutes revival and distinguishes his revival work from other manifestations commonly attributed to him. The Spirit exalts Jesus and the doctrines of his saving grace. Thus Jesus, not the Holy Spirit, will be the hero and focus of attention in every genuine revival. That is one reason why I have called this book 'Firestorm of the Lord' rather than 'Firestorm of the Spirit'.

The definition also insists that revival is not for the church only. Revival is for the greatest good of the wider community in which the church is incarnated as salt and light. Because my primary discipline is history and not biography, I have been concerned to highlight the social and community aspects of revival as well as the psychological and personal aspects. Another way of putting this is that I am concerned, not only with the intensive work of the Spirit of God in the human soul, but with the extensive work of the Spirit in propagating Christ's kingdom within the nations and cultures of the earth, in order to transform them. I share the belief of the eighteenth-century evangelicals that revival is the engine of history, the most powerful gift of God for the expansion of his church and the renovation or reform of human society. Chapters 2–7 deal with the above objections.

The difficulties encountered in producing a biblical, as distinct from a historical, view of revival are acknowledged in Chapter 2. But the language, the experience and the theology of revival are all to be found primarily and formatively in the Bible. The Old Testament not only gives us the pattern, but also, as the theologians say, the 'type' of revival. The Old Testament repeatedly depicts the recurring pattern of decline and revival in terms of the cycle of sin, judgement, repentance and restoration within the historic experience of the people of God. Israel's chronic forgetfulness of her mission to occupy Canaan and establish God's kingdom there is a type of the church's failure to engage exclusively in the extension of the kingdom in obedience to her ascended King. We need revival in our

---

[1] Tony Sargent, *The Sacred Anointing: The Preaching of Dr Martyn Lloyd-Jones*, p. 261.

day (between the two comings of the Lord) to recall God's people
to that exclusive mission. The Bible's picture of the escalating
experience of renewal following judgement of the people of God
underlines the fact that revival is concerned with the moral reform
of the wider community as much as with the spiritual refreshment
of the individual.

To say that the Old Testament experience of the people of God is
a type of its experience in the New Testament is to say that it looks
forward to ever greater fulfilment. So revival needs to be understood
as part of the promise-fulfilment theme in the Bible. Especially in
their experience of the Holy Spirit, the people of God under the
new covenant will be superior to that of the old. Under the old covenant, the Spirit gifted individual leaders. In the new covenant,
beginning at Pentecost, God pours out the Spirit on all his people,
creating the prophethood of all believers. The nature and the timing
of Pentecost, where the Lord Jesus Christ is the focus of attention, is
the church's prototype of revival, and demonstrates that every
genuine, Spirit-sent revival will be a revival of Christlikeness. That is
another reason why I have entitled this book 'Firestorm of the Lord'
rather than 'Firestorm of the Spirit'.

Chapter 3 addresses the objection that revival is the product of
unhealthy emotionalism, that it results in delusion and error, and
that it is incompatible with vigorous evangelism. We address these
issues by looking at the Great Awakening of the 1740s. First, the long
spiritual pedigree of the Awakening is explained to show that the
revival was consistent with the tested traditions of the mainstream
exponents of vital orthodoxy. The Great Awakening was not a spontaneous irruption from peripheral, unstable, heterodox fanatics.
Jonathan Edwards' five distinguishing marks of genuine revival are
then reviewed, demonstrating that this revival produced useful tools
for the rational assessment of any spiritual movement. Finally, an
analysis of the essential contribution of the Great Awakening to the
development, 50 years later, of the modern missionary movement, shows
that, far from jeopardizing evangelism, revival is a key to its success.

Chapter 4 surveys the wide-ranging experience of revival in the
nineteenth and twentieth centuries. There is plenty of evidence
here to justify the criticism that revivals are the pathetic response of
helpless communities to unmanageable stress, especially if that
response is manipulated by technicians experienced in the field of

human emotions. The Americanization of revival and the decline of historic Calvinism accompanied the development of the technology of 'revivalism'. Revivals became identified with highly organized evangelistic campaigns.

History, however, is never as neat as the theologians who dislike revivalism would like it to be, and genuine revivals were sufficiently common in revivalistic circles to encourage the revivalists to continue in their ways. But the most amazing scenes of revival were witnessed in places where they were least expected. Revivals remained 'surprising works of God'.

The range of human need addressed in these awakenings was such as to underline the community dimension of all genuine revival: working-class miners as well as middle-class stockbrokers; the bereaved in disaster or war; Africans and Asians engaged in nation-building; Australian Aborigines and New Guinea natives fighting for their very survival; Christian college students at the beginning of a lifetime of ministry. Revivals are the coming down to earth of the glory of the Lord, but they always meet desperate human need.

Chapter 5 contrasts evangelical and charismatic positions on revival. The basic reason why evangelicals have difficulty with the charismatic understanding of revival is that the evangelicals formed their theology of revival at a time in church history when soteriology (the understanding of the way we are saved) was the primary concern of the church, and Christ the Saviour was the person of the Trinity to whom evangelical preaching directed the sinner in need of salvation. The charismatics, who now speak of revival far more than evangelicals, have forged their theology of revival at a time when the church is most focused on pneumatology, the study of the work of the Spirit, and more attention is paid to the Spirit than to the Saviour. The evangelical contends that revival is more concerned with soteriology than with pneumatology, and therefore insists that genuine revival should not be equated uncritically with the charismatic movement. The marks of authentic revival are not the same as the gifts of the Spirit or extraordinary 'manifestations' characteristic of such movements as the 'Toronto Blessing'.

But the work of revival is not done in a corner, a fact correctly understood by the charismatics. The genuineness of revival may only be tested long-term by its fruit. This fact justifies the evangelical emphasis on fruit as the key to revival. But the fruit itself cannot be the essence of revival. The essence of revival is that which produces the fruit, and that is the activity of the Holy Spirit. In revival, that activity is so intense and conspicuous that those outside the church may observe it, and that is why revivals lead to the conversion of outsiders and why they make an impact on the community. It is also what makes them so controversial.

The lessons which the charismatic movement has to teach are critical to the future of the church. Just as earlier crises in the history of the church led to rethinking the areas of Christology (the nature of the human and divine in Christ and his role in the Trinity) and soteriology (the way we are saved), so the experience of the Spirit in the twenty-first century highlights the poverty of much current pneumatology (the study of the Spirit). The Bible does distinguish between the fruit and the gifts of the Spirit, and it is helpful to maintain this distinction in any attempt to assess the genuineness of any spiritual movement. But the division can be too schematic, and a mature church, Chapter 6 contends, will be one where both gifts and fruit are in evidence. The gifts of the Spirit are given to subserve the gift of salvation in Christ.

The first and most distinguishing mark of genuine revival, Jonathan Edwards taught and the evangelical would concur, is that, through the preaching of the gospel, Jesus is exalted as Lord and Saviour.[2] Just as the charismatic obscures this whenever he or she fails to preach the gospel (as too often occurs in charismatic gatherings), so churches in the sacramental tradition – Catholic, Orthodox and Anglican – also inhibit revival by not preaching the gospel as plainly as they might. Chapter 7 discusses this issue and reviews the Spirit-quenching characteristics of such churches – formalism, a set liturgy, clericalism, traditionalism, nominalism and even sacramentalism itself. The sovereignty of God in revival, however, is established by the fact that revivals have sometimes visited such churches. And sometimes, as we shall see, the very party of the church that has sought to eliminate such Spirit-quenchers, namely, the evangelical Anglicans, have themselves erected barriers against revival.

---

[2]   Jonathan Edwards, 'The Distinguishing Marks of a Work of the Spirit of God' (1741), in *The Great Awakening*, p. 249.

Before discussing what we *might* do to foster revival in church and community, it is necessary to look at what we *can* do in view of the fact that genuine revivals are sovereign works of God. This is the subject of Chapter 8, which reviews the important issue of divine sovereignty and human responsibility in revival with special reference to the thought of Edwards and Charles Finney. In the first half of the nineteenth century, Finney's 'New Measures' moved the church away from revival – God's sovereign act, to revivalism – a human edifice. This chapter stresses again the community aspect of revival as we look at the little-explored relationship between revivals and community disasters, sometimes understood in popular religion (and in insurance policies) as 'acts of God'. The critical importance of revival to the church and nation follows from my conclusion that communities will be visited either with revival or disaster. If communities do not turn to God, they invite disaster – which is a solemn warning, all too obvious for those with the eyes to see, that if individuals do not accept the salvation offered by Christ, they invite eternal disaster.

The responsibility of church leaders in encouraging Christians to long, pray and work for revival is the subject of the next section of the book, Chapters 9 to 12. Here we address preaching, praying, paying and planning for revival.

Chapter 9, 'Preaching for Revival', is based on a study of the sermons of Jesus, George Whitefield, Jonathan Edwards and Billy Graham on the grounds that they have deliberately and with great skill set their sights on revival as the outcome of their preaching. Preaching for revival stresses justification by faith alone as the antidote to self-sufficiency, and the blood of Christ as the antibiotic that kills guilt, the stain of sin. The chapter deals not only with the anatomy of the revival message, but also with the delivery and the deliverer of the message. The biblical principles governing the relationship between prayer and revival, a history of prayer movements for revival, and how to pray prevailingly for revival, are the three matters surveyed in Chapter 10. Chapter 11 explores the cost of revival, with special reference to 2 Chronicles 7:14, the Old Testament's most celebrated revival text. The final chapter reiterates the price we have to pay for revival. While suggesting a tentative strategy for revival, it draws attention to the destructive attitudes of which we shall have to repent if we are to see revival in our own experience.

What might the next Great Awakening in the church look like? That is the question I put to my class at Regent College, Vancouver, at the end of the 1995 Summer School course on revival at which I gave the lectures on which this book is based. I incorporate some of their answers in the conclusion of this book. Revivals are always the surprising work of the sovereign God, and it would be a foolish person who would dare to imagine the characteristics of the next great revival. But genuine revivals are marked not so much by amazing manifestations the likes of which no one could prophesy, but by the accentuation of the doctrines of grace as revealed in the word of God. Jesus and his gospel will be the twin foci of the next great awakening, just as they have been of all genuine revivals in the history of the church. But Jesus will deepen our understanding of the love of the Father and heighten our vision of the power of the Spirit. The next great awakening will reawaken the church to the glory of the Holy Trinity. And it will thereby revitalize the church with its threefold mission of caring for the Father's creation, propagating the Son's gospel and reflecting the Spirit's nature in holiness of life.

1

Revival Defined

When the Reverend Thomas Angwin, Methodist minister, disembarked at Kiama Harbour on the New South Wales south coast in Australia in 1864, curious onlookers could see that he was not long for this world. His frame was emaciated, and he coughed up blood. He was dying of tuberculosis. When he spoke he wasted no time in directing his hearers to the deep things of God. He preached with all the fervour of an apostle. Like the angel messenger of Psalm 104:4, he was a flame of fire. One Sunday in July 1864, shortly after his arrival, a strange phenomenon broke out during the evening service in the Methodist church. Each night for a week and a half, the townspeople flocked to the church. From the youngest to the oldest, men and women, boys and girls, they crowded the communion rail, confessing their sins, weeping and seeking the Saviour.

Some of the elderly members of the congregation had seen a similar phenomenon before in 'the old country', in Wales in 1859. This was a genuine revival, they explained, and the hearers, as they came under conviction, were experiencing 'a breaking down'.

Forty years later a massive revival swept Wales, adding 162,000 members to the churches. Once again, among those who enjoyed this great visitation of the Lord were some who had witnessed the great awakening in Wales of 1859. At the beginning of the 1904 revival, two old pilgrims leaped to their feet in a prayer meeting and, with arms uplifted, shouted: 'Here it comes! Old "59"!'[1] This experience of revival kept an understanding of God's greatest

---

[1] R.O. Roberts (ed.), *Glory Filled the Land: A Trilogy on the Welsh Revival of 1904–1905*, p. 5.

instrument for the advancement of his kingdom alive in their minds and hearts.

But in late twentieth-century North America or England or Australia or New Zealand, how many have witnessed a genuine religious revival? Who among us has been a member of a community that has experienced a sudden, awesome and overwhelming flood of God's power? It is outside the experience of most of us. Judges 2:10 says, 'another generation grew up, who knew neither the LORD nor what he had done for Israel'. Therefore it is necessary at the outset to define revival for such a generation as our own.

But this is not as easy as it sounds. Religious revival is an issue that has evoked more prejudice than is healthy and less reflection than is desirable. There is no consensus among theologians on how to understand it, or among historians as to how it functions in society or among Christians as to what it is or whether it is essential for the church.

Admittedly, there is an understanding of revival that many mainstream evangelicals accept. This view owes everything to the church's greatest theologian of revival, Jonathan Edwards (1703–58). His 'classic' understanding is that revival is waking up to reality, which is God's perspective on his own character and that of sinners, and which comes when a new affection, given by the Spirit of God, takes possession of the heart. Edwards' view was disseminated to some extent in the twentieth century, chiefly through the published sermons and writings of the renowned evangelical preacher, David Martyn Lloyd-Jones (1899–1981).

But this 'classic' understanding of revival in the Protestant tradition was questioned by nineteenth-century, largely American, practitioners of 'revivalism'. Pentecostal Christians challenged it in the late twentieth century. And it has been denied by secularists who see 'revival' as the first resort of scoundrels.

Revival is such a historical phenomenon that historians seem to be incapable of defining it without also commenting on its cause. What causes revivals? They are sovereign outpourings of the Holy Spirit sent from heaven; they are 'merely the routine activities of evangelists enthusiastically in pursuit of souls';[2] they are caused by

---

[2] Roger Finke and Rodney Stark, *The Churching of America, 1776–1990*, p. 238.

the business cycle and social and natural disasters;[3] they are interludes of hysteria attributable to psychic insecurities;[4] they are attempts to resolve anxiety, including the sexual tension of the young.[5]

Revival – my definition

My own definition of revival is also based on my understanding of its cause:

> Revival is a sovereign work of God the Father, consisting of a powerful intensification by Jesus of the Holy Spirit's normal activity of testifying to the Saviour, accentuating the doctrines of grace, and convicting, converting, regenerating, sanctifying and empowering large numbers of people at the same time, and is therefore a community experience.
>
> It is occasionally preceded by an expectation that God is about to do something exceptional; it is usually preceded by an extraordinary unity and prayerfulness among Christians; and it is always accompanied by the revitalization of the church, the conversion of large numbers of unbelievers and the diminution of sinful practices in the community.

The definition calls for a theological understanding of revival (the first paragraph of the definition), but it allows (the second paragraph) for historical analysis of revivals in terms of the six antecedent and accompanying characteristics.

This is a definition that insists that historians should not ignore the theological dimension of revival, and that theologians or churchmen and women should not ignore the community dimension of revival. One of the major points I want to emphasize in this book is that revival is not for the church only, but is for the transformation of the

---

[3] William G. McLoughlin, *Revivals, Awakenings and Reform*; J.F. Wilson, 'Perspectives on the Historiography of Religious Awakenings'; R.C. Gordon-McCutchan, 'Great Awakenings'.

[4] R.C. Gordon-McCutchan, 'The Irony of Evangelical History'.

[5] Michael J. Crawford, *Seasons of Grace: Colonial New England's Revival Tradition in its British Context*, p. 7.

community in which the church is located.[6] The very fact that, whatever else they may be, revivals are historical movements, means that the social and cultural context is critical to the understanding of revival. It would be unfortunate if theologians were to find the social and cultural dimension to revival less than exciting, because it is this dimension which gives scope for theological reflection beyond the narrow confines of much theological enterprise in our churches.

As far as theological issues are concerned, revival raises two matters at the forefront of evangelical religion. First, to what extent is revival so understood consistent with biblical categories of thought? And, secondly, how is the work of the Spirit implied by revival phenomena to be understood? The theology of revival, then, raises problems of hermeneutics, or the study of biblical interpretation, and also of pneumatology, or the study of the Spirit.

For the purpose of this study I would want to identify 'revival' with 'awakening', and distinguish between 'revival' and 'renewal' and 'reformation'. Renewal applies to the spiritual refreshment of God's people, and reformation refers to the restoration of God's people to the pure doctrines of grace and to godliness. According to these definitions, revival includes renewal and reformation, but it is larger than either one because its influence reaches beyond the people of God to the wider community.[7]

Now let us begin to unpack our definition.

---

[6]   In the *New Schaff-Herzog Encyclopedia of Religious Knowledge* published at the beginning of the twentieth century and reprinted fifty years later, the entry on revival emphasizes this community aspect. The author applies the term 'revival' to 'the spiritual condition of a Christian community' in which attention to religion increases, believers grow in grace, backsliders return to duty and sinners convert. The author of the entry explains that just as an individual may become distracted from the pursuit of holiness by worldly concerns, so may a community. The only remedy for such a decline is spiritual revival resulting from 'a special and peculiar effusion of the Holy Spirit'.

[7]   Iain H. Murray, *David Martin Lloyd-Jones: The Fight of Faith*, p. 549 refers to an address to the British Evangelical Council Conference by Roland Lamb, the General Secretary, on 'Revival and Reformation'.

Revival is a work of God

God makes bare his arm. In biblical terms, it is 'a visitation from on high' (Isa. 32:15; Lk. 1:78); a time of refreshing *from the Lord* (Acts 3:19); it is a *heavenly* light; a *divine* fire; a river of water *from God's sanctuary*; a dayspring from *on high*; a revival is *one of the days of the Son of Man*, in which the exalted redeemer rides forth in his glory and majesty, on the white horse of the pure gospel, conquering and to conquer (Rev. 6:2). Genuine revival cannot be worked up from below. It must come down from above. The authentic prayer for revival is 'Come down, Lord. Come down from where your glory fills the heavens and let your glory fill the earth.'

That is what revival is. In August 1969, a mission entitled 'Free Indeed' was held at Wudinna, a little town in South Australia. A revival in which the glory of the Lord was perceived to descend to the earth, in this case very literally, accompanied this meeting. There was a sense of the presence of God brooding over the whole geographical area. A farmer who had not been going to the meetings, although his wife was, was out on his tractor ploughing when great conviction came upon him and he got down in the dust and gave his life to the Lord.[8]

One of those transformed in a great revival among Aboriginal people in Australia that began in 1979 also testifies to God's descent to be with his people on earth:

> . . . the glory of the Lord was so low – it really came and lived with people, spoke with people. When I say low – the glory of the Lord covered the whole area – it came right down to earth. Kids can tell you they received the touch. Old ladies can tell you [about] that first touch. People are saying today, Why can't we go back . . . to that first step – that time of glory. The Lord Jesus had magnified Himself through common people – would you like to call us third world people? It wasn't somebody that told them to be like that, but God chose these people for His own glory to be the witness for Him concerning the baptism of the Holy Spirit and people need to get back to the first touch.[9]

---

[8] Trevor Faggotter, 'Revival Fire at Wudinna'.

[9] John Blacket, ' "I Will Renew the Land": Island on Fire'.

Revival is a sovereign work of God coming down and spreading his glory in the dust and in the hearts of the poorest and the humblest. A revival is really a theophany, an appearance of the glory of God. We cannot work it up. We can only pray it down.

To say that revival is a work of God is to say that it is not a human work. Jonathan Edwards no more thought of promoting a revival than of flying to the moon. Revival, then, must be distinguished from organized evangelism. An evangelistic campaign is not a revival. Occasionally, as we shall see, an evangelistic campaign can be accompanied by revival or be the means of encouraging Christians to pray earnestly for revival. But most such campaigns have witnessed neither. Using man-made programmes and series of meetings to promote revival is akin to King David believing he was able to bring the presence of God into the centre of the nation by bringing the ark to Jerusalem (2 Sam. 6). God objected to the manipulation (v. 7), and David responded with hurt, bewilderment and anger (vv. 8,9). So our theology should not let us suppose that we can control the holy and sovereign God. Such a presumption will only bring disappointment and hurt. Revival is an *outburst* of *God's* power: it is not a conglomerate of mere human energies.

Revival is an intensification by Jesus of the Holy Spirit's normal activity

I have called this book *Firestorm of the Lord* rather than *Firestorm of the Spirit* because it is Jesus who is the author of revival. Revivals are outpourings of the Spirit, but the Spirit is poured out by Jesus (Acts 2:33).[10] Jesus is the one who kindles fire on the earth (Lk. 12:49) and who baptizes with the Holy Spirit (Jn. 1:33).[11]

What Jesus does in a revival is to pour out the Holy Spirit in an unusual and remarkable way. But it is unusual and remarkable only in the sense that it is an unusually powerful manifestation of the *normal* work of the Holy Spirit – which is to awaken, convict, convert and confirm. It is not an *abnormal* manifestation of the

---

[10] 'Exalted to the right hand of God, he has received from the Father the promised Holy Spirit and has poured out what you now see and hear.'
[11] ' "The man on whom you see the Spirit come down and remain is he who will baptise with the Holy Spirit." '

power of the Spirit through his *extraordinary* gifts: healing, prophecy, tongues, and so on. These may or may not accompany revival, and therefore they are not the essence of revival. The essence of revival is, again, an intensification of the Holy Spirit's normal work of awakening, convicting, converting, and confirming.

If revival is an intensification of the normal work of the Holy Spirit, it follows that revival yields a bumper harvest of the fruit of the Holy Spirit (Gal. 5:22). The greatest of that fruit is love (1 Cor. 13:13). And that is why, if you have the love of God in your heart, you will dedicate yourself to pray for revival. For you are praying for the bringing down from heaven to earth, not so much the love of God, but the God of love. You are praying that the God of love will set up his tabernacle with people on the earth and dwell with them. That is another way of describing revival. Revival is the God of love, who is in heaven, coming down and dwelling with us on earth.

It follows that revivals may also be understood as foretastes of heaven. In heaven the Holy Spirit will be 'poured forth in perfect love into every heart'.[12] Revival is an outpouring of the Holy Spirit of love, and therefore it is a foretaste of the heavenly outpouring. In heaven there will be no need for the gifts of the Spirit. Only the fruit of the Spirit will be there in evidence. If revivals are literally anticipations of heaven, they will be characterized not primarily by amazing gifts, but rather by the fruit.

Another dramatic way of understanding the nature of the outpouring of the Holy Spirit in revival is to look at what is happening in the heavenly places while the Spirit is doing the work of grace on earth. Revival constitutes a massive assault, the unleashing of an angelic host, against the powers of darkness. The angels are given charge over the churches (Rev. 2 and 3) and they long to attack the cohorts of Satan. The angels are magnificent, beautiful warriors and they long to strike a deadly blow for their Lord. When unleashed they pack a lethal punch, which explains why in revival the powers of darkness, which many had come to accept as integral to society, are exposed for what they are and are driven into such unexpected retreat. That is why revivals make such dramatic, sudden advances on seemingly entrenched and invincible evil – not just in the church,

---

[12] Jonathan Edwards, *Ethical Writings*, p. 367.

but also in the community and nation. 'No situation is hopeless with God. He can change a nation in a few days.'[13] The forces of darkness, which are the foundation of entrenched evil, are suddenly put to flight, and the evil edifice collapses – sometimes very quickly.

But the forces of darkness are first provoked into retaliation, and that is why revival is concerned with spiritual warfare. Revival is a concerted invasion of territory held by the enemy, and Satan at first will counter-attack viciously. This explains why revivals are accompanied frequently by such undesirable features that frightened Christians in positions of leadership are tempted to abort the revival before it brings great blessing.

Revival accentuates the doctrines of grace and hence is a waking up to the reality of the Lordship of Jesus, the Saviour

One of the reasons why revival is often characterized by tremendous conviction of sin, such that it can leave the soul in distress for days on end, is that the affected person wakes up to the reality of Jesus as Saviour for the first time. In Belfast in 1859 the Revd Samuel Moore, in observing amazing scenes of conviction accompanying the Ulster revival, found himself wondering:

> Do these emotions, whether gentle or confounding, result from a consideration of sin issuing in the soul's everlasting destruction, and of the long, unseen, and slighted Saviour – His love, His charms, His power to save to the uttermost – to save me?[14]

In genuine revival the soul finds the beauty and excellence and love of Christ electrifying. The Holy Spirit works to that end in the soul. We are brought to high and exalting thoughts about Christ. He is 'outstanding among ten thousand . . . he is altogether lovely' (Song 5:10,16). He has won my heart, and he keeps drawing it to himself:

---

[13] George Strachan, *Revival – Its Blessings and Battles: An Account of Experiences in the Solomon Islands*, p. 59.
[14] Patrick Dixon, *Signs of Revival*, p. 149, quoting the author's *The Great Revival in Ireland*, 1859.

It is most wonderful to know,
His love for me so free and sure;
But 'tis more wonderful to see
My love for Him so faint and poor.

And yet I want to love Thee, Lord;
O light the flame within my heart,
And I will love Thee more and more,
Until I see Thee as thou art.

To be with Christ – to be present with him and to commune with him; to explore more of his dying love for me, who had no love for him; to be more like him; to do everything for him, even suffer; to bring others to him; to be with those who share my love for him; to learn more of him from them – these are among the longings of the revived soul. One Solomon Islander who experienced revival said 'Revival is Jesus': it is what 'goes on in the soul when Jesus comes into right focus'.[15] Revival is a firestorm of Jesus.

Further, we can say that revival is a waking up to the reality and relevance of the finished work of Christ. A revival is *a manifestation in this world of a divine victory in the supernatural world*. A revival is an outbreak in the present world of the great victory over satanic and demonic forces which took place in the past on the cross and which will receive its most visible and permanent manifestation when Christ returns again to bring in a new heaven and a new earth. Revivals, then, are re-enactments, not of Calvary, but of the victory won at Calvary. Therefore revivals are always associated with the preaching of the gospel, which is the message of the cross.

Revivals may also be understood as anticipations of the unfinished, but certain, future work of Christ. A revival is an anticipation of the second coming. The victory over sin, the world and the devil which, at the second coming, will be evident for all to see, is evident to those who experience a revival.

---

[15] Strachan, *Revival*, p. 2.

The always-present elements of revival

In subsequent chapters we will discuss those elements included in our definition which have generally preceded revivals throughout history – namely the expectation that God is about to visit his people in an exceptional way and extraordinary unity and prayerfulness among Christians. While they are pre-revival characteristics, our concern in this chapter is to examine revival characteristics. So we turn now to consider three vital aspects of revival: revitalization of the church, the conversion of large numbers and the decline of sinful practices.

The revitalization of the church

The first characteristic of revival is that church members are awakened from their deadness. D.M. Panton defined revival as 'an inrush of divine life into a body threatening to become a corpse'.[16] That which has never been alive cannot be revived. Therefore revival is first and foremost *the enlivening and awakening of church members* who have fallen asleep or who are just about to nod off. They begin to be moved by and get excited about the doctrines that hitherto they have believed intellectually. They begin to get distressed about their behaviour, which hitherto they thought God would tolerate. They are resensitized to the corruption in their own hearts and they receive new energy to struggle for holiness. They are transformed by a new vision of the glory of God and they are renewed by a transfusion of the power of God. They begin to wait on God and really pray that God will give their minister a message which satisfies their new hunger for the word.

Hence, revival is first and foremost a revitalization of Christians. 'Will you not revive *us* again?' (Ps. 85:6). Revival is the extraordinary work of God's Spirit in God's people. It is needed because, left to ourselves, our spiritual life runs down. John Bunyan depicted Satan as the one who makes it run down. Satan threatens:

---

[16] Quoted by Selwyn Hughes, 'Heaven-Sent Revival'.

I will cool you insensibly, by degrees, by little and little. What care I . . . though I be seven years in chilling your heart if I can do it at last; continual rocking will lull a crying child asleep.[17]

Christmas Evans, a Welsh preacher used of God in a number of revivals, said:

Revival is God bending down to the dying embers of a fire just about to go out and breathing into it until it bursts into flame.[18]

Revival has been well defined, then, as 'the work of the Holy Spirit in restoring the people of God to a more vital spiritual life, witness, and work by prayer and the Word after repentance in crisis for their spiritual decline.'[19]

If the Lord sent a revival to your church, what would happen to you? You would experience five things:[20]

- A *greatly enhanced sense of God's presence.* In a revival the holy, omnipotent, majestic God comes down and draws near. God visits his people. But what a visitor. You would never be the same again after such a visit.
- A *heightened responsiveness to God's word.* It would pierce you to the division of soul and spirit. You would discern the thoughts and intentions of your heart (Heb. 4:12). That would lead on to:
- An *increased sensitivity to sin.* Because this sensitivity would so contrast with your present insensitivity, you would experience such conviction that it would almost certainly frighten you. But that deep conviction leading on to thorough repentance would do a great work in your soul that you would come to enjoy:
- An *unprecedented sense of personal liberation.* You would become assured in your faith to the point of boldness; your church-

---

[17] *Grace Abounding to the Chief of Sinners*, p. 35.
[18] Hughes, 'Heaven-Sent'.
[19] E.E. Cairns, *An Endless Line of Splendor*, p. 22.
[20] J.I. Packer, *God in our Midst: Seeking and Receiving Ongoing Revival*, pp. 26–35.

going would fill you with delight as you are set free to praise
him; your witness would become spontaneous and natural,
and you would see:

• *Unparalleled fruitfulness in your testimony for Christ* – both in
soul-winning and in standard-setting as you stand fast for the
law of God.

A revived church will be alert to its responsibility to evangelize the
world. Christ did not die for the church, but for the world (Jn. 3:16).
A local church, therefore, cannot be content to live for itself. Revival
awakens the local church to the spiritual plight of the community in
which it is located. The church has to take the nation – each local
church has to take its community.

Revivals also quicken the church in worship, singing, preaching,
praying and in attendance. Worship is an unalloyed joy. Eternity
pervades the services in terms of atmosphere rather than in terms of
time. Of the 1734 revival in Northampton, Massachusetts, Jonathan
Edwards wrote in a classic passage:

> God's day was a delight, and his tabernacles were amiable [Ps. 84:1].
> Our public assemblies were then beautiful; the congregation was alive
> in God's service, everyone earnestly intent on the public worship,
> every hearer eager to drink in the words of the minister as they came
> from his mouth; the assembly in general were, from time to time, in
> tears while the Word was preached; some weeping with sorrow and
> distress, others with joy and love, others with pity and concern for the
> souls of their neighbours.
>
> Our public praises were then greatly enlivened; God was then
> served in our psalmody, in some measure, in the beauty of holiness
> [Ps. 96:9]. It has been observable that there has been scarce any part of
> divine worship, wherein good men amongst us have had grace so
> drawn forth and their hearts so lifted up in the ways of God, as in sing-
> ing his praises. Our congregation excelled all that ever I knew in the
> external part of the duty before, generally carrying regularly and well
> three parts of music, and the women a part by themselves. But now
> they were evidently wont to sing with unusual elevation of heart and
> voice, which made the duty pleasant indeed.[21]

---

[21] Edwards, *Great Awakening*, p. 151.

Robert Murray McCheyne, a Scottish preacher, was overseas when revival swept through his church in Dundee in 1839. He observed on his return that the singing was not only more joyful. It was also sweeter: 'so tender and affecting, as if the people felt that they were praising a present God'. Yes, revivals work miracles: they actually improve singing.

Preaching is more powerful and authoritative in a revival. A revival preacher will sometimes report that his whole frame is electrified by spiritual energies. His hearers say that his voice pierces each heart like a knife and his face is radiant. He is to them an angel of God. As in Psalm 104:4 (KJV), '[God] maketh his angels spirits; his ministers a flaming fire.'

The conversion of large numbers of unbelievers

As a result of all this new life, unbelievers are caught up and get converted to Christianity in large numbers. This is the second element which is present without exception in a genuine revival. It is not that they just 'come to Christ' in a 'flush of affection', as Jonathan Edwards would say. But unbelievers count the cost, take Christ's yoke upon them, and follow him. They drastically alter their behaviour as they 'prove their repentance by their deeds' (Acts 26:20).

True revival reaps a new harvest of souls. If revivals are dramatic manifestations of the glory of God, they show that God's glory is found chiefly in the salvation of sinners. In the 1859 revival in Wales 110,000 were added to the church; a further 162,000 in the 1904/5 revival. Twenty-five thousand were added to the churches in a revival in New South Wales in 1902/3. These figures are a net gain for the church. They do not refer to the transfer of the old harvest from one church to another. Small churches today often empty into large ones, and we have commuter congregations rather than community impact. Our churches house wandering mobs looking for blessing without commitment. Our congregations are made up of the saved, but restless. In the book of Acts, congregations were armies which made a stand and captured a neighbourhood. If our churches don't really want souls and won't make room for them, then God won't give them souls. Would you put babies into a freezer?

Hence revival is a waking up to the fact that the church is asleep to the power of God, living on the memory of God and not the power of God. The church is not asleep to methods and techniques; it is not asleep to the need for change; it is not asleep to the need for experimentation. It's just asleep to God. It's a very common sickness. Calvin said, 'The whole history of the Church is one of sleep, sometimes deeper, sometimes lighter, with a few waking moments.'[22]

But while it is true that the sleepiness and deadness of the church is a very common condition, we should not be lulled into the complacent attitude that it is not a serious condition. From God's perspective, which is reality, we need to do something about it. Do not doubt for one moment that God's hand is raised against the deadness of the church. He is stung by it: like smoke in his eyes, he wants to rub it out. It is distasteful to him: like vinegar on his teeth, he wants to spit it out. 'Woe to you in Zion who are complacent' (Amos 6:1). 'A curse on him who is lax in doing the LORD's work!' (Jer. 48:10).

God's perspective is reality. And my favourite definition of revival, in agreement with Edwards' understanding, is that it is waking up to reality. It is seeing God, yourself and your nation from God's perspective. It is seeing the fundamental problem, which is sin, wrath and eternal death. All the problems that distract and torment us are but symptoms of that one fundamental problem. Nothing helps us to see the problem and the divine answer as clearly as revival. As one Scottish pastor reported of the revival in Edinburgh in 1905:

> There was nothing, humanly speaking, to account for what happened. Quite suddenly, upon one and another came an overwhelming sense of the reality and awfulness of His presence and of eternal things. Life, death, and eternity seemed suddenly laid bare.[23]

The decline of sinful practices in the community – the healing of our nation

The third element that is always present in a genuine revival is that sin in the community is curbed as even unbelievers see the power of

---

[22] Quoted in a sermon by the Revd Tony Lamb, Christ Church, St Ives, Sydney, in the 1980s.

[23] Winnie Kemp, *Joseph W. Kemp*, p. 32.

goodness and holiness. While, wrote Jonathan Edwards, 'none are converted but what are reformed', yet 'some men are reformed that are not converted'.[24] This is why in many revivals the wider community has historically taken notice of the church and many outside the church have acknowledged that Christian morality is in the best interests of the community.

It follows from the fact that revival is a massive assault on the powers of darkness that revival results not only in the forgiveness of sin, but also in the healing of our land (2 Chron. 7:14). In the Welsh Revival of 1859, the morals of whole communities were improved. In the 1905 revival in Wales the police were almost put out of work, and the graph showing children conceived out of wedlock fell almost to zero. In 1959 in Australia, the Billy Graham Crusade temporarily reversed Australia's headlong descent into crime, slowed the rate of increase of illegitimate conceptions in a permissive age, and reduced the per capita consumption of liquor.[25]

In a revival God rises and scatters his enemies. In the absence of revival, the forces of darkness make gains. The tension is just part of the age in which we live. We experience potential, inaugurated, occasional victory, rather than achieved, permanent and complete victory. On the cross, God reined in the demonic powers (Col. 2:15), but the social evils (slavery, gender, race) take longer to abolish. If we are to follow God's rhythm we will, at times, be patient with long-standing evil and be prepared to lay deep foundations for its eventual overthrow. At other times we will act with the conviction that the time has come for a decisive victory over the enemy. We will know that now is the hour of our deliverance. We shall feel that it is our turn to do something great for God – that this is our *kairos* – our anointed opportunity to witness the action of God in his revival power.

England experienced such an opportunity in the 1740s when the Evangelical Revival changed the direction of the nation and under-girded unprecedented social reform. China has had this opportunity in the last generation, with 50 million Christians born in an age of persecution – since the beginning of the cultural revolution. There are currently reports that 200 million now attend house churches in

---

[24] Jonathan Edwards, sermon on Acts 19:19.
[25] Stuart Piggin, 'Billy Graham in Australia, 1959 – Was it Revival?'

China. Newspapers even report a quickening of revival since the Tiananmen Square massacre. It was the turn of the Soviet Union in the late 1980s, thanks to the revolutionary impact of a modern Cyrus called Gorbachev. Unprecedented scenes of revival were then witnessed in Russia. The Eastern Bloc underwent rapid revolution accompanied by amazing religious revival. New governments committed to the freedom of worship were sworn in with the blessing of the churches and accompanied by the prayers of Christian people everywhere – in Poland, East Germany, Czechoslovakia, Hungary, Romania, and, to a lesser extent, Bulgaria. Romania's Ceausescu, after 24 years in power, fell in a moment and was executed on Christmas Day – the significance of which was not lost on those who suffered in his atheistic regime. In Revelation 18:10 at the return of the Lord, Babylon, 'that great city', fell in an hour. So in revivals, which are anticipations of the Lord's return, evil that is entrenched and apparently invincible can collapse in a moment.

When will it be your nation's turn for a Great Awakening? Do we have to be crushed like Israel was in days of old because we refuse to serve the Lord joyfully in the time of prosperity (Deut. 28:47)?

That is our challenge in this interim age: our life in Christ is vibrant with instant possibilities and yet fraught with long-term expectations. Christians are to long for revival, be alert to 'the brightness of [God's] dawn' (Isa. 60:3), and watch, 'for his wrath can flare up in a moment' (Ps. 2:12). But it may take ages for that moment to come; it may take more than a generation for that day to dawn. Both the 'sudden' and the 'slow' are in the mind of God, that mind which responds to our urgent, importunate prayer for rain, rain, rain.

Conclusion

Revival, then, is an outburst of the divine energy, like a firestorm from the sun. It flares up to scorch Satanic forces in heavenly places and it blazes out across the earth. It cannot be contained – either within the individual heart or within the four walls of churches. It is God himself in the wider community. Revival is when the community, made up of the saved and the unsaved, wakes up to the reality of the glorious and holy presence of the God who is at once a consuming fire and an overflowing love.

2

Revival in the Bible

The problem

There are surprisingly few scholarly studies on revival in the Bible.[1] This fact raises the critical question of whether revival is a biblical concept at all or just a recent historical phenomenon devoid of biblical justification. The problem becomes even more acute when the very recent development of the usage of the word 'revival' is taken into account. As a noun denoting 'awakening', it is about as recent as Jonathan Edwards himself.[2]

The theology of revival is also far less developed than might be expected given the great interest in the subject at certain stages in the church's history – including the renewed fascination with revival today. It is as if the whole subject of revival – its nomenclature and vocabulary, its biblical basis and its theological interpretation – are sewn up in a single pair of breeches, namely those of Jonathan Edwards. He is the church's theologian of revival *par excellence*, and the church has not only failed to produce anyone like him, but few have dared to attempt sustained reflection on the area where he so dominates. In spite of the many writings about Edwards, I am not aware of any study that answers the question, 'Edwards on revival: How biblical is he?' An answer to this question would have to take into account the fact that modern scholars tend to interpret the Bible very differently from the way Edwards did. Edwards interpreted the whole Bible in the light of Christ (that is, Christologically), emphasizing redemption and the role of

---

[1] See Geoff Stacey, ' "Revival" in the Old Testament?', p. 36.
[2] Stacey, 'Revival', p. 36.

revival in restoring Israel to its hope in future redemption by God. Many modern scholars prefer not to interpret the whole of the Old Testament in the light of Christ, and they tend to stress 'creation' as more foundational than the new creation. Because they do not see Christ and redemption everywhere, they have some difficulty seeing revival anywhere.

Biblical vocabulary and the experience of revival

Edwards certainly sounds biblical! He was actually far more likely than twentieth-century theologians to express himself in biblical vocabulary, even if he did not share the same understanding of biblical concepts as modern scholars. In the eighteenth century evangelical clergy, including Edwards, developed a vocabulary to describe the amazing movements of the Spirit which they witnessed. The vocabulary was scriptural and imparted to many a religious gathering a dramatic sense of the presence of God, which is one of the hallmarks of revival – for example, 'The Lord whom we have sought has suddenly come to his temple.' This was the language of hymns and other literature that exercised a formative influence on society and culture.[3]

Modern theologians who doubt that revival is biblical need to reckon with the fact that the vocabulary used to describe the Evangelical Revival of the 1740s was thoroughly biblical. Converts then had no way of expressing and therefore understanding their religious experience apart from the language of the Bible. Hymns, in particular, identified scriptural images with the experience of the modern convert. Revival is the welding together, in the soul, of biblical history, national history and personal experience. *Revival is the Bible lived in the modern world.* The effect is to make the people of God in the modern world see themselves as continuous with the people of God in the Bible and therefore as part of God's sacred history. Here is an example of such a use of the Bible in a Welsh hymn:

---

[3] Derec Llwyd Morgan, *The Great Awakening in Wales.*

Lo, a poor and wretched pilgrim,
Knowing naught but years of strife,
Back and forth, confused, I wander
Through the wilderness of life.

Pi-hahiroth beckons thither
And Baal-zephon beckons there,
Egypt on my mind, about me,
Makes me fear and despair.[4]

It is not surprising, therefore, that the antidote to this 'fear and despair' should also be cast in biblical language, and that, for example, the people of Northern Tasmania in Australia, when revival came to them in 1874, gave over thirty Bible place names to their local geographical surrounds – including Paradise, Beulah, Garden of Eden and the Promised Land.[5]

The Bible is used similarly, but on a far greater scale, in the Aboriginal revival which began in Australia in 1979. The leaders had not witnessed anything like this before, and white missionaries did not seem to be able to give any help. Therefore Aboriginal pastors became extraordinarily dependent on the Bible to guide them to know what to do next. They read what Jesus and his Spirit did in the Gospels and the Acts and they believed that Jesus was doing it all over again in Australia. They read the Bible with excitement and expectation, because they needed a map to guide them over this exciting new terrain. One said, 'we were like explorers who came to Australia to explore the new territory, and who found out where the rivers run'.[6] They turned to the Bible to find out where the rivers run. They interpreted the Bible literally and pictorially and they expected to witness miracles and to see visions.

Some biblical images have been more evocative of revival than others. The image of Edom from Isaiah 63 was particularly popular in the Welsh revivals of the eighteenth century. Such an image was

---

[4] Morgan, *Great Awakening*, p. 281.
[5] Alan F. Dyer, *God was their Rock*, p. 16. The names are taken from the official Lands Department maps.
[6] Quoted in Blacket, 'I Will Renew'.

capable, through much repetition, of accumulating a richness and a ripeness such that the initiated soul would thrill with the vibrations and overtones of a fugue, thus energizing praise and spontaneous ejaculations of admiration for God's superabundant love and goodness.

Another powerful image has been that of the little cloud like a hand. On 24 November 1858 before a revival sermon in Wales, David Morgan cried out in prayer:

> We thank Thee, O Lord, that there are indications of a rising cloud. It is but a little one, like a man's hand, but it is a *cloud*, and it arises from the *sea*. Let the whole sky grow black! *Let the whole sky grow black!* LET THE WHOLE SKY GROW BLACK![7]

Perhaps, then, the experience of revival is better grasped by the imagination than by the intellect. The imagery of the Bible appeals hauntingly to the imagination, encouraging us to hope and to pray. Biblical imagery usually becomes a vehicle for revival through its incorporation in our hymns, the words of which are probably better known to most Christians than the words of Scripture because they are sung so often. Perhaps one of the reasons for the great popularity in our own day of the hymns of Graham Kendrick is that they arise from the experience of revival and the lyrics are so thoroughly clothed with biblical imagery that the Christian soul thirsting for revival instinctively identifies with them.

> Shine, Jesus, shine
> Fill this land with the Father's glory.
> Blaze, Spirit, blaze,
> Set our hearts on fire.
> Flow, river, flow,
> Flood the nations with grace and mercy.
> Send forth your word, Lord,
> And let there be light.

---

[7] Quoted in E. Evans, *Revival Comes to Wales: The Story of the 1859 Revival in Wales*, p. 58.

We must not be fixated by the words, however. We must get to the concepts behind the vocabulary. If revival is an outpouring of the Holy Spirit which awakens whole communities to spiritual reality, especially to the holiness of God, then the basic question we must answer here is, does the Bible encourage us to believe that God sometimes acts in this unusual way?

Jonathan Edwards does not answer that question definitively for the modern scholar. There is no doubting that he always strove to be biblical. But one cannot make eighteenth-century theology normative. Edwards used a Puritan interpretation of the Bible, a hermeneutic that today's biblical scholars no longer use. Prevailing twentieth-century hermeneutics may not be any more accurate to the word of God than Edwards', but if a theology of revival is to have any sway in our day, it must be consistent with this modern hermeneutic.

Modern hermeneutics and revival

What are some of the major themes in the modern study of the Old Testament and how might the issue of revival be related to them? We have space to deal very briefly with just two themes: 'the people of God' and 'promise and fulfilment'.

The people of God

The Bible has as one of its major themes the experience of the people of God, that is as Israel in the Old Testament and as the church in the New Testament. Three aspects of the Old Testament experience of the people of God appear to have a strong bearing on the issue of revival: their recurring experience of decline and revival; their experience of deliverance or redemption; and their experience of the absence of God.

The pattern of decline and revival
The historic experience of the people of God was one of a recurring pattern of decline and revival. To use more biblical vocabulary, they experienced the cyclical pattern of sin, judgement, repentance and

restoration. We might study many examples of this cycle.[8] But the pattern is perhaps found in its purest form in the book of Judges. This is a harrowing story of recurring apostasy, followed by divine chastisement through foreign oppressors, the raising up of leaders or deliverers known as judges, and the restoration of the land to peace. The book of Judges is a particularly promising Old Testament book on which to base a biblical theology of revival because of the following features:

- The purity of the pattern. It is most briefly encapsulated in Judges 2:10–19, but it just continues on and on, gathering speed with constant and regular undulations.
- The apparent parallel with the church in the time between the two comings of the Lord. For the church today is the product

---

[8] For example:

1. Exod. 32–36: The people declined into gross sin and idolatry while Moses was away receiving the Ten Commandments. The denunciation of their apostasy, repentance, restoration and the building of the tabernacle followed his return.

2. The book of Judges (see discussion above).

3. 1 Sam. 7: A period of spiritual doldrums, in which the Ark of God languishes at Kiriath Jearim and Israel's enemies rage undefeated, is followed by 'all the people' mourning and seeking after the Lord. Samuel challenged the people with the insistence that returning to the Lord with all their heart involved putting away everything that competed with the Lord for their affections. Their repentance and cries for deliverance were followed by the defeat of the Philistines at Mizpah.

4. 2 Sam. 4–7: Decline accompanied the capture of the Ark by the Philistines and its 20-year sojourn at Kiriath Jearim. David's bringing the Ark to Jerusalem precipitated a crisis and an awakening.

5. 2 Chron. 7:14: The famous verse speaks of the Lord's coming to his people and healing their land on condition that they humble themselves and pray and seek the Lord's face and forsake their wicked ways.

6. 1 Kgs. 16–18: Declension in the days of Ahab and Jezebel is arrested and reversed by Elijah's challenge to the people to choose between God and Baal.

7. 2 Chron. 15–17: Decline in the days of Rehoboam and Abijah was followed by renewal under the godly kings Asa and Jehoshaphat.

There were similar reversals of decline in the times of Hezekiah, Josiah, Ezra and Nehemiah.

of the many fulfilments of the promises of God in Christ and has now no responsibility but to engage in the extension of the kingdom in obedience to her ascended King. Likewise, the Israelites in the book of Judges had entered Canaan, and were thus enjoying the fulfilment of many of the covenant promises given to the patriarchs. They had nothing to do but to occupy and to establish God's kingdom on the earth. Israel's chronic forgetfulness of her mission and her consequent corruption is a model or type of the church's failure, and her restoration is a type of the church's revivals.

- The human role of repentance in revival. It is repeatedly after the suffering people cry out that the Lord sends deliverance and restoration (see 2:18; 3:9,15; 6:6,7; 10:10). Instructively, the pattern in the book of Judges is a downward spiral. It is about the downward decline of a people, because they had not fully repented.
- The sovereignty of God in revival. Far more conspicuous than the role of the people in repentance is the role of the Lord in his covenant faithfulness. The gift of salvation and restoration are the dependable results of God's patience and long-suffering. That is why we may confidently call on the Lord to restore his church. He is always faithful, patient, and long-suffering.
- The role of the Holy Spirit in deliverance and restoration. The age of the church is sometimes called the age of the Spirit, and it has been observed of Judges that it is 'in a special way the Old Testament age of the Spirit'.[9]

There is a pattern evident, then, in the history of Israel. The spiritual cycle consists of decline, crisis or judgement, the addressing of the crisis by the word of God heard through a chosen leader, repentance and revival.

The exodus experience
A second and even more fundamental experience of the people of God is their experience of salvation, or redemption as it came to be

---

[9] *NIV Study Bible*, p. 326. See Judges 3:10; 6:34; 11:29; 13:25; 14:6,19; 15:14.

known, because God redeemed them, or bought them, out of slavery in Egypt in the exodus. So the exodus motif appears throughout the Bible. The most important point for our purpose is that it is in the life of the people of God, the church, that the exodus motif is most extensively developed in the New Testament. This theme was developed in part as a way of confronting the sinfulness and rebellion of Christians who were in constant danger of corruption just as Israel was in the days of the Judges. Just as Israel had manna from heaven and water from the rock to sustain them in the wilderness, so Christians too have their supernatural food and drink.[10] And just as the generation which came out of Egypt, in spite of all these blessings, never entered the promised land because of rebellion against God, so Christians should take heed lest they too fall into disaster. To make this point Paul gives us one of the basic texts for the use of the Old Testament in the New: 'For these things happened to them by way of example *(typikos)*, but they were written down for our instruction, upon whom the end of the ages has come' (1 Cor. 10:11; cf. Rom. 5:14).[11] Similarly, the writer to the Hebrews reminds his readers that the children of Israel had a promised rest before them, but failed to enter it because of unbelief, and that 'brothers' may suffer the same end if they have 'a sinful unbelieving heart which turns away from the living God' (Heb. 3:12).

That the house of God is in fact at risk of such contamination leading to the death and destruction of Christians is clear from Jude 5 and 23 and 1 Peter 4:17. The church, then, needs to be delivered and restored or revived in its historic experience, as did Israel.

The absence of God

A third point about the theme of the experience of the people of God is that revival seems to be necessary because of the painful experience of the absence of God. In the Bible God's transcendence in heaven is never doubted. But the feeling that God is not with them in their earthly plight frequently troubles the people of God.

---

[10] 1 Cor. 10:3f.

[11] L. Goppelt, *Typos: The Typological Interpretation of the Old Testament in the New*, p. 4.

Now you have rejected and humbled us;
you no longer go out *with* our armies. (Ps. 44:9)

> I will forsake them and I will hide my face from them, and they shall be
> devoured, and many evils and troubles shall befall them; so that they
> will say in that day, 'Are not these evils come upon us, so that our God
> is not among us?' And I will surely hide my face in that day for all the
> evils which they shall have wrought. (Deut. 31:17,18)

The effect of Israel's disobedience has been to grieve the Holy Spirit
(Isa. 63:10) and he has turned away. And his people miss him. Where
is he? Where is he? 'Where is he who brought them through the sea.
. . where is he who set his Holy Spirit among them?' (v. 11). Where is
he? He is in heaven (v. 15). And the complaint now arises from the
prophet in his prayer that the Lord is bottled up in his heaven. The
God who has always been a father to Israel is no longer acting like
their father and redeemer in the world. He is an absent father. That is
why the most heartfelt prayer in the Bible for revival is that of Isaiah
63 and 64, 'Come down Lord, we miss you.'

The theme of promise and fulfilment

These experiences of the people of God are not only patterns which
recur and are therefore useful examples to Christians, who although
living in a new age, are also in danger of spiritual decline and in need
of constant reviving. These experiences are also types. That is, they
are events on a small scale destined by God to be repeated on a much
greater scale. The small revivings of the Old Testament (e.g., Ezra
9:9) are anticipations of much greater revivals to come. The experiences of God's grace by his people in the Old Testament are preg-
nant with the promise of greater blessing in the future. So revival
needs to be understood as part of the promise-fulfilment theme in
the Bible, especially with reference to the prophecies of revival and
to covenant renewal.

Prophecies of revival

The most celebrated Old Testament prophecy of revival is that
found in Ezekiel 37, the valley or plain of the dry bones. The bones

are those of a decimated army who probably suffered carnage at the hands of Nebuchadnezzar in one of his whirlwind campaigns.

> Then he said to me, 'Prophesy to the breath, prophesy, mortal, and say to the breath: Thus says the Lord God: Come from the four winds, O breath, and breathe upon these slain, that they may live.' I prophesied as he commanded me, and the breath came into them, and they lived, and stood on their feet, a vast multitude (Ezek. 37:9,10)

This is a prophecy of Pentecost, when a great wind came upon the large crowd (a vast multitude) of Jews from every nation, who, on hearing Peter preach, were cut to the heart, repented and were baptized.

Pentecost, that greater fulfilment, is also prophesied in Joel 2:28,29:

> And it shall come to pass afterward, that I will pour out my spirit upon all flesh; and your sons and your daughters shall prophesy, your old men shall dream dreams, your young men shall see visions: And also upon the servants and upon the handmaids in those days will I pour out my spirit.

The Old Testament contains prophecies of the future outpouring of the Holy Spirit on the people as a whole, but it does not report any historical occurrences of it. We have to wait for the New Testament for that fulfilment. In the Old Testament the Holy Spirit is poured out on individuals, especially the judges (as we have seen) and the prophets (1 Sam. 10:10; Isa. 61:1; Ezek. 2:2; Micah 3:8). Moses did not have his wish fulfilled when he said, 'I wish that all the Lord's people were prophets, and that the Lord would put his Spirit on them!' (Num. 11:29). The Lord did not put his Spirit on all the Lord's people in Old Testament times.

But in spite of the difference between the Old Testament and the New with respect to the work of the Spirit, our definition of revival remains true for both dispensations. Revival is an outpouring of God's Holy Spirit, which awakens whole communities to spiritual reality. In the Old Testament the whole community was awakened not through the Holy Spirit in the soul of every member of the community, but through the Holy Spirit in the leader through whom the community was awakened.

The renewal of the covenant

Another major element in the promise-fulfilment theme, covenant renewal, is of major relevance to the biblical understanding of revival. The concern in the Old Testament for the renewal of the covenant after it has been broken by the rebellious people of God is a concern for the restoration of a vital faith. The renewal is of the heart, not of the outward forms. This is especially true of those prophets who are sometimes significantly labelled revival prophets: Isaiah, Jeremiah, Ezekiel, Amos and Hosea.

To come to a biblical understanding of revival it is important to understand first of all that it is God who takes the initiative in covenant renewal, in restoring the relationship broken by human sin. For once the covenant is broken, the people are dead. Resurrection or revival is required, and any renewal that takes place does so only by the grace of God. This is clear in Hosea 6:1, 2, a text which is perhaps part of a covenant renewal ritual:

> Come let us return to the Lord. He has torn us to pieces but he will heal us; he has injured us, but he will bind up our wounds. After two days he will revive us. On the third day he will restore us, that we may live in his presence.

It is also significant for a biblical understanding of revival that covenant renewal is not something primarily prophesied for the end time. That is, it is not to be understood eschatologically so much as historically. With the possible exception of Daniel, which is an apocalyptic book and therefore different from the rest, the prophets are concerned with what happens in history. So Micah 4, for example, is concerned about the restoration of the people of God and the house of God within history. True, the chapter begins with the words 'In the last days', but those words really mean 'in the afterwards days', sometime afterwards in time. Within human history, 'many nations' will come to the Lord. The same may be said of Zechariah 8:22, 'Many peoples and strong nations shall come to seek the LORD of Hosts in Jerusalem, and to pray before the LORD'. Clearly, covenant renewal and return to the Lord by whole communities, even nations, which is part of our definition of revival, is prophesied in the Old Testament as an expectation for the people of God within time.

Furthermore, covenant renewal is always accompanied by the exposure of sin, another feature of covenant renewal relevant to revival. Witness especially the call for national repentance by Amos, a prophet much concerned with the righteousness of God and therefore with social justice. Amos is interested in a dramatic improvement in national or community morality, and that again is an aspect of our definition of revival. Indeed, the Bible will not have us separate the quest for social justice from spiritual renewal. That would be to overestimate 'man's unaided capability to effect real and lasting change'.[12] That is an error to which liberation theology is prone, and it makes that error because it is based on Marxism, which sees the solutions to social injustice coming wholly from within the historical process. Revivals, however, are acts of God 'within history that, at the same time, sovereignly select and go beyond the human political processes of this age'.[13]

A fourth aspect of covenant renewal relevant to a biblical understanding of revival is that it is accompanied by the refreshment of the people of God. This is the first of the three ever-present characteristics of revival according to our definition – the revitalization of the church – and it is well prefigured in Hosea. The book of Hosea is largely about a protracted period of spiritual decline in the history of Israel. Right at the end (14:4,7) revival is promised to Israel. And what would the people of Israel then be like? Fresh as morning dew; fresh as newly blossomed flowers; fresh as the most delicate fragrance; fresh as new growth in the shade. The freshness, however, is not that of fragility and vulnerability. The people of Israel would also be stable and vigorous. They would be stable: as firmly grounded as the poplar trees or the cedars and mountains of Lebanon. They would be vigorous, like the spreading shoots of new growth. Those are the marks of a revived church: freshness, stability, vigour.

Finally, the prophets show that covenantal blessing and renewal was not to be found in national Israel and its king. It was to be sought, rather, in the coming of the Messiah, who came to be understood not only as the anointed leader of the nation, but also as the lover of each soul, which can be in union and communion with him in the most unprecedented intimacy. This blessing will not be

---

[12] Goppelt, *Typos*, pp. xiiif.
[13] Goppelt, *Typos*, p. xiv.

associated with Jerusalem, but with the heart (Jer. 31:33), and it will be accompanied by the pouring out of the Holy Spirit on all, including non-Israelites (Joel 2:28–32).

The Old Testament, then, does teach much about spiritual revival. It evocatively anticipates revival in imagery and songs. It vividly depicts the pattern or cycle of decline and revival. It contains many examples of the elements of revival: repentance, return, restoration, replenishment, refreshment and renewal. It shows the Spirit coming chiefly upon leaders to call the people of God to repentance. It prefigures and prophesies greater outpourings of the Holy Spirit, and it points to the coming Messiah as the one through whom the fullest blessings of the covenant are to be received. It points to the firestorms of the Messiah.

Revival in the New Testament

Some find it difficult to find revival in the New Testament fundamentally, I think, because it is everywhere. The entire New Testament is really an account of revival. God enlivens his people by pouring out his Spirit on them, quickening their consciences, making their sins plain to them and exalting his solution, namely his Son, that they might turn and be saved. This is the great subject matter of revival and it is the great subject matter of the New Testament. The pattern for the revived church will always be New Testament Christianity. Accordingly, every church does well to return to the New Testament to catch fire and to understand the revival pattern.

The New Testament depicts a new era inaugurated by the emergence of a new reality, namely the coming in power of the Holy Spirit. The Spirit came first on Jesus, who was the first prophet after Haggai, Zechariah and Malachi to bring the Spirit back in an extraordinary way. The Spirit then came on the people of God as a whole. The Holy Spirit was poured out on God made flesh and then on all flesh. This new reality was an experience of renewal. For the individual, this experience was said to mean that he was a 'new creation' (2 Cor. 5:17), that he was 'born anew' (1 Pet. 1:3) or 'born from above' (Jn. 3:3). This is the experience of personal renewal: to be a Christian is to become part of a redeemed fellowship among whom the Spirit is vital both individually and corporately. New Testament Christianity is a firestorm of the Lord in the sense that the joy and liberty which it brought in the Spirit was accompanied by an extraordinary awareness of Jesus Christ as Lord, who though risen, ascended and glorified was nevertheless present in the heart. Spiritual renewal accentuates the lordship of Christ. The apostle Paul attempts to convey this new reality with the extraordinarily evocative words in 2 Corinthians 3:17, 'Now the Lord is the Spirit, and where the Spirit of the Lord is, there is freedom.' To be precise, 'the Lord' here refers to Jesus, and Jesus is, of course, not the Spirit. So when Paul says that 'the Lord is the Spirit', he witnesses to the truth that the work of the Spirit is never to be separated from that of Jesus. Paul here speaks of the Lord of the new covenant of the Spirit. The Lord Christ is the Spirit-giver, the Spirit is given in consequence of hearing a message about Christ, and walking in the Spirit is living in the light of Christ's lordship.[14]

Revival under John the Baptist and Jesus

The New Testament speaks of two mighty spiritual movements, the one inaugurated through John the Baptist, the second by Jesus. Under John there was a generalized and widespread movement of repentance (Matt. 3:5; Lk. 3:7). It divided the people as genuine revivals nearly always have done. First the chief priests and the elders of the people did not believe. Because the Pharisees saw this repentance by the people, but did not themselves repent, they earned the condemnation of Jesus (Matt. 21:32). The common people, typified by tax collectors and prostitutes, did believe. Tax collectors repented of their extortion, soldiers of their abuse of power. There was also that wonderful reunification of divided families which has been so often remarked in later revivals (Mal. 4:5: 'He will turn the hearts of the fathers to their children, and the hearts of the children to their fathers').

---

[14] In this I follow the argument of Paul Barnett, *The Second Epistle to the Corinthians*, pp. 195–209, rather than that in Gordon D. Fee, *God's Empowering Presence: The Holy Spirit in the Letters of Paul*, pp. 309–20. Fee's argument seems to owe a lot to his conviction that this passage (2 Cor. 3:16–18) is pneumatological rather than Christological, which seems a bit circular.

This revival of repentance under John the Baptist was a preparation for the greater revival inaugurated by Jesus. 'He who comes after me is mightier than I,' said John the Baptist, '. . . he shall baptise you with the Holy Spirit and with fire' (Matt. 3:11). After John baptized Jesus in the Jordan, the movement under John faded and was superseded by that of Jesus. Multitudes followed Jesus, sometimes thousands. Wherever Jesus went he took revival with him because the Holy Spirit was upon him. As in all great religious revivals, some regions of the Holy Land were more receptive to Jesus' message than others. In Galilee, Samaria and Perea the fields were white unto harvest, and Jesus could have inaugurated a great national revival which might have swept the Romans from Palestine. But Jesus was after a different sort of revival, a revival which would inaugurate the kingdom of God on earth and which would create a church against which the gates of hell would not prevail. He therefore concentrated, not on the multitude, but on the Twelve, training them for future leadership. In Luke 10:1–20 we learn of his sending out 72 missionaries who exorcised demons, thus prefiguring both the future explosive expansion of the church and the fall of Satan, two marks of revival. Because the Twelve and the 72 were trained in this way, when Holy Spirit revival did break out as it did at Pentecost, there were commissioned officers ready to train the thousands of revival troops recruited for God's army. So, before Pentecost, Jesus generated the spirit of revival, but he contained its manifestation until Pentecost when the confined energies burst forth in a spiritual explosion.

Pentecost (Acts 2:1–47)

A fundamental question posed by Pentecost is to what extent was it unique and in what way is it the paradigm of all subsequent revivals? As to its uniqueness, it was not the only outpouring of the Holy Spirit in the book of Acts. There was another outpouring on the apostles after Peter and John appeared before the Sanhedrin. In Acts 4:31 we read of what has been labelled 'the little Pentecost':

> After they prayed, the place where they were meeting was shaken. And they were all filled with the Holy Spirit and spoke the word of God boldly.

Then there was an outpouring on the Samaritans (Acts 8:14–17) and another on the gentiles (Acts 10:34–48; 11:15–18). Revivals, then, continued in the early church.

To what extent were the apparent physical phenomena (the wind and the flames) at Pentecost unique? The mode of reception – namely the tongues of fire descending on each individual – has been reported in subsequent revivals.[15] Other revivals, too, have reportedly experienced the wind noise heard at Pentecost. In the Solomon Islands, for example, on 27 August 1970, the Holy Spirit came on a congregation like a mighty wind, as one who was present explained:

> In the silence I heard what I thought was a plane a long way off. That seemed unusual. Planes came nowhere near that isolated spot in those days. I continued praying, then became conscious of the noise of a big wind coming. I was concerned for our ship anchored nearby among reefs. (The anchor had dragged the previous day.) I looked out to see the effect of the wind, and to my amazement there wasn't a movement in the trees. Then it occurred to me that this was the Holy Spirit coming as on the Day of Pentecost.
>
> As I closed my eyes again the sound changed and became like a myriad of angels hovering over us, flapping their wings. These sounds were quite distinct and were heard by us all.
>
> Some people literally writhed and groaned under deep conviction of sin. Others were worshipping the Lord. Many saw visions. One older pastor sat enraptured, with arms uplifted, worshipping the Lord. He had the light of God on his face. I said to him later, 'You had a good time'. He replied, 'I saw Jesus'.[16]

Pentecost, then, was the first general outpouring of the Holy Spirit, but it was not unique either in its generality or in the phenomena which accompanied it. So understood, it is not inappropriate to pray for another Pentecost.

But what about our second and more important question: In what way is Pentecost the paradigm of all subsequent revivals?

---

[15] For example, Indonesia 1960s, the Kampuchean revival, and the Aboriginal revival in Australia.

[16] Strachan, *Revival*, p. 10. See also Alison Griffiths, *Fire in the Islands: The Acts of the Holy Spirit in the Solomons*, p. 175.

Revival, although not the normal experience of the church, is the means of going back again to the God-given norm for the church. Pentecost was the God-given norm for the church in that it was then that the church was endowed with spiritual power. This power was given in fulfilment of Jesus' promise ten days earlier, 'You will receive power when the Holy Spirit has come upon you.' This transformed the hitherto timid disciples into men ablaze and invincible. Their ministry now became so powerful that multitudes were swept into a close and life-changing relationship with God. This power in ministry is not common in the church, but it must be the ideal for which the church always longs in prayer and faith.

But if Pentecost is indeed the norm for revival in the church, why is that so? Why do revivals in the church not have Old Testament examples of revival as the norm? The answer must be that, since revival is an outpouring of the Holy Spirit, the Holy Spirit could not be fully given until Jesus was glorified:

> Why should this be so? It was because only through the life and death of Jesus could God's power be properly seen and understood. Eternal power must be seen not only in the context of signs, wonders and miracles, but at work on a cross, dying, suffering and overcoming sin. The power that fell at Pentecost, if it is to be the pattern for the centuries to come, must not be just power – but *Christlike* power.[17]

The conclusion is obvious, but so thrilling that it must be spelt out: Every true revival is a resurgence of the power of Christlikeness, and every genuine movement of the Holy Spirit has the power to make people like Christ. That is why the Holy Spirit could not be given fully until Jesus came, because Jesus had to reveal first just what kind of Spirit the Holy Spirit is: 'The Incarnation has to come before the Indwelling.'[18] It was Jesus, the crucified Saviour, who inaugurated Pentecost, the first full revival, and, as our definition says (Ch. 1) he inaugurates every subsequent revival. And just as Pentecost was close to the cross, there is a sense in which every revival must look back to the cross. But the crucified Lord inaugurated the age of full revivals so that the church would be empowered to fulfil its missionary

---

[17] Hughes, 'Heaven-Sent', 8 May.
[18] Hughes, 'Heaven-Sent', 10 May.

responsibility (Acts 1:8). So revival stands between the cross and the church's mission, and it is a response to the former which enables the achievement of the latter. Revival is a firestorm of the Lord Jesus Christ.

Conclusion

In this biblical overview we have had, of necessity, to omit much of relevance to this subject. But enough has been said to conclude that, far from being an unscriptural and therefore quite unnecessary experience for the church, revival is what much of the Old Testament and most of the New is all about. It is the word of God, which speaks more clearly than any other words of the absolute necessity for revival. Outside of a relationship with God, the human condition is one of death. Hence covenant renewal, or restoration of the relationship, that is, revival, is a prerequisite for life. The Bible shows that it is the sovereign God who takes the initiative in covenant renewal. This is consistent with the first clause in our definition of revival (Ch. 1) that revival is a sovereign work of God.

Further, the Old Testament prophesies, and the New Testament records, how the Messiah is the one through whom the fullest blessings of that covenant relationship are to be procured. This, too, is consistent with our definition that it is Jesus who sends the Spirit, and that it is to Jesus as Saviour that the Spirit testifies in revival, and it is the doctrines of his saving grace which the Spirit accentuates in revival. Just as it is the Messiah who is the hero of the Bible, so it is the Messiah who is the hero and the goal of every genuine revival.

It is in the Bible, too, where we learn of the promise and of the pouring out of the Spirit leading to the conviction and repentance and conversion of multitudes, which we have characterized in our definition as the 'normal activity' of the Holy Spirit. The periodic need of believers for revival is also more clearly seen in the Scriptures than anywhere else as the recurring pattern of decline and revival in God's people in both the Old and the New Testaments is described and prophesied. The model of the revived individual Christian and of the revived church congregation are both found in the New Testament and anticipated and promised in the Old.

Finally, by dwelling on the communal nature of the covenant renewal of the people of God and by insisting on the interdependence of national righteousness and personal holiness, the Bible spells out the insistence found in our definition that all genuine revivals will have as their effect the reformation of society as well as the salvation of the individual.

3

The Great Awakening and the Marks of Genuine Revival

The most celebrated of all the Lord's firestorms since Pentecost fell in the first half of the eighteenth century. The story of the Evangelical Revival in Britain, the Great Awakening in America, and the Reveille in continental Europe in the late 1730s and 1740s has been told often, and well, and with increasing detail. Far from discrediting the Great Awakening, the thrust of the best modern scholarship establishes the centrality, utility and fruitfulness of this remarkable spiritual movement. These are very significant findings. They discredit the commonest charge against religious revival, namely that it is essentially a counter-productive side-track down which the church was led by over-emotional, unstable, heterodox fanatics.

We will argue first that this, the best known of the revivals of history, was the outcome of vital orthodoxy, a proven and broad-based tradition within the church. This is an argument based on the solid foundations of the past. I will then argue that the Great Awakening produced mature and rational theological criteria for its own evaluation, namely Jonathan Edwards' five distinguishing marks of a genuine work of the Spirit of God. This argument is based on a biblical interpretation of present experience. The chapter concludes with an evaluation of the contribution of the Great Awakening to the development of the modern missionary movement, the most sustained and energetic evangelistic movement in the history of the church. This is an argument for the usefulness of revival to the church based on its future, long-term fruit. The Great Awakening, then, drew deeply on the best from the past, transformed the present and shaped the future.

It is customary for church historians[1] to begin any account of the revivals of the 1730s with a catalogue of those known as the forerunners or 'precursors'. On the Continent there were the Pietists, Spener and Francke, and the Moravians, Zinzendorf and Peter Bohler; in England, Anthony Horneck and Josiah Woodward; in Wales, Griffith Jones and Howell Harris, that aristocrat of the Spirit; in Scotland, John Balfour; in America, Solomon Stoddart, Theodorus Frelinghuysen and William Tennent.

Such an approach narrows the foundation on which we can assess the revivals, because it gives the impression that revivals were the unusual work of unusual men who were on the fringes of orthodoxy and the edge of sanity. History is the discipline of context, and this is too straitened a context on which to base our study.

Revival and the tradition of vital orthodoxy

Recent research has greatly broadened our understanding of the deeply flowing currents which came together to produce the river of revival. In particular it has shown that Edwards' theological position has a very long pedigree,[2] and that Edwards was only one of many working on these issues.[3] W.R. Ward, in the most important recent historical study on the Evangelical Revival, traces its genesis back through the Pietism of Europe and the Puritanism of Britain, to Reformation and Counter-Reformation fountains of spirituality.[4] He and others establish that the view that the Great Awakening

---

[1] For example, R.E. Davies, *I Will Pour out my Spirit: A History and Theology of Revivals and Spiritual Awakenings*, ch. 5.

[2] Charles Hambrick-Stowe, *The Practice of Piety: Puritan Devotional Disciplines in Seventeenth-Century New England*, pp. 132, 255.

[3] 'The sermons of Mather's group, and also those of the Connecticut River Valley preachers, "constituted a concerted campaign," a movement to produce revivals of religion, and when their sermons finally bore fruit in regional and then colonial harvests of souls, their professional networks provided the context for the revivals' surprisingly rapid transmission,' Michael J. Crawford, 'The Invention of the American Revival: The Beginnings of Anglo-American Religious Revivalism, 1690–1750', p. 40.

[4] W.R. Ward, *The Protestant Evangelical Awakening*.

came out of nowhere unexpectedly is a mythology that should be seriously questioned.[5] But they also question the view that revival is some sort of aberration which blossoms suddenly at a certain point in history due to unique and unrepeatable circumstances outside the mainstream of the great tradition of Christian thought and practice. As Jonathan Edwards was to argue so persuasively, true revival is in the great tradition of vital orthodoxy.

Ward contends that there are four major tributaries flowing into the river of evangelical piety which emptied into the sea of revival: Catholic mysticism, Reformation spirituality, Puritanism and Pietism. The first tributary – Catholic mysticism – we shall leave until Chapter 7, 'Revival in Anglican and Catholic Churches'. The second tributary flowing into the river of evangelical piety was Lutheran writing. It nourished the devotional movement known as Pietism as much as the intellectual movement known as scholasticism.

The third stream of influence on vital orthodoxy was Puritan devotional writing. Puritanism was a movement not only for church reform and doctrinal precision, but it was also a movement for the spiritual revival of the people of God. The Puritans understood that it is critical to vital faith to win the affections, because the affections will have their way at the last. When the chips are down, we will do what we most love to do. Said John Owen, 'affections are in the soul, as the helm is in the ship; if it be laid hold on by a skilful hand, it turneth the whole vessel which way he pleaseth'.[6] But how does one win the affections? The Puritan says, quite unequivocally, that the godly affections must be stirred and steered through the mind. And the way to the mind is through the clear teaching of God's written word.

---

[5] Crawford, *Seasons of Grace*, is a very useful study of the long road along which the pneumatology in the Great Awakening developed. See also Marilyn J. Westerkemp, *Triumph of the Laity: Scots-Irish Piety and the Great Awakening, 1625–1760*; Gerald F. Moran, 'Christian Revivalism and Culture in Early America: Puritan New England as a Case Study'; Jon Butler, 'Enthusiasm Described and Decried: The Great Awakening as Interpretative Fiction'; Jon Butler, *Awash in a Sea of Faith* (reviewed *JEH* 44.4 [Oct. 93], p. 754); Finke and Stark, *Churching*.
[6] J.I. Packer, *Among God's Giants: The Puritan Vision of the Christian Life*, p. 256.

Jonathan Edwards, the last of the Puritans and the first of the evangelicals, was not embarrassed by the direct appeal to the affections, just so long as those affections reinforced the truth and arose from the truth. Modern rational evangelicals give the emphatic thumbs down to that approach, and the modern charismatics often appeal to the emotions independent of the truth, believing that the stirred emotion is an end in itself. The Puritan balance of mind and heart needs to be recovered at this point. Truth that does not appeal to the affections is ineffective.

A fourth stream of influence on the development of vital orthodoxy was Pietism. The religious wars of the sixteenth and early seventeenth centuries had a deadening effect on the people, as did the arid dogmatizing of the disputing theological parties. Pietism was a revival after this death. Pietism relegated doctrine to a secondary position; it elevated experiential piety, personal assurance and high moral and devotional life.[7] Randall Balmer says that Pietism was essentially a renewal movement, seeking 'the infusion of spiritual ardour into religious traditions that had grown stuffy and cold',[8] while Middlekauff has demonstrated that Pietism was 'a strategy, and a well-conceived one, to produce the reformation which virtually every minister in New England had cried out for over two generations'.[9]

The creative energy and influence of Pietism is only now being given the recognition it warrants by English-speaking historians. Pietism, they now see, made a significant contribution to worship and hymnody, preaching, pastoral work, social outreach and concern, education, ecumenism (because of its emphasis on *praxis pietatis* rather than doctrine), and, above all, missions (it bequeathed to the Protestant world a new vision of a world in need of the gospel of Christ).

Having successfully navigated the four lively streams that flow into the river of vital orthodoxy, Ward is in a position to discuss with understanding the value of that river for irrigating church and

---

[7] P.C. Erb, *Pietists: Selected Writings*.

[8] Randall Balmer, 'Eschewing the "Routine of Religion": Eighteenth-Century Pietism and the Revival Tradition in America', p. 6.

[9] Robert Middlekauff, *The Mathers: Three Generations of Puritan Intellectuals, 1596–1728*, p. 306.

society. His daring, authoritative conclusion is that vital orthodoxy has been more fertile than rationalist scholastic orthodoxy, not only spiritually and evangelistically, but also intellectually and socially.

Because the vital orthodox were committed to seeking the proof that God was with them to bless, they were exceptionally open to learning about and from contemporary Christianity. They were intrigued by what God was doing all over the world and they were therefore very eager to learn about 'the leadings of God'. They were also open to the leadings of God in the individual soul. In opposition to the scholastics, they insisted that a prerequisite for sound theology was the gracious gift of the new birth. The Great Awakening, then, owed its emphasis on the seminal doctrine of conversion, the felt experience of being born again, to vital orthodoxy.

Vital orthodoxy, Ward demonstrates, had much greater mass appeal than scholastic orthodoxy and was more successful in Christianizing its age. What did Baxter, the Puritan; Spener and Francke, the Pietists; Isaac Watts, the nonconformist hymnwriter; Doddridge the nonconformist theologian; and John Wesley all have in common? They were all middlemen who mediated between the world of theological and ecclesiastical precision and the world of 'spiritual nutriment'.[10] They were able to put many of the intellectual developments of the age at the disposal of the revival.[11] The understanding of vital Christianity in terms of the affections, for example, was, in view of the philosophy of John Locke, an intellectually acceptable way of formulating Christian truth, and Wesley and Jonathan Edwards were entirely at home in that academic environment.

It is from this tradition of pietistic vital orthodoxy that the Great Awakening came. It was a great tradition, both in breadth and depth. The following summary of the substantial contributions of vital orthodoxy to the expansion of the church and to predisposing it to revival lays the foundation for a consideration of the marks of genuine revival. The chief lessons are that the Christian faith will only be infectious on a large scale when it:

- Communicates a sense of the divine presence.
- Fosters an interest in the leadings of God in the present world.

---

[10] Ward, *Protestant*, p. 49.
[11] Ward, *Protestant*, p. 11.

- Gives greater recognition to the role of the emotions in worship and life. Truth that does not appeal to the affections is ineffective.
- Encourages the enterprise of advancing the evangelical gospel in the academic and intellectual paradigms of the present age.

The marks of genuine revival

The next argument in defence of the theological and psychological validity of the Great Awakening is that it was itself capable of producing theological reflection of lasting value to the church. In particular, it resulted in a rational and useful instrument for the evaluation of purportedly spiritual movements, namely Jonathan Edwards' five 'distinguishing marks'. We have defined revival as an intensification of the normal activity of the Holy Spirit. What is the normal work of the Holy Spirit? Edwards returned to that issue time and again, and in the process he wrote a number of very important studies of revival, including *A Faithful Narrative of the Surprising Work of God in the Conversion of Many Hundred Souls in Northampton* (1736); *The Distinguishing Marks of a Work of the Spirit of God* (1741); *Some Thoughts Concerning the Present Revival of Religion in New England* (1742); and *The Religious Affections* (1746).

Edwards wrote these books to refute those who argued that the Great Awakening was not a genuine work of the Holy Spirit. The year after the Great Awakening began in Massachusetts he wrote *The Distinguishing Marks of a Work of the Spirit of God*.[12] The text on the title page, John 10:4,5, testifies to the pre-eminence of Christ in revival: 'And the Sheep follow him: for they know his voice; and a Stranger will they not follow, but will flee from him: for they know not the Voice of Strangers.' It is the word of Christ that brings revival. But the five critical tests of genuine revival are based on the exegesis of 1 John 4, and he begins the study by citing verse 1: 'Beloved, believe not every spirit, but try the spirits whether they are of God; because many false prophets are gone out into the world.'

---

[12] The best text is found in Edwards, *Great Awakening*, pp. 213–88.

The first part of the *Distinguishing Marks* is devoted to disarming the critics of the Great Awakening who argued that, because of all the strange phenomena that accompanied the revival, it could not have been a genuine work of the Holy Spirit. Edwards insisted that all these strange, even unprecedented, phenomena – the intensity of feeling and conviction; effects on the bodies of converts, including 'the failing of bodily strength';[13] the fact that they may become very noisy; that human means have been used to produce emotional states; the fact that some are guilty of imprudent conduct, or are judgmental or hypocritical; that some of the converts are deluded or later fall into scandal – all such phenomena 'are not evidences that a work that is wrought among a people is not a work of the Spirit of God'.[14] Throughout this section, Edwards lists a vast number of untoward practices by the first Christians as reported in the New Testament to establish that there never has been a revival free of undesirable elements, and there never will be this side of eternity.

This section does reveal where Edwards' sympathies lie. He was actually quite intolerant of the opposition to the Awakening, suspecting that the hyper-caution of those who stood aside and questioned whether it was of God raised serious doubts about their own Christian experience. Those who wanted to wait until the whole movement was cleared of all imperfections were as foolish as a person who stands on a riverbank and waits for all the water to pass.

In all this Edwards becomes quite difficult to follow, but it's fun to work through it. Objectively, he is arguing that these phenomena prove nothing either way: he is treating as he says in his difficult prose 'what are not signs that we are to judge of a work by, whether it be the work of a Spirit of God or no'.[15] But subjectively, he is far more interested in establishing that these things do not prove that God is not in this movement than he is in establishing that they do not prove that God is in it. Have you got that? Go over it again until you have! Edwards is interested in showing 'especially, what are no evidences that a work that is wrought amongst a people, is not the work of the Spirit of God'.[16] Those who have been eager to use Jonathan Edwards

[13] Edwards, *Great Awakening*, p. 230.
[14] Edwards, *Great Awakening*, p. 248.
[15] Edwards, *Great Awakening*, p. 228.
[16] Edwards, *Great Awakening*, p. 228.

to attack the 'Toronto Blessing' have not always understood Edwards' main thrust here.[17] He would say of all the wildest manifestations reported in the Toronto Blessing and more, 'they do not prove that God is not in this movement'. He would be far more interested in making that point than in making the equally undeniable point that these manifestations do not prove that God is in it. Edwards was far more worried by those who were in danger of quenching the Spirit than by those who unwisely refrained from testing the spirits.

In the second part of the study Edwards gives the marks, or signs or tests, which do prove something, namely that the Great Awakening was undoubtedly from the Spirit of God. The five marks or conclusive proofs that he gives are really five aspects of the normal work of the Holy Spirit. We may be confident that a revival is a genuine work of the Holy Spirit if it:

1. Raises our esteem for Jesus as Son of God and Saviour of the world.
2. Leads us to turn from our corruptions and lusts towards the righteousness of God.
3. Raises our esteem for the Bible.
4. Establishes our minds in the great, central truths of the gospel.
5. Increases our love for God and humankind.

And genuine revival will have not just one but all five of these distinguishing marks. Let us look at each in turn.

The first conclusive proof of the genuineness of a revival is that Jesus is glorified as Saviour and honoured and obeyed as Lord (1 Jn. 4:2,3)

John Blacket, a Uniting Church missionary to the Aboriginal people in central Australia, has written a marvellous account of the amazing phenomena which have accompanied the revival among Aboriginal people since 1979.[18] To his surprise, he found that the

---

[17] The inclusion of Gary Benfold's article 'Jonathan Edwards and the "Toronto Blessing"' in *Briefing* 152, 7 March 1995, seems to be based on this misunderstanding.

[18] John Blacket, *Fire in the Outback*.

Aboriginal people do not appear to think of these amazing, supernatural events as the work of the Holy Spirit so much as the work of Jesus himself.

On at least two occasions during the Aboriginal revival there was a manifestation of that phenomenon sometimes described as 'slaying in the Spirit'. But one leader said he did not like the term: he preferred 'resting in Jesus'.[19] Jesus is very real to them. He is the hero of the revival. It is Jesus who will end injustice and put history right. Visions of Christ were the most commonly reported of all the visions in a revival characterized by many visions – perhaps because they have a visual rather than a verbal culture.[20]

Aboriginal Christians thus affirm that it is Christ himself, rather than a phenomenon called revival, who is liberating them from a world which had been death to them. It is Jesus who is giving them a new life. Revival is his firestorm. The first distinguishing mark of real revival, then, is that the Lord Jesus is exalted.

The second conclusive proof of genuine revival is that it leads us to turn from our corruptions and lusts towards the righteousness of God (1 Jn. 4:4,5)

It is Satan who encourages and establishes sin, and it is the world that cherishes sin. Therefore every genuine revival is a revival of holiness, as cherished sins are resisted and cast aside. Every genuine revival enables us to see reality, which is God's perspective on the world. And the reality is that our God is holy and he will have a holy people.

Revival came to Thornleigh Anglican Church, Sydney, Australia, in 1962 at a teaching mission taken by the Revd Geoff Bingham, who had just returned from Pakistan where he had witnessed amazing scenes of revival. A prayer meeting for the mission, with about thirty people, was held in the home of Fred George, a returned missionary from Tanzania. Geoff Bingham read from Psalm 24, 'Who shall ascend to the hill of the Lord? He who has clean hands and a pure heart.' And then he suggested that those present should

---

[19] Blacket, *Fire*, p. 211.
[20] John Harris, *One Blood: 200 Years of Aboriginal Encounter with Christianity: A Story of Hope*, facing page 783 and p. 850.

come to the Lord and ask him to reveal himself to them. They all knelt down in a circle, and then someone began to weep, and a great conviction came over all of them. Some tried to pray but dissolved in sobs. And then there came over one present, John Dunn, an incredible sense of his own depravity in the sight of God. He saw something extraordinary. It was as if he were standing outside himself, looking at himself. And he wanted to flee from himself as fast and as far as he could because of the horrific sight he had of his own sin. He was crushed and he broke down and sobbed convulsively, and the others around him were prostrate on the floor, broken-hearted. Then a gentle quietness came over the whole group, and then a wonderful sense of God's total forgiveness. Then they sang and sang until they were hoarse. The singing and intercession just went on and on, until someone said, 'It's half past four in the morning.' Everyone was astonished that so much time had elapsed.

In genuine revival the Spirit convicts of cherished and secret and unacknowledged sins. We see God in his holiness and repent with tears.

The third conclusive proof of genuine revival is that it raises our esteem for the Bible (1 Jn. 4:6)

The Bible is the record of the truth that comes from God. Satan has always raged against and hated this holy book, says Edwards. Through many ages he has experienced its power to defeat his purposes and baffle his designs. It is the main weapon that the saints use in their war with Satan. Revelation 12:11 says, 'They overcame him by the *word* of their testimony.' It is the sword of the Spirit which pierces him and conquers him (Eph. 6:12). Every text of the Bible is a dart to torment and sting the old enemy. He hates every word of it.

Iain Murray put Edwards' third test this way:

> God works in accordance with his Word. Without Scripture there is no 'sword of the Spirit'. The test whether experience is of the Spirit of God or of 'another spirit' is whether or not it brings greater understanding of the Bible and a closer obedience to it.[21]

---

[21] Iain H. Murray, *Revival and Revivalism: The Making and Marring of American Evangelicalism, 1750–1858.*

One who had a positive experience in the Toronto Blessing testifies to her new appreciation of the Scriptures: 'This outpouring has somehow made the Word real in my heart and mind; it's alive and fleshly for the first time ever. The Bible now seems to me to be an autobiography of my closest friend and passionate lover so I want to read more and more to know him more and more.'[22]

The fourth conclusive proof of genuine revival is that it establishes our minds in the objective truths of the gospel (1 Jn. 4:6)

It is so important for ministers to have the confidence that what they are saying is from the Lord, that their message is from God, when they preach. In 1987, I was given the opportunity to preach a series of three sermons on revival at my own church. Led by God, I determined to preach not *about* revival, but *for* revival. But I didn't really know how to do this. I recalled that the first sermon Jonathan Edwards preached at Northampton, Massachusetts, in 1734, when revival broke out in that town, was on justification by faith alone. Edwards explained that:

> justifying faith . . . is that by which the soul, which before was separate and alienated from Christ, unites itself to him . . . it is that by which the soul comes to Christ, and receives him.[23]

The soul's unity with the *crucified* Saviour – that, I concluded, is at the heart of the revival message. The word of the cross, I realized, is the gospel. And this gospel is the power of God (Rom. 1:16).

So, I preached first on Christ's cross – its answer to our guilt, hurts and pain. Some claimed that they were helped by this sermon. Then I preached on the cross as the answer to our sleepiness and deadness (Eph. 5:14). The temperature was decidedly higher. A few wept. Finally, I preached on the cross as the power over our enemies: sin and guilt, Satan and the powers of darkness, and the flesh or the world. The emotion did not seem to be high, nor the sermon particularly well delivered as I had barely finished writing it before I

---

[22] Greg Beech, 'The Outpouring of the Holy Spirit at Randwick Baptist Church, 6 November 1994'.
[23] Edwards, *Works*, I, 1974, pp. 625f.

preached it. But the theology was right. For the first time in my life, I really felt that the theology was right. This gospel of the cross was the wisdom and the power of God.

So I made an appeal. Ten people responded. When I asked them what they understood they had done, most replied, and some with tears, that they had seen their sin and were now trusting Christ to give them release from its penalty and therefore some hope of winning occasional victories over its power. The guarantee of forgiveness robs Satan of his power to accuse us.

Later that week I received a letter from one member of the congregation who reported thus on her reaction to the preaching:

> As I arrived home I knew that I was going to cry. It was unlike any urge to cry that I had ever experienced, it was an irrepressible urge. I stepped through the front door and the tears started, they continued for over an hour. Then an amazing thing happened! For the first time since I've been a Christian (7 years) I got down on my knees and I prayed, confessed and wept before my Lord and Master.
>
> . . . My tears continued to fall as one by one I confessed hurts, jealousy, pride, anger, bitterness. People who had hurt me appeared in my mind and I would confess, then another, then another, then another. As I confessed, the crying got more violent and I felt more and more humbled.
>
> Then your sermon would flash in my mind and I began to cry again as I was humbled once more at the words the Lord had spoken through you.
>
> I felt for the first time that the Lord was speaking to me and working through his Holy Spirit in my life. I had desired it for a long time but the Lord had to break me first. He did it in such a loving, tender way. Oh how I love my Lord Jesus now and desire His Holy Spirit to be at work in me.
>
> The experience has changed my attitude to a lot of things including my ministry, my marriage and my worship . . .

Revival preaching must come from God's word, the Bible. And it must come from God's gospel: the cross of Christ. Revival establishes our minds in the great, central truths of the gospel.

The fifth conclusive proof of genuine revival is that it increases our love for God and humankind (1 Jn. 4:7–15)

This is the most excellent way in which the Holy Spirit leads the sons and daughters of God. Superior to special gifts, it is the way of God by which he imparts his true nature to his people, a nature that will last for eternity. It is this divine love which constrains us to deal with needy brothers and sisters, giving them what they really need rather than what we imagine they need.

William McLeod, in whose church in Saskatoon, Canada, a remarkable revival began in 1971, testifies that love was the principal characteristic of that revival. This love led to forgiveness and the healing of broken relationships, with many ministers reporting the reconciliation between them and their co-workers in churches where relationships had been strained. 'In all kinds of human relationships,' McLeod said, 'the sand has been removed from the works. Love has become the basis upon which all questions are settled.'[24]

Edwards makes the important observation that these five evidences are not things that are the characteristics of any work in which Satan is involved. He never does them, because he cannot. He does not have the power to do them. And if he could, he would not. Satan would not confirm men and women in a belief that Jesus is the Son of God and the Saviour of sinners. Satan would not lead us to see our wretched state because of our sin and our need for a Saviour. Satan would not convince us that the Scriptures contain all that is necessary to salvation. Satan would not establish our minds in the great, central truths of the gospel. Satan would not fill us with love for God and the rest of humankind.

Some might object that surely Edwards' list is not complete. Surely there is yet another normal work of the Holy Spirit. Surely he gives gifts to his people. Won't revival be characterized by remarkable manifestations of the gifts of the Spirit? This is a big issue, but we shall postpone discussion of it until Chapter 5, 'Revival and the Charismatic Movement'. My conclusion, to anticipate, is that spiritual gifts are commonly in evidence in revivals, but that they are not of the essence of revival since they do not have to be always present as do Edwards' five evidences. The essence of revival is the fruit of

---

[24] Kurt E. Koch, *Revival Fires in Canada*, p. 32.

the Spirit, which Satan never imitates as we have just seen, and which is different from the gifts of the Spirit that Satan can and does imitate.

Rather than add to the essential evidences of revival, Edwards actually condensed them. Five years after writing the *Distinguishing Marks* Edwards wrote what many regard as his greatest work on true spiritual religion, the *Religious Affections*. The excitement over the manifestations of the Great Awakening had subsided. Here Edwards considers how we can identify with confidence the work of the Spirit in our own lives, whether in a time of revival or elsewhere. He boils it all down to three essential tests:

1. Is the joy we have in our hearts the result of our wonder at the excellence of the work and person of Christ? (The primacy of the gospel.)
2. Are our convictions consistent with Scripture? (The primacy of the Bible.)
3. Is the profession of our faith finding expression in consistent Christian behaviour? (The test of tests is our Christian practice.)

Edwards' tests of a work of the Spirit of God – first the distinguishing five and then the essential three – are a scriptural, simple, workable and so far unrefuted guide to the church in the increasingly common task of evaluating religious movements which lay claim to divine inspiration. Not the least of the blessings of the Great Awakening is that it produced such an instrument for the guidance of the church that is at once so rational and so scriptural. Edwards himself embodied this fruit to such ripeness that his thought is itself one of the surest indications that revival is among the greatest of Christ's blessings.

Revival and the development of the modern missionary movement

Our third and final argument against the view that revival is an emotional counter-productive side-track for the church is that it resulted in the most energetic and sustained evangelistic enterprise in the history of the world, namely the modern missionary movement. At first sight this looks like an unlikely argument: fifty years separate the Great Awakening from the birth of modern Protestant missions in 1792 by William Carey, 'the father of missions'. But the gap should not obscure the very strong – I contend essential – links between the two. I want to suggest that:

- Modern Protestant missions were born of revival, specifically the Great Awakening of the 1740s.
- Modern Protestant missions developed their theology and strategy from the experience of revival.
- The revival theology of Jonathan Edwards had a formative impact on Protestant missions.

Missions born of revival

That the gospel is the power of God for all humankind was learned in practice and not just in theory through the experience of revival when, especially in North America, Blacks and Indians were converted as well as Whites, slaves as well as free, children as well as adults.

God clearly loved to work through slaves. That was already known from Paul's letters, but it was seen in practice as Black slaves were converted in the Great Awakening along with their masters. Some of them even did a pretty good imitation of the chief human instrument of that revival, George Whitefield himself. One of the most 'entertaining' of such stories came from Boston.

A 'gentlemen being a great hater of religion' thought he heard Whitefield preaching in his own home in the very room next to him. He eventually plucked up sufficient courage to investigate and, on opening the door, found one of his Negro slaves doing a very good imitation of Whitefield. The next day he invited some friends for dinner. Pipes, tobacco, glasses and bottles were brought in, as was the Negro, to entertain them.

He prayed using the very phrases of Mr Whitefield and then preached, reducing his congregation to hysterical laughter. 'I am now come to my exhortation,' he said, 'and to you my master after the flesh: But know I have a master even Jesus Christ my Saviour, who has said that a man cannot serve two masters. Therefore I claim Jesus Christ to be my right master. You know, Master, you have been given to cursing and swearing and blaspheming God's holy name, you have been given to be drunken, a whoremonger, covetous, a liar, a cheat etc. But know that God has pronounced a Woe against all such, and has said that such shall never enter the Kingdom of God. And now to conclude . . . except you all repent you shall like-wise perish.'

'The negroe spoke with such authority,' the account continued, 'that struck the gentlemen to the heart. They laid down their pipes, never drank a glass of wine, but departed every man to his own house: and are now pious sober men; but before were wicked profane persons. Such is the work of God by the hands of poor negroes.'[25]

The frequently reported experience of Christ's making 'freemen of the poor slaves in their bondage' and of genuine revival among Indians (best reported in the most famous missionary diary of the eighteenth century, that of David Brainerd), must have reinforced the evangelicals' conviction that the gospel was divinely designed for the renovation of all, a conviction of considerable missionary significance.

Missionary theology and strategy developed from the experience of revival

For the eighteenth-century evangelical the great evidence of divine activity was conversion, not miracles. Jonathan Edwards, in his extremely influential *Faithful Narrative of the Surprising Work of God in the Conversion of Many Hundred Souls in Northampton* (1736), set out the morphology or pattern of evangelical conversion. Hencefor-ward, those who mixed in evangelical circles would expect to be converted in that way, especially in seasons of revival. This under-standing of conversion was reinforced by the revival chronicles, or magazines, which contained reports of hundreds of conversions. For example, the *Christian Monthly History* and the *Faithful Narrative of the Extraordinary Work of the Spirit of God at Kilsyth*[26], both of which were edited by James Robe of Kilsyth in Scotland, report scores of

---

[25] *Weekly History* 28, 17 October 1741.
[26] Published Edinburgh, Glasgow, and London 1742, Glasgow 1790 and 1840. The 1840 edition is entitled *Narrative of the Revival at Kilsyth*.

conversions in minute detail. Such reports reinforce the pattern of
conversion experience delineated by Edwards, and they left
evangelicals in no doubt that conversions were the chief end of
awakenings. It was therefore inevitable that the primary aim of the
missionary movement as it took shape in the womb of revival was to
make converts.

The revival magazines, while mostly devoted to reporting on
contemporary revivals, also devoted a significant and increasing
amount of space to missions to the heathen. In the *Christian Monthly
History*, for example, we find accounts of the Danish mission to
Tranquebar in India in 1739; of the baptism of some Negroes on the
American Island of St Thomas by Moravian Brethren; and of the
rise of the Scottish Society for Promoting Christian Knowledge and
the correspondence of its missionaries to the American Indians.
Robe's stated aim was threefold: to preserve records of this significant work of God's Spirit which otherwise would be lost; to defend
the validity of the revival; and to encourage Christians to support
the new missionary movement.

Here we observe, close to conception, the evangelical commitment to missions as interest in revivals at home and abroad was
quickened into zeal for the propagation of the gospel throughout
the whole world by more institutionalized means. The finest and
most permanent institutionalization of historic evangelicalism is the
missionary movement. The evangelical revival magazines of the
1740s were destined to pass away with the cessation of revival, but
they would be replaced within half a century by the missionary
magazine.

The revival theology of Jonathan Edwards and its impact on Protestant missions

Edwards himself made a multifaceted contribution to the birth and
nurturing of overseas missions. In 1739, the year before the Great
Awakening came to New England, he gave a series of sermons
which were published posthumously in Scotland in 1774 under
the title *The History of the Work of Redemption*. Missions to the
heathen are therein depicted as part of God's grand design for the
accomplishment of redemption throughout the whole world.

In 1747 Edwards wrote *A Humble Attempt to Promote Explicit Agreement and Visible Union of God's people in Extraordinary Prayer for the Revival of Religion and the Advancement of Christ's Kingdom on Earth*. It is a study of the relationship between revival, prayer and missions. Edwards here proposes that Christians commit themselves to pray monthly for seven years for the worldwide extension of the kingdom. In 1789 John Sutcliff, a British Baptist, wrote a preface to a new edition of the *Humble Attempt*. This caught the attention of those who later founded, in 1792 and 1795 respectively, the Baptist Missionary Society and London Missionary Society.

Then, in 1749, Edwards published the journals of David Brainerd, missionary to the American Indians – the first missionary biography ever published. It was an apologetic for the revival and, to a lesser extent, for missions which were questioned by the settlers. This missionary biography shows by way of example what the power of godliness and 'vital religion' truly is. The Christian life is God-centred living. It means giving reverence to all the commands of God, and it is 'not rapture but habit'. The Christian has an experience of God which is 'of an increasing nature' even when 'a general deadness returned' in the land. The motivation is to be 'conformity to God', not a longing for experiences as such. The concluding 'Reflections and Observations' on Brainerd are said by Iain Murray to be possibly the most important descriptive pages on the Christian life which Edwards ever wrote.[27]

Edwards does not mention Brainerd in *The Nature of True Virtue* (1755, published posthumously in 1765), but Brainerd is certainly the model of the true saint in this work. Here Edwards identifies true sainthood with total commitment to making the condition of humankind as 'excellent' or 'beautiful' as God had intended. Brainerd was willing to abandon all comfort for the sake of redeeming society. It was Brainerd's benevolence to being in general, not his benevolence to the Indians, which finally mattered. For the mission to the Indians was merely an example of what could be done on a larger scale for all of God's people, all over the world.

Evangelism and mission have become the most honoured of evangelical commitments. It is worth recalling what this

---

[27] Iain H. Murray, *Jonathan Edwards: A New Biography*, p. 308.

commitment to missions, which has done so much for the conversion of the world, owes to the world-conquering visions emanating from revival. The large number of conversions that occurred in the Great Awakening gave evangelicals the confidence that such expansion could happen all over the world, among people of all races. The revival magazines contained missionary intelligence, a feature that led eventually to the development of the missionary magazine. Jonathan Edwards, the church's leading theologian of revival, was also the main architect of both modern missionary ideology and the spiritual vitality essential to the successful prosecution of missions. He saw that missions were integral to God's plan of redemption; that the expansion of the church was a sign of the eschatological last days; he fostered prayer for revival and the spread of the gospel; and he showed that missions would be the work of saints such as David Brainerd, who cared naught for his own comfort.

Conclusion

The Great Awakening, then, is best understood not as an emotional and counter-productive side-track for the church, but 1) as the apogee of the rich tradition of vital orthodoxy, 2) as the source of some of the church's most treasured reflections on the nature of true Christianity, and 3) as the foundation of the modern Protestant missionary movement. It was a revival that shaped American culture, energized great social reforms in Europe and Britain, forged evangelicalism as a major movement within the church, and was to become institutionalized in overseas missions. It was evidently one of the most powerful of the Lord's firestorms, and when it passed over it left the church stronger and the world a better place.

4

Revival and Revivalism in the Nineteenth and Twentieth Centuries

The numbers of revivals and of people transformed by them have multiplied amazingly in the last two centuries. Far from being impervious to revival, twentieth-century men and women have probably been more open to revival than any previous generation. This century has witnessed the greatest growth ever in the Christian church, and revival in Africa, Asia and South America is endemic. The present revival in China may be the greatest religious awakening yet in the history of revivals.[1] Neither has Eastern Europe been exempt. In recent years there have been astonishing mass movements into the Christian church in places formerly ruled by Communist regimes.

The most conspicuous features of revivals in the west today are associated with the charismatic movement. We shall explore that association in the next chapter. In this chapter we will identify the main developments in the revival tradition since the Great Awakening and distil something of what we might learn from them. For the purpose of analysis within this vast field, we shall divide these developments into four periods. First, in the half-century or so after the death of John Wesley (1791), revivals were experienced most frequently among Methodist churches. Second, the century from 1850 to 1950 was the age of 'revivalism', a human methodology of revival that is usually attributed to the 'new measures' of Charles Finney (1792–1875). Third, overlapping the age of revivalism, from the beginning of the twentieth century, highly significant revivals broke

---

[1] See Tony Lambert, *The Resurrection of the Chinese Church.*

out in places in which Protestant missionaries had a significant presence: India, China, Korea and Africa. Finally, since the end of the Second World War revivals have broken out among peoples who are attempting to establish their own national identity following the departure of the colonial powers, or among those marginalized, minority peoples struggling to survive the onslaught on their own cultures of western materialism and secularism.

From the association of revival with Methodism and revivalism we could conclude that revivals came where they were expected and longed for and made the subject of earnest prayer. In our definition of revival (Ch. 1), we observed that two common pre-revival characteristics are heightened expectation and extraordinary prayerfulness. From the prevalence of revival in developing nations and among the marginalized, we could conclude that revivals came where they were needed. Either way, revivals are evidence of the love and mercy of the sovereign Lord who answers heartfelt prayer and meets the desperate needs of whole communities as well as individuals.

Methodism and revivals

To evangelicals, especially in the Wesleyan Methodist tradition, revival is the 'engine of history' and scriptural holiness is 'the leaven of history'.[2] For much of the nineteenth century in England, the USA, Canada, New Zealand and Australia, revivals were experienced most commonly in the Methodist denomination.[3] In Australian Methodism, for example, revival in the nineteenth century is mainly associated with John Watsford, the first Australian-born Methodist clergyman. Strong emotion accompanied Watsford's ministry wherever he proclaimed his Wesleyan message of entire sanctification and the duty of evangelism. In the city of Sydney and its suburbs, and in the country towns of NSW, Watsford was used to ignite the fires of revival. Of a service in the Bourke Street Methodist Church, Sydney, in 1860, Watsford reported:

---

[2] J.D. Bollen, *Religion in Australian Society*, p. 43.
[3] Don Wright, *Mantle of Christ: A History of the Central Methodist Mission*, p. 45; Robert Evans and Roy McKenzie, *Evangelical Revivals in New Zealand*.

To a congregation which packed the building I preached from 'Quench not the Spirit'. What a time we had. The whole assembly was mightily moved, the power was overwhelming; many fell to the floor in agony, and there was a loud cry for mercy. The police came rushing in to see what was the matter; but there was nothing for them to do. It was impossible to tell how many penitents came forward; there must have been over two hundred. The large schoolroom was completely filled with anxious inquirers.[4]

Local revivals were relatively common in nineteenth-century Australia,[5] and, consistent with our definition, they had an impact on the wider community. In Australia they were one of the most powerful means by which a godless, convict society was transformed into a God-fearing, Sabbath-observing, church-going community.

What was it about nineteenth-century Methodism that so fostered revival? David Hempton has argued that Methodism was well calculated for advance by its combination of evangelistic innovation, discipline, urgency, central direction and local participation.[6] Arnold Hunt, historian of Australian Methodism, argues that the Methodists came closest to revival because they were the denomination most confident that the church of Christ must grow and that God was at work in their movement. He lists four characteristics of Methodism which predisposed it to revival:

- They were a successful missionary organization.
- They had a message which they believed was pure gospel.
- They were a spiritual rather than a bureaucratic or liturgical movement.
- They were a warm fellowship in which laity as well as clergy were expected to evangelize.

---

[4] John Watsford, *Glorious Gospel Triumphs*, p. 123.

[5] See Stuart Piggin, *Evangelical Christianity in Australia: Spirit, Word and World*, pp. 41, 62.

[6] David Hempton, *Methodism and Politics in British Society, 1750–1850*, p. 76; Robert Currie, Alan Gilbert and Lee Horsley, *Churches and Church-Goers: Patterns of Church Growth in the British Isles since 1700*, pp. 56, 90.

Hunt's last point raises an interesting issue. In nineteenth-century Methodism, evangelistic rallies and campaigns commonly followed, and did not precede, outpourings of the Holy Spirit.[7] That guaranteed the success of evangelistic enterprise. All those interested in evangelism should ponder the significance of that fact and make prayer for revival an integral part of any evangelistic campaign. It would be wrong, however, to make revival a precondition of evangelism. Revival, an extraordinary manifestation of the normal work of the Holy Spirit, is never to be taken as normative for the life and labour of ministers of the gospel, without which they feel they can do nothing.[8]

It is also significant that Methodist revivals most commonly broke out in normal services of worship or in prayer meetings. They resulted from an emphasis on believing prayer and fasting not found in our churches today. Church membership was then prized as a privilege and discipline was exercised in the maintenance of its purity: there was trial membership in the Methodist Church. Sin was taken seriously, and the gospel preacher believed the whole Bible and preached the whole gospel. He sought to bring his hearers under the conviction of sin. Then he let the Holy Spirit deal with the sinner. He did not seek to terminate quickly this period of conviction, for that would short-circuit the cleansing work of the Holy Spirit and leave the sinner relieved but unsaved. In all this, Methodism looked back to the experience of its founder rather than forwards to the techniques of the revivalists.

Revivalism

'Revivalism', or human techniques and programmes designed to foster revival, is usually traced to Charles Finney's 'new measures' which he developed out of his own amazing experience and success in the so-called 'Second Great Awakening' in New York State from

---

[7] J.E. Orr, 'Evangelical Revival in Australia in the Mid-nineteenth Century', p. 2; *Wesleyan Magazine*, 1858, p. 468, letter of the Revd Isaac Harding, 15 February; Iain Murray, 'Lessons from Australia's Evangelical Heritage'.

[8] Murray, *Revival*, pp. 384f.

1789 to 1830. His new measures, the theological significance of which will be analyzed in Chapter 8, reflect the moderation of Calvinism in the direction of Arminianism, with its emphasis on human responsibility. After Finney, revivals were no longer quite such 'surprising works of God'.

Yet in Finney's autobiography are reports of the most astonishingly powerful and frequent experiences of God's Spirit, beginning with his conversion in 1821:

> I received a mighty baptism of the Holy Ghost . . . without any recollection that I had ever heard the thing mentioned by any person in the world, at a moment entirely unexpected by me, the Holy Spirit descended upon me in a manner that seemed to go through me body and soul.[9]

So common are the incidents of prevailing prayer and sinners falling under powerful conviction as he preached that his biography is fairly described as 'perhaps the most remarkable account of manifestations of the Holy Spirit's power since apostolic days'.[10] It is, therefore, significant that these 'manifestations' are far more frequently dramatic expressions of the Holy Spirit's normal activity of convicting and converting than they are of the remarkable 'manifestations' of a kind associated with movements such as the Toronto Blessing.

Just as Finney's success was truly astonishing – his converts must be numbered in the hundreds of thousands – so the achievements of the revivalism which he pioneered were by no means negligible. The 1859 Prayer Revival in America, which should be understood partly as an outworking of Finney's ministry, spread to Britain and Ireland and harvested a million souls. Foundational to its phenomenal success in Ulster were three great truths: 'The Sovereignty of the Holy Spirit, the Sufficiency of the Holy Scripture, and the Secret of the Holy Supplication'.[11] Revivalism fostered the sad habit of developing such slogans whose very correctness became a substitute for the reality. The 1859 revivals were followed by the revivalist campaigns of Moody and Sankey and by the influential holiness

---

[9] Charles G. Finney, *The Memoirs of Charles G. Finney*, p. 23.
[10] James G. Lawson, *Deeper Experiences of Famous Christians*, p. 243.
[11] Ian R.K. Paisley, *The 'Fifty-Nine' Revival*, p. 17.

movements emanating from Mildmay and Keswick in Britain. Dwight L. Moody (1837–99), characterized by J. Edwin Orr as 'the greatest of world evangelists',[12] conducted campaigns in London in 1875 and in Cambridge in 1882 at which the churches were greatly encouraged by an unprecedented response to the preaching of the gospel. It is estimated that Moody travelled more than a million miles and preached to more than a million people on his evangelistic campaigns.

The spiritual floodtide created by the energies of revivalism was soon to lap the shores of the British Empire. Australia, along with other English-speaking countries, was considered favourable soil for evangelistic and revivalistic experiments, and many of international evangelicalism's most celebrated evangelists visited Australasia. Most of these evangelists drank deeply at the wells of revivalism: William 'California' Taylor, Henry Varley, Dr A.N. Somerville of Glasgow, John MacNeil, Thomas Spurgeon, Dr Harry Guinness, George Müller, Hudson Taylor, Henry Drummond, Francis E. Clark, the founder of Christian Endeavour, Thomas Cook, Gypsy Smith, John R. Mott and the Revd Charles H. Yatman from New York, T. Champness and R.A. Torrey. Among the most successful was George Grubb, a 'rip-roaring wild Irishman'. Under their ministries the showers of blessing fell on the parched land, and evangelical institutions were established as channels for the effective irrigation of the new growth.

There was a problem. The gospel according to Moody was less exacting than that of Edwards and Wesley, and preaching was made more palatable: more entertaining and simpler. Strongly reasoned, doctrinal sermons and catechizing all but disappeared.[13] Iain Murray, in his sustained critique of revivalism,[14] contends that in the first half of the nineteenth century evangelism became a means of filling declining churches instead of a necessity in itself. Evangelistic preaching oversimplified the gospel so it could be understood by the increasingly uncatechized masses. As theology became simpler, technique became more critical, and pragmatism more highly

---

[12] J.E. Orr, *Evangelical Awakenings in the South Seas*, p. 44.
[13] Robert Evans, 'Collecting for Revival: Library Resources Relating to the Study of Revival', pp. 58–74.
[14] Murray, *Revival*.

valued. The emphasis on powerful and sudden conversion gave way to nurturing faith through education. Too much trust was placed in human organization, in 'charismatic' preachers, and in mechanical means of procuring converts. Christians adjusted to the absence of God's power and presence and learned to live without them. In due course, the study of the Puritans and of revivals fell out of the curriculum of theological colleges, particularly as the manipulations notorious in revivalism brought all talk of revival into disrepute.

Revivalism has been described as 'an Americanisation of revival'.[15] This is seen clearly in the music of revivalism. From the 1870s, evangelical Christians worldwide sang more American revival songs and listened to singing American evangelists. Most popular were Ira D. Sankey and Charles Alexander. Sankey's *Sacred Songs and Solos* sold 80 million copies worldwide by 1900, and the study of its songs is therefore a rewarding way to analyze the theology of revivalism. It was a gentle, sentimental theology, far from the hellfire preaching of earlier revivalists. There is great stress on the power of human choice: to choose salvation, and to choose blessing. A robust biblical theology of the kingdom of God is wanting, but the imagery of the songs is consistently biblical.

If the theological developments associated with revivalism were regrettable, they are understandable enough. Here is a theology sensitive to the emotional stresses of common folk in a difficult world. In their desire to simplify the gospel as much as possible, revivalists were motivated by a praiseworthy desire to bring to faith those, especially in the working class, among whom the churches had a dismal record. A prominent feature of capitalist society in the age of revivalism was industrial warfare. Strikes and lockouts caused bitterness that could last for decades. Revivals – some associated with the revivalists, some not – seem to have averted such wars occasionally or brought healing after them. The 1904 Welsh revival, for example, brought healing to communities embittered and fractured by industrial strife.[16]

In the Depression years there were more such dramatic stories to tell. In 1929, the NSW coalfields had been the subject of first a coal

[15] W.W. Sweet, quoted in Bollen, *Religion*, p. 24.
[16] Eifion Evans, *The Welsh Revival of 1904*, p. 110.

miners' strike and then a lockout by the management. Conditions were desperate: miners and their families were living on rabbits; the Communist leaders of the Miners' Union stirred up the miners to use direct action to promote the rule of the proletariat. The commanding officer of the 35th Infantry Battalion contemplated calling out the militia.

In the midst of this anxiety, the Protestant churches of Cessnock (Baptist, Methodist, Presbyterian, Salvation Army) promoted an evangelistic campaign with J.B. Van Eyk and Albert Banton as evangelists. The meetings were phenomenally successful, with hundreds converted. Many of the 'red' activists were converted and revealed their caches of explosives stored in readiness for the insurrection. The loss of so many men from supporting the cause defused the situation and deprived the unions of so many Communists that they never recovered their influence. It is the opinion of the son of the commanding officer at the time that this revival may have saved Australia from bloody revolution.[17]

Van Eyk and Banton were professional Pentecostal revivalists. No one could pin that label on Martyn Lloyd-Jones. Yet revival came to his church at Aberarvon in South Wales during the Depression. Church membership climbed from 80 to over five hundred, and this revival, too, appears to have saved the impoverished and disaffected miners from going over to Communism. The Communist Party's local official was among those converted, and he joined Martyn Lloyd-Jones' congregation.[18] Community impact such as this is a feature of every genuine revival.

Revivals in India, China, Korea and Africa

Revivals in India, China, Korea and Africa in the first decade of the twentieth century were part of what J. Edwin Orr has called the 'fifth great awakening'. He characterizes it as:

. . . the most extensive Evangelical Awakening of all time, reviving

---

[17] Piggin, *Evangelical Christianity*, p. 91.

[18] T. Sargent, *Sacred Anointing*, p. 43; Iain H. Murray, *David Martyn Lloyd-Jones: The First Forty Years, 1899–1939*, pp. 203–27.

Anglican, Baptist, Congregational, Disciple, Lutheran, Methodist, Presbyterian and Reformed churches and other evangelical bodies throughout Europe and North America, Australasia and South Africa, and their daughter churches and missionary causes throughout Asia, Africa, and Latin America, winning more than five million folk to an evangelical faith in the two years of greatest impact in each country.[19]

The high point of this decade of revival was, of course, the Welsh revival of 1904/5, which may have harvested a hundred thousand souls, made a massive impact on the crime rate, and was exported all over the world. Young Evan Roberts, the most prominent name in the revival, was something of a mystic, most conspicuous for his habit of not preaching at meetings, which has led to much speculation since on the relationship between the neglect of preaching and religious aberrations, occasionally evident in the Welsh and subsequent revivals.[20] The distinctive emphases of Evan Roberts were 'obedience to the Holy Spirit's leading, confession and restitution, together with the full assurance of faith, the priority of prayer, and the pre-eminence of Christ in all things'.[21]

In this same decade, very remarkable scenes of revival were also witnessed in India, Korea and China. India then gave to the Christian world such remarkable names as Pandita Ramabai, John 'Praying' Hyde, and Sadhu Sundar Singh. The Indian revivals owed much to the Welsh Revival, but the Indians passed on what they received. From India, revival rolled across Korea in three waves of increasing magnitude in 1903, 1905 and 1907. These revivals brought social and political, as well as spiritual, salvation. The Japanese protectorate, established in 1905, increased its stranglehold on an impoverished and demoralized nation. Buddhism, which was then hiving off into mysticism, and Confucianism, because it lacked a supernatural dimension, seemed powerless to help. There was widespread desperation. The Korean revival of 1907 saw amazing scenes of simultaneous public praying and confession of sins. An eye- and ear-witness account of how this practice began makes fascinating reading:

---

[19] Orr, *Evangelical Awakenings*, p. 97.
[20] Davies, *Spirit*, p. 178.
[21] Evans, *Welsh Revival*, p. 73.

After a short sermon, Mr. Lee took charge of the meeting and called for prayer. So many began praying that Mr. Lee said, 'If you want to pray like that, all pray,' and the whole audience began to pray out loud, all together. The effect was indescribable. Not confusion, but a vast harmony of souls and spirit, a mingling together of souls moved by an irresistible impulse of prayer. The prayer sounded to me like the falling of many waters, an ocean of prayer beating against God's throne.[22]

Another who witnessed the 1907 manifestation of revival in Korea was Jonathan Goforth, a Canadian Presbyterian who had been a missionary in China since 1887. In 1905 he was set ablaze by reading Finney's lectures on revival and his memoirs. He returned from Korea to China and shared his experience of the wonder-working results of repentance and confession. In 1908 and 1909 the fires of revival raged throughout China and Manchuria. Reflecting on his experience of revival in his autobiographical *By My Spirit*, Goforth affirmed his conversion to Finneyism:

We wish to state most emphatically as our conviction that God's re-vival may be had when we will and where we will . . . Our reading of the Word of God makes it inconceivable to us that the Holy Spirit should be willing, even for a day, to delay His work. We may be sure that, where there is a lack of the fullness of God, it is ever due to man's lack of faith and obedience. If God the Holy Spirit is not glorifying Jesus Christ in the world today, as at Pentecost, it is we who are to blame.[23]

Then, for a decade after 1927, another wave of spiritual blessing swept across China, deepening the spiritual life of Christians and bringing many of the unconverted to Christ. This response was in spite of, or probably because of, the political unrest.[24] This revival

---

[22] W.N. Blair, *The Korean Pentecost and the Sufferings which Followed*, p. 403, cited in L. George Paik, *The History of Protestant Missions in Korea, 1832–1910*, p. 371.

[23] Jonathan Goforth, *By My Spirit*, p. 131.

[24] The following is based on the doctoral research of Valerie Griffiths, which I read in early draft form.

movement is very interesting, highlighting the valuable contribution to the history of revival made by women missionaries. Leslie Lyall says that,

> . . . the pioneer of the spiritual 'new life movement', the handmaiden upon whom the Spirit was first poured out, was Marie Monsen of Norway. Her surgical skill in exposing the sins hidden within the church and lurking behind the smiling exterior of many a trusted Christian – even many a trusted Christian leader – and her quiet insistence on a clear-cut experience of the new birth set the pattern for others to follow.[25]

Arriving in China in 1902 just after the Boxer Rebellion, Monsen's first term was inauspicious as she wrestled with chronic sickness. She was charged with the responsibility of pioneer evangelism in a city in the Henan province (central north-east China), but she felt the hopelessness of it all. When she asked why the experience of the early church was not replicated, she was told that the times were different now. But she refused to accept this. After reading about revivals elsewhere, she took a longer-term view of things, accepting that spiritual vitality might only come after a long period of laying gospel foundations in a culture which had not experienced it before.

After her first furlough, Monsen gave a lot more time to prayer and to teaching the Bible to Christian women. Then, in her third term in the 1920s, she began to reap – largely through the revolutionary change wrought in the lives of Chinese women through learning how to read. At a school for 'Bible women', who were commissioned to take the Scriptures to their fellow Chinese, great conviction of sin came upon the women who had gathered to study the Bible. They confessed to infanticide and other sins. Monsen did not encourage the public confession of sin, but she worked with each Bible woman individually, urging her to fully confess her sins and receive the new birth. For five years she ministered in this way. The movement spread right across the provinces of north and central China, with people bursting to come to meetings to learn and pray. She left China in 1932, but at that time there were over six

---

[25] Leslie T. Lyall, 'Historical Prelude', pp. 20f.

thousand baptisms annually,[26] and the quiet prayer revival under Marie Monsen prepared the church for the coming of the Japanese in 1937[27] and the Communist takeover of 1949.

Anna Christensen from Denmark succeeded Marie. Christensen spent 35 years in China and ministered in 19 of its 24 provinces. She had already shared in the blessing under Marie, and she now held meetings for the deepening of the spiritual life, which were carefully planned and yielded much fruit.[28] Victory over sin in daily life was not seen as an unattainable ideal, but as a real possibility in the power of the Holy Spirit.[29] An unnamed editor in *China's Millions* characterized Christensen as one of God's skilled workmen, 'commissioned with a special message of radical repentance, living faith and entire sanctification'.[30] She encouraged missionaries who felt defeated not to make difficulty an excuse for lack of blessing, she fostered their faith that God could work in their areas in a special way, so that they would pray with more faith, preach with more power, and see more results.[31] When the Japanese invaded the north and coastal areas of China she ministered to the poorer and more needy churches of the western provinces. She retired in 1950.[32]

Revivals in non-western countries raise the interesting and important question of whether a spiritual movement in a Christian tradition and culture such as in Wales was in some way different from a movement which battled against a background of animism, Buddhism, Hinduism or Islam. Revivals have often been caught rather than taught, and they have been exported from one country to another. But revivals in non-western countries, even when western missionaries shared in them, frequently caused problems when attempts were made to import the blessing to the west. The

---

[26] H.S. Cliff, 'Revival Blessing', *China's Millions* (March 1933), pp. 50f.

[27] Leslie T. Lyall (ed.), *The Clouds His Chariot: The Story of 1937*, pp. 56f.

[28] Sofie Romcke, 'Times of Refreshing in Shansi', *China's Millions* (Dec. 1930), p. 193.

[29] T.E. Benson, 'A Campaign in Retrospect', *China's Millions* (Dec. 1937), pp. 228f.

[30] Preface to G. Vinden, 'Miss Anna Christensen in Western Szechwan', pp. 45–8.

[31] Vinden, 'Miss Anna Christensen', pp. 45–8.

[32] Eileen Crossman, *Mountain Rain*.

reflex influence of revivals in mission areas on the home or sending church is well illustrated by the East Africa Revival.[33]

The influence of this revival, which began in 1933 in Gahini, in the Rwanda CMS Mission, was immense, and it continues to this day. The revival resulted in the outflanking of Islam in Africa and in much constructive nation-building in the post-colonial era in the 1950s and 1960s. Secular employers felt secure in entrusting great responsibility to the 'Revival Brethren', who have a reputation for high moral character. The effects of the revival were also felt throughout the evangelical world. This influence was mediated chiefly through returning missionaries who took news of the revival back to their sending countries; through African pastors, such as William Nagenda, Yosiya Kinuka and Festo Kivengere, who became international evangelists, speaking at missions and conventions; and through a great classic of evangelical spirituality produced by the revival, namely Roy Hession's *Calvary Road*. The west's profound interest in the East African Revival, arising primarily from the fact that many missionaries were so influenced by it, raises acutely the question of how possible it is to reproduce in another culture a revival which has met the needs of peoples in an entirely different culture.[34]

The chief principle of this revival was 'walking in the light', being open with one another, mutual confession. Its theme text was 1 John 1:7: 'If we walk in the light, as he is in the light, we have fellowship one with another, and the blood of Jesus Christ cleanseth us from all sin.' The revival produced a repentant church with 'a high level of spirituality and practical holiness'.[35] It produced a people of such joy that they were able to withstand the misery and despair of famine. The institution of marriage was honoured; government, administration and commerce were all transformed through the infusion of honesty; the consumption of alcohol dropped.

The revival divided the missionaries into three parties: 1) those who were themselves blessed in the revival and trusted the Holy

---

[33] F.B. Welbourne, *East African Christian*.

[34] H.H. Osborn, *Fire in the Hills: The Revival which Spread from Rwanda*, ch. 9; J.E. Church, *Quest for the Highest: An Autobiographical Account of the East African Revival*, ch. 15.

[35] A.C. Stanley Smith, *Road to Revival: The Story of the Ruanda Mission*, p. 103.

Spirit to sort out the problems; 2) those who were gladdened by all the new life but who reserved their judgement over some of its features; and 3) those who considered it owed more to evil spirits than to the Holy Spirit. Missionaries in the revival commonly identified four problems:

- Unedifying expressions of joy such as wild singing and dancing.
- False doctrine.
- The breaking of fellowship with those believed to be at a lower level of spirituality.
- The problems created by the public confession of sin.

As to the first, it is now better understood that revivals give communities permission to express joy in ways congenial to their culture. As to the second, the revival, like all revivals, accentuated key doctrines hitherto neglected. This emphasis of the revival on sanctification gave rise to the charge of perfectionism. 'The overwhelming emphasis in the revival was on the sins of the Church, the need for repentance, and the efficacy of the Blood of Christ for cleansing and life-giving power.'[36] The third issue is one found in all revivals, namely the division among believers caused by the new understanding that means everything to some and bewilderment to others. Division within the church, however, only detracted from a more marvellous unity, namely that between tribes, as the revival worked against deeply entrenched racial hatred. This, of course, raises the most obvious question: 'How can a nation which enjoyed such deep revival, as did Rwanda, just a half-century later suffer such genocide?' As to the fourth problem, western Christianity in particular struggled with the practice of the public confession of sin, which has been a characteristic of American college revivals, but less to the liking of the inhibited British. So the East African Revival is a good case study of the problems identified by the unsympathetic in all revivals.

---

[36] Stanley Smith, *Road to Revival*, p. 105.

Revivals among indigenous peoples

If revivals may be understood as God's initiative in times of community crisis, then one should expect to find revivals among those indigenous minority groups whose needs and cultures have been steamrolled by the inexorable advance of western capitalism. It has been so in Australia. One of the most significant revivals in Australia's history began among Aboriginal people in the Uniting Church in Elcho Island (now Galiwin'ku) in late 1978. According to their pastor, Djiniyini Gondarra:

> . . . people were starting to feel that something strange was happening, through dreams, through being woken up at night and seeing something wonderful. Some people were just going and praying for sick people and those people were being healed. They were starting to wonder.[37]

On 14 March 1979, about thirty people gathered with Djiniyini Gondarra, who thanked those few who had been praying for renewal. He said that he too had been praying for revival. He describes what happened next:

> I asked the group to hold each other's hands and I began to pray for the people and for the church, that God would pour out His Holy Spirit to bring healing and renewal to the hearts of men and women, and to the children. Suddenly we began to feel God's Spirit moving in our hearts and the whole form of prayer-life suddenly changed and everybody began to pray in spirit and in harmony. And there was a great noise going on in the room and we began to ask one another what was going on. Some of us said that God had now visited us and once again established His kingdom among His people.[38]

Nightly meetings were held with upwards of two hundred in attendance, some of which went on until 2 a.m. Few on the island were

---

[37] Terry Djiniyini, cited in Max Hart, *A Story of Fire: Aboriginal Christianity*, pp. 49f.
[38] Cited in Jeanette Boyd, 'The Arnhem Land Revival of 1979: An Australian Aboriginal Religious Movement'.

left untouched. In one weekend, 128 people either accepted Christ or rededicated their lives to him. Not only was the worship reportedly sweeter, but there was also a change in the tone of the community: less drunkenness, petrol sniffing and fighting; greater conscientiousness in work; an increased boldness in speaking out against social injustices. Males took over leadership of the church and of the singing in worship from women, an event of great significance in Aboriginal society.

Unlike most of the revivals in Australian history, the Aboriginal revival was neither localized nor short-lived. Using the facilities of the Missionary Aviation Fellowship the Elcho Islanders spread their good news all over Arnhem Land, and north and north-western Australia. At the Anglican Roper River Mission (Ngukurr) in eastern Arnhem Land, which had been reduced to a social disaster area by the granting of a liquor licence, the revival came as a form of social salvation, including the renouncing of alcohol, petrol sniffing and immorality.

Amazing phenomena, which owe far more to the charismatic movement than to traditional Reformed evangelicalism, have accompanied the revival. John Blacket reports miracles, sightings of angels, and numerous visions – of fire coming down from heaven igniting spotfires all over the continent, of a great river flowing from Elcho Island to towns in south-western Australia, of signs in the sky telling the Aboriginal evangelists and their teams where to go next.[39] They also experienced many dreams in fulfilment of the prophet Joel who prophesied that sons and daughters would prophesy, old men would dream dreams and young men would see visions.

Such manifestations, which made many whites cautious at first, have come to be seen as time-honoured features of Aboriginal culture. This was especially true of the visions which preceded the revival and which continued to feature as the years passed. Djiniyini Gondarra himself had a remarkable vision of crows and flying foxes (which are totems of himself and his wife) and of a beautiful girl wearing lots of bangles, namely Queen Jezebel. Gondarra called out to his wife, 'Go to Jerusalem, get the blood and wash the cross.' She

---

[39] Blacket, *Fire*; see also his " 'Rainbow or the Serpent?" Observing the Arnhem Land Aboriginal Revival, 1979 and Now'.

did so and, when she washed the cross with the blood, it turned into a flaming two-edged sword. She thrust it through Jezebel, who turned back into a flying fox and exploded. Then God said to Gondarra:

> You lay down every totem and ceremony. In each of them there is good and bad. All of them must come under my Lordship, be washed by the blood of Jesus Christ, and then you will see a new Aboriginal culture. I don't want to destroy and leave you empty. I will restore and renew what is good.[40]

It would be totally inadequate to view this experience as a mere bout of Pentecostal delirium. Djiniyini's vision gave him the clear cultural message that Christianity comes not to destroy but to fulfil the aspirations of traditional Aboriginal law. The revival is thus a dramatic step by the Aboriginal people towards self-identity. Once – during the two centuries of subjugation – they were not a people; now they are a people, God's people. The revival is the power by which the Aboriginal people are moving away from subjugation towards autonomy and a genuinely independent Aboriginal church. For a start, the revival itself was completely led by Aboriginal people. It was when white missionaries were away or had just left an Aboriginal community that the revival came.

Revivals are often associated with the political empowerment of a social group, leading to economic progress and cultural integration.[41] Revival is the power sufficient for the indigenization of Christianity in minority cultures leading to the empowerment of adherents of those cultures who had hitherto been demoralized unto death. This is how anthropologist and Uniting Church minister, Robert Bos, interprets the Aboriginal revival.[42] It was one of the means by which Aboriginal people were able to persevere in their campaign for land rights and for a just recompense for the land from

---

[40] Blacket, *Fire*, p. 248.
[41] Richard Carwardine, 'The Second Great Awakening in Comparative Perspective: Revivals and Culture in the United States and Britain', p. 84.
[42] Robert Bos, 'The Dreaming and Social Change in Arnhem Land'.

which they had been dispossessed. On 3 June 1992, in the case of Mabo v. State of Queensland (a famous land rights case named after one of the plaintiffs, Eddie Mabo), the High Court of Australia buried the fiction that, at the time of white settlement, Australia was *terra nullius* (belonging to no one). Therefore indigenous peoples had a legal communal title to land. The state governments, mining and pastoral interests howled with hysteria, but the Aboriginal people, now strengthened by revival and strongly supported by the churches, were able to persuade Australians to seek truth and justice in this issue, rather than be ruled by self-interest. The Aboriginal people, together with the churches, have been in the vanguard in the matter of land rights, and together they have changed the national mood, which has become one of a desire for reconciliation between black and white and atonement for past wrongs.[43] The Mabo verdict is an achievement of the Spirit.

Conclusion

Any survey of revivals in the past two centuries reveals how indispensable they have been to communities struggling against great odds: war; disease; migration; industrial, class or cultural struggle; marginalization; demoralization. The history of revival richly illustrates God's love for the poor and the oppressed and the fact that he is on their side. Revivals are evidently for the moral strengthening of communities. Yet if all the communities in the world were to be visited with revival whenever they were immoral or demoralized, we would have nothing else in the experience of the world. Great and amazing as they have been, revivals have not been as frequent or as long-lasting as many ardent Christians have wished. Such zealous souls have developed a technology to make it happen more often: revivalism.

There is a tantalizing contradiction in revivalism. It attaches a lot of importance to human programmes, but they are programmes that

---

[43] See, for example, *Social Issues Update* 3.2 (Oct. 1993), the occasional newsletter of the Social Issues Committee, Anglican Diocese of Sydney.

must demonstrate the Spirit's power. Jonathan Goforth concluded his autobiographical account of revival in China with the words:

> Brethren, the Spirit of God is with us still. Pentecost is yet within our grasp. If revival is being withheld from us it is because some idol remains still enthroned; because we still insist in placing our reliance in human schemes; because we still refuse to face the unchangeable truth that 'it is not by might, but by my Spirit'.[44]

At its best revivalism insists that revival is a work of God's Spirit, and not of the human spirit. Revivalism organizes for revival, whilst insisting that it cannot produce it. Human might cannot produce revival, revivalism asserts, but it can organize for it, and it can block it. Finney and Goforth are proof that God honours the faith and zeal which revivalism has produced at its best. But this does not prove that revivalism has a lot going for it: God often graciously works through defective vessels. Revivalism is defective because it does not give the Lord the honour that is due to him: he will not be organized, and he cannot be blocked. Surely Martyn Lloyd-Jones was right to insist, 'You cannot stop a revival any more than you can start it. It is altogether in the hands of God.'[45]

The purest, most amazing revivals of the past century have not had much to do with revivalism. They have been, as ever, 'surprising works of God'. Great conviction of sin and heartfelt repentance and an awesome sense of the presence of God have been the most conspicuous human aspects of these revivals, just as they were in the Great Awakening. The Welsh and Aboriginal revivals were both accompanied by an enduring sense of the presence of the Lord as he came down from glory to shed his glory on the earth and to encourage his needy people. In all of this one is impressed with the sovereignty of God in revival. One is left with the conviction that any human blueprint to produce a revival ignores both the critical importance of the sovereignty of God and the difficult-to-reproduce context of need which God habitually relieves when he pours out his Spirit.

---

[44] Goforth, *By My Spirit*, p. 138.
[45] D. Martyn Lloyd-Jones, *Revival*, p. 236.

But those same Welsh and Aboriginal revivals were also characterized by remarkable manifestations of the Spirit. In its emotionalism, its spontaneity, its clear departure from anything which recalled organized evangelism, in the intense and lasting impressions of the divine presence, the Welsh Revival of 1904 looked backwards to the Great Awakening and forwards to the preoccupation with extraordinary manifestations of the Spirit reported in modern Pentecostal revivals, among which the Aboriginal revival must be numbered. To these we must now turn.

5

Revival and the Charismatic Movement

The conservatives put the emphasis on the 'fruit of the Spirit', with Christian character to the fore. In charismatic teaching the main emphasis is on the 'gifts of the Spirit', stressing power for ministry. The word and the Spirit combined to form God's provision for his people to live for him in this world. In Ephesians 5:18 we are told to go on being filled with the Spirit, while in Colossians 3:16 we are told: 'Let the Word of Christ dwell in you richly'. One gives power, the other gives light. Each complements the other. Both are needed in correct balance.[1]

He who has no religious affection is in a state of spiritual death. True religion consists so much in the affections that there is no true religion where there is no religious affection – even while there is no true religion where there is nothing else but affection. On the one hand, there must be light in the understanding as well as an affected, fervent heart; where there is heat without light, there can be nothing divine or heavenly in that heart. So, on the other hand, where there is a kind of light without heat, a head stored with notions and speculations and a cold and unaffected heart, there can be nothing divine in that light.[2]

Our definition of revival (Ch. 1) has led us to assess revival in terms of its outcomes or fruit (revitalization of the church, the conversion of large numbers of unbelievers and the reduction of sin in the community). From these measurable outcomes we have inferred a theological understanding of revival in terms of what is required to produce them. As we have seen, revival is an intensification of the

---

[1] Strachan, *Revival*, p. 60.
[2] Jonathan Edwards, *Religious Affections* (Banner edn, 1986), p. 49.

normal work of the Holy Spirit in exalting Jesus, in accentuating the doctrines of grace, and in convicting, converting, regenerating, sanctifying and empowering. And we have followed Jonathan Edwards in contending that the only real proofs that a genuine work of the Spirit in revival has occurred are that those influenced actually come to love Jesus, the Bible, the doctrines of grace and other people more, and that they hate their sins more. The only test of the genuineness of a revival is its fruit.

Gifts and manifestations

But how does all of this help us to assess the relationship between revival and the gifts of the Spirit or manifestations of supernatural power which have been reported so frequently in revivals, especially those in the recent past? The fruit of revival helps us to assess its long-term genuineness. Indeed, it is the only long-term test. But that is not to say that a revival is, in essence, fruit. By definition a revival cannot itself be the fruit if it produces the fruit. The fruit is the fruit of the Spirit, whose activity produces the fruit. So the essence of revival is the activity of the Spirit. But a revival produces a lot of fruit. A revival is a bumper harvest. So the Spirit must do something different either in kind or intensity from what he normally does. We have emphasized the latter. Revival is an intensification of what the Spirit normally does.

But does the very intensification of the normal work of the Spirit present itself, at least in the short term, in unusual, uncommon phenomena or extraordinary manifestations? If his normal activity is to convict and regenerate sinners and this is normally unobserved, would an intensification of this normal activity cause it to be conspicuous? Does the human instrument that is subject to this intensified divine influence sometimes respond in striking and unusual ways? Is one demonstrable difference between a work of the Holy Spirit in revival and a work of the Holy Spirit outside of revival that the former is public and prominent and the latter is normally quiet and unobserved? And if that is true, what is the purpose of this unusual manifestation of the Spirit's power?

This brings us to the most difficult area in the matter of revival: gifts and manifestations. This is the area where Bible-believing

Christians most disagree. In this chapter we will examine a number of issues over which charismatic and conservative evangelicals are in dispute. First, were the extraordinary gifts of the Holy Spirit and other manifestations of the divine, such as miracles, in evidence in the revivals reported in the book of Acts? If so, were they an integral part of those revivals or incidental to them so that, had they been omitted, it would not have affected the outcome? Have such signs and wonders survived the apostolic era and do they feature in the later history of the church? How are we to assess reports of 'manifestations' today, such as those claimed for the 'Toronto Blessing'? Are they 'signs of revival'? What is the 'the baptism of the Spirit' and what is its relationship with revival?

Martyn Lloyd-Jones, the influential Bible expositor who taught thousands of engrossed listeners at great length on revival and the baptism of the Spirit at Westminster Chapel in London, was sadly conscious that this was the area where he was most in dispute with many of his evangelical contemporaries. He believed strongly that evangelicals tend to be a lot weaker in this whole area than they are in many other areas of biblical theology, and that many of the arguments which they have advanced against the reality and place of exceptional outpourings of the Spirit's power in the modern church are less than biblical. He believed that much evangelical thinking on revival, or rather the lack of it, is of a type that is in danger of quenching the Spirit, is calculated to rationalize a lack of faith, and explains why many orthodox churches are so dead. On the other hand, many charismatics may have put so much emphasis on the baptism of the Spirit and on gifts and 'manifestations' that they tend to lose sight of the one who does the baptizing, namely Jesus, and the primary purpose of the gifts, namely to witness to the gospel.

Signs and wonders in the first revivals

Were signs and wonders features of the revivals reported in the book of Acts? The model church created at Pentecost was prayerful, faithful to the apostles' doctrine, generous and compassionate, and united (Acts 2:44–47). These are all fruit of the Spirit. On the basis of such fruit alone, we would conclude that the first Christians had experienced genuine revival. But these early movements of God's Spirit

were not quiet affairs. They were conspicuous, public and prominent. It was evident to outsiders that something amazing and
extraordinary was going on before their very eyes and in their very
hearing: they could *see* and *hear* these outpourings of God's Spirit
(Acts 2:33). Great fear of God came in the wake of what they heard
and saw, and, if there is no evidence of supernatural gifts among the
new Christians themselves,[3] many signs and wonders were being
done by the apostles (Acts 2:43–47). The accounts of the subsequent
revivals in Acts continue to report these miracles (4:30; 5:12; 14:3).

The apostle Paul affirmed that he won the Gentiles to Christ 'by
word and deed, by the power of signs and wonders, by the power of
the Spirit of God', which had enabled him fully to proclaim the
good news of Christ (Rom. 15:18,19; cf. 2 Cor. 12:12).[4] The writer
of the letter to the Hebrews says that God himself bore witness to
the gospel of salvation by signs and wonders and various miracles,
and by gifts of the Holy Spirit, distributed according to his will (Heb.
2:4). There can be no doubt that miracles and manifestations of
supernatural power accompanied these first revivals and that demonstrations of the Spirit's power accompanied the apostolic preaching of the word. Furthermore, the very suggestion that these
manifestations of supernatural power might be incidental to the real
means of establishing faith, such as the preaching of the gospel, is
tantamount to blasphemy. For nothing in the word of God, let alone
such explicit references to God's own work on behalf of the gospel
of his dear Son, is incidental. It does no honour to the word of God
itself to make such a suggestion, and it grieves the Spirit.

Post-apostolic signs and wonders

Most Bible-believing Christians would not want to deny that miracles and spiritual gifts were integral to the proclamation of the gospel
in the apostolic church, nor do they have much heart for the com-
moner enterprise of seeking to exalt the word preached by diminish-
ing the significance of signs and wonders. But what many Bible-
believing Christians do deny is that these wonders or special gifts

---

[3] But see Gal. 3:5 and Jas. 5:13–16.
[4] See also 1 Thess. 1:5; 1 Cor. 2:3–5.

continued past the apostolic age. Some argue that such supernatural demonstrations were necessary to authenticate the gospel at first, but, with the establishment of the church, that is no longer required. Others argue that, with the completion of the New Testament canon, there was no longer a need for divine signs to authenticate the word because the word preached is self-authenticating. Such opponents to the continuing of signs and wonders are known as cessationists,[5] and Martyn Lloyd-Jones contends that there are no grounds for their beliefs, 'save prejudice'.[6] His antipathy to cessationism was pronounced, for he believed it produced 'an intellectualism devoid of Holy Ghost power'.[7]

Have the special, extraordinary gifts of the Spirit continued into the ongoing life of the church or not? What do theologians make of the evidence? It seems that they are commonly tempted at first to answer that question in the negative and then to revise their thinking in the light of further reflection or evidence. Saint Augustine, for example, first argued that miracles had ceased, as they were no longer necessary. Then, in one two-year period, he was confronted with the evidence of 70 attested miracles. In *Retractions*, which was written in 427 AD, three years before his death, he withdrew his endorsement of the view that the age of miracles had passed.[8] Jack Deere, an Old Testament professor at Dallas Theological Seminary, is another example.[9] Like many conservative evangelicals he had been wedded to the view that miraculous signs and wonders were confined to the New Testament era and are not to be expected today. But he has now repented of that view. The argument from Scripture itself that the gifts have come to an end with the apostolic foundation of the church seems to many scholars to be weak. The

---

[5] On cessationism, see William DeArteaga, *Quenching the Spirit: Discover the REAL Spirit behind the Charismatic Controversy.*

[6] Sargent, *Sacred Anointing*, pp. 66–9, 143. In 'Spiritual Gifts' (i), Sermon on Romans 12:6 (tape 3312), Martyn Lloyd-Jones says, with reference to Paul on knowledge, tongues and prophecy, 'we cannot go along with the argument that the latter two are rendered void with the completion of this canon without applying that to the former . . . that is not interpretation. It is prejudice.'

[7] Sargent, *Sacred Anointing*, p. 69. The words are Sargent's.

[8] Francis MacNutt, *Healing*, p. 58.

[9] Jack Deere, *Surprised by the Power of the Spirit.*

view seems to owe most to an unbiblical Dispensationalism, which divides church history into different eras, whereas the scriptural position is that from Pentecost we are all in the indivisible 'last days' (Acts 2:17) until the Lord returns. Even John Wimber, who did more than anyone to promote the interest of charismatics in signs and wonders, held a cessationist view of the gifts until he enrolled in Peter Wagner's church growth course at Fuller Theological Seminary. There his cessationism was buried under the weight of contemporary accounts of healings and deliverances in South America.[10] But it is probably still a hallmark of conservative evangelicalism to adhere to cessationism. Peter Masters, for example, has condemned Martyn Lloyd-Jones' 'unthinking criticism' of cessationism.[11] The jury on this theological debate is still out.

Is it, then, a question for the historian to settle rather than the theologian? Have such gifts of the Holy Spirit always been in evidence in past revivals or not? That should be a simple question to answer. What verdict is reached by the historical evidence? The charismatic party, for want of a better term, is probably right to insist that evidence of post-apostolic manifestations of the Spirit have been suppressed, and that they have been present in every age of the church. Church bureaucrats always have been and always will be irritated when God does a new thing outside of the 'guidelines'. But the problem is that records of revivals, like any other historical documents, only record material which people at the time thought was important. Tongues may have been present in the evangelical revivals of the eighteenth century, but speaking in tongues does not appear to have been as highly prized then as it is today. For whatever reason, there is little evidence of the gift of tongues in the Evangelical Revival.

Exorcisms were reported in the Evangelical Revival. For example, for 29 October 1739 we read in Wesley's *Journal* that he cast a demon out of a woman. Healings, raisings from the dead and angel visitations were reported in the Indonesian revival of the 1970s and in the current revivals in China and South Korea.[12] Tongues, visions,

---

[10] Nigel Scotland, *Charismatics and the Next Millennium*, p. 181.

[11] See Sargent, *Sacred Anointing*, p. 69.

[12] George W. Peters, *Indonesia Revival: Focus on Timor*, pp. 57–85; Carl Lawrence, *Against all Odds: The Church in China*, pp. 73–82; Arthur Wallis, *China Miracle*, pp. 57, 163–84; Colin Whittaker, *Korea Miracle*, pp. 93–112.

prophecy, healings and the casting out of demons were reported in the Solomon Islands revival which began in 1970, and one who experienced that revival argued that 'a new dimension' of the Spirit was evident.[13] The Aboriginal revival, beginning in Australia in 1979, has been marked by reports of countless manifestations of remarkable gifts and signs and wonders: miracles, sightings of angels, visions, deliverances and healings (especially after road accidents).[14]

Evaluating manifestations

It may be significant that such manifestations are more commonly experienced among those communities that are being penetrated by the gospel for the first time. That would suggest that God tends to permit every new people group to enjoy its own 'pentecost'. It may also be that such experiences are more common among those who have a worldview that is open to the spirit dimension. Western culture, based on a scientific worldview that excludes interventions from the spirit world, may be more impervious to revivals. Much of the opposition to revival, even by Bible-believing Christians, may result from the fact that they are essentially secularized and really believe western science more than they do the Bible.

Apart from these cultural factors, Christians tend to respond to claims about manifestations in three different ways. Some accept them, look for signs and wonders to be repeated in their own experience, and explore further what significance ought to be attached to them. Some keep an open mind and look for further evidence to establish or supplement these claims. Others remain sceptical about them, pointing out that these reported signs and wonders are often hard to establish, and they deplore the interest in them as a side-track or they bewail the fact that they so easily discredit the church.[15]

Charismatics are commonly among the first group. They take comfort from the labours of their historians who have discovered that there have long been those who have insisted that such manifestations are of God and that they are for his good purpose. They are

---

[13] Strachan, *Revival*.

[14] Blacket, *Fire*.

[15] Davies, *Spirit*, p. 233.

distressed that reports of 'manifestations' can be thought of in any other way. William Blair, Minister of Dunblane Presbyterian Church, went to Belfast in August 1859 to witness the great revival there. After reporting on such manifestations, he concluded robustly:

> I care not what sceptics may say or little-faith Christians, who have no confidence in the extraordinary influences of the Spirit. I believe, as firmly as I believe in my own existence, that the Holy Ghost would never have permitted His work to be entangled with such perplexing and seemingly incredible phenomena, had He not had a most important end to serve by them.[16]

Similarly, Dr James Carson, a medical doctor, wrote an open letter on 20 September 1859 from Coleraine, Ireland, where the manifestations were manifold:

> I conclude that physical manifestations were a most important part of the work, as they entered into God's design, and were no mere accidents of the Revival. They were essential or God would not have sent them.[17]

Again, Bramwell Booth, son of the founder of the Salvation Army, while insisting that he had an aversion to manifestations, nevertheless conceded that they had been a part of the earliest work of the Salvation Army in the 1870s. He testified that medical opinion found very few such manifestations to be insincere and suggested that 'the fact that their new lives dated from so extraordinary a beginning no doubt helped their faith'.[18]

I found that a number of the very sane evangelical students I taught at Regent College had experienced 'manifestations' associated with the Toronto Blessing and were frankly wondering how they should understand these experiences. The purpose that God might have in allowing such manifestations is a matter to which the leaders and recipients of the Toronto Blessing have given much attention. Some testify as follows:

---

[16] Dixon, *Signs*, p. 146.

[17] Dixon, *Signs*, p. 155.

[18] Dixon, *Signs*, p. 160.

I felt like God was shaking off a lot of sin . . . It was like some deliverance from the power of sin.

. . . the laughter anointing seemed as if God in mercy 'shook off' all the physical and emotional debris in a much happier and more effective way than grief/sorrow.[19]

. . . when God gave me a shaking anointing, I felt He had shaken me out of my 'boxes' and broken the boundaries I'd built around me from HIM, as well as from other people.

I felt affirmed – God is real, and can be seen and felt by me in my body and emotions in an earthly way, as well as in my mind and spiritually.

It seems to me that nothing but moans, chatterings and bellows can express the joy, healing and love that I have so suddenly discovered dwell within me and I just cannot shape the words to fit around this thing that is not of me that is churning my stomach . . . and blowing out of my mind the dust of too many books, too many arguments and too much logic.

God was taking me from victim mode to victory and authority. No, I'm not going to take this any more. I'm going to fight.[20]

Martyn Lloyd-Jones was such a skilled diagnostician of the soul, and he was so interested in any reported movings of God's Spirit, that it would be very valuable to have had his assessment of such reports. The fact that these manifestations were felt in bodies and emotions and could be witnessed by outsiders would have been no problem to him at all. He believed that revival would commonly exhibit such features. The felt, physical, emotional dimension, evident to all, was what differentiated revival from other genuine works of the Holy Spirit.

---

[19] Historically, as we have observed in Ch. 3, godly sorrow is the normal foundation in revival to repentance and joy. But God is sovereign, and no two revivals have ever been identical, and it is conceivable that God might revive a stressed and abused person, who has suffered sorrow for much of his/her life, through laughter and rejoicing rather than sorrow and lament.

[20] Beech, 'Outpouring'.

Gifts sidetrack us if they do not lead us to Jesus

But there is a feature of such manifestations which would have
worried Lloyd-Jones greatly: they often seem to have very little to
do with Jesus. To be signs of revival, they must have everything to do
with Jesus (1 Jn. 4:2).[21] In our definition of revival (Ch. 1), we
observed that revivals accentuate the doctrines of grace. The Holy
Spirit is committed to that same work. But the manifestations conspicuous in such movements as the Toronto Blessing do not appear
always to point to and highlight and honour the doctrines of grace.
In fact, there appeared to be very little attention paid to the doctrines of grace in the Toronto Blessing. Barry Chant, Pentecostal
teacher and writer, observed:

> . . . there is a relative absence of the preaching of the cross. In some
> meetings, the redeeming work of our precious Saviour and the for-
> giveness that is ours through His atoning sacrifice is virtually over-
> looked. I have personally sat in several gatherings where people are
> invited to receive the 'blessing' but little or no mention is made of the
> fundamental teaching that all blessings are ours only through Christ.[22]

Barry Chant is even concerned that, far from accentuating the doctrines of grace, the emphasis on manifestations threatens to give
people the impression that there is another gospel altogether:

> . . . we now seem to have a new means of grace. Whereas once we
> would come to God, by faith, trusting only in the merits of his Son, our
> Saviour (Romans 5:1ff.; 8:1ff.), now we come to God by having an
> experience of being slain in the Spirit or 'holy laughter' or some other
> bodily extravagance which is normally administered to us by someone
> else. Do we now have a third sacrament?[23]

It is clearly very easy, even for professing Christians, to seek the
power of the Spirit apart from the cross of Christ. Those who have

---

[21] See D.A. Carson, 'The Purpose of Signs and Wonders in the New Testament'.
[22] Barry Chant, 'The "Toronto Blessing": Priestly or Prophetic?', p. 5.
[23] Chant, 'Toronto Blessing', p. 6.

sought and found help in the Toronto Blessing frequently testify to anxiety in the work place, unhappiness at home, the limitations of human rationality, the deprivation of love and exhaustion from working too hard. They confess to stressed, joyless lives and a lack of self-esteem. The manifestations appear to have addressed needs such as those. Now we may be confident that a loving heavenly Father would be interested in giving his family the resources to address such needs, and critics of the Toronto Blessing need to be concerned that the church has not helped people to cope better with these genuine human problems. But, as Lloyd-Jones said of similar movements, many such needs could be as well addressed by a psychologist or by a course in positive thinking. 'There are many agencies that can give men wonderful gifts,' Lloyd-Jones declared, 'but unless these gifts are directly related to the Lord himself, they are not of God.'[24] He added:

> Feelings come and go, gifts come and go, you can become devout and careful in your life without him, but the hallmark of the work of the Holy Spirit is that he presents the Lord Jesus Christ to us, and brings us to an ever-increasing intimacy with him, and an enjoyment of his glorious presence. The Spirit sanctifies us by bringing us to the word, the word that brings us to a knowledge of him.[25]

A tenuous commitment to the word and to doctrine was what Martyn Lloyd-Jones most lamented among charismatics. Like them, he was prepared to accept that the gift of 'prophesying' could be experienced in the church today. But he insisted that it must be tested by Scripture, whereas some charismatics put it in addition to Scripture or as an alternative to Scripture. Some even put it above Scripture. Having experienced what they label the baptism of the Holy Spirit, many then interpret the Bible in terms of the experience rather than interpreting the experience in terms of the Bible.[26] Because of the emphasis today on listening to the Spirit rather than heeding the timeless word of God, charismatics are less concerned

---

[24] D. Martyn Lloyd-Jones, *Growing in the Spirit*, ch. 4 'The Work of the Holy Spirit', p. 54.
[25] Lloyd-Jones, *Growing*, p. 55.
[26] M. Hamilton, *The Charismatic Movement*, p. 36.

with doctrinal precision. This lack of doctrinal commitment means that charismatics lose their focus on the centre of the gospel and obscure the great gospel truths which genuine revivals always highlight – namely sin, redemption, regeneration and sanctification. Far from fostering genuine revival, charismatics, when they ignore doctrine, actually reduce the opportunities for it.[27]

The gifts of the Spirit and the marks of revival

The emphasis on spiritual gifts can be unhelpful if people become fixated on them for their own sake, rather than using them to strengthen their relationship with Christ or to increase their understanding of his word. So easily detached are the extraordinary gifts from a concern for the gospel that it must be observed that those gifts *in themselves* have little to do with revival. The marks of revival and the extraordinary gifts are not the same thing:

Gifts of the Spirit	Marks of revival[28]
Word of wisdom	Profound conviction of sin
Word of knowledge	Deep repentance
Special faith healings	A fervent laying hold of Christ for salvation
Working of miracles	Fearless witness
Contemporary revelation	Liberty and joy in the Lord
Discerning of spirits	Love in fellowship
Tongues	Repudiation of sin
Interpretation of tongues	Growth in grace

Jonathan Edwards even insisted that there is no scriptural warrant for believing that extraordinary gifts would characterize any glorious future time of prosperity for the church. In *Distinguishing Marks* he condemns the desire for such gifts as 'childish': the church in its adult state has no need for such. In *Charity and its Fruits* he argues that the most glorious way in which the Holy Spirit can be poured out is in his ordinary saving operations to fill hearts with grace and empower Christians to lead holy lives. This is more glorious than any outpouring of the extraordinary gifts of the Holy Spirit. The

---

[27] Murray, *Lloyd-Jones: Fight*, pp. 663f.
[28] In this table, items on the two lists do not correspond to one another.

absence of such gifts in the future glorious times of the church will not make those times any less glorious than the apostolic church when those gifts of speaking in tongues and working miracles were present. The glory of the church in the last days will be more glorious than that of any previous age – not because of the presence or absence of extraordinary gifts, but because it will be most like the church in heaven where there will be no extraordinary gifts, just the gift of love.[29]

It is an instructive idea, even if it is wrong. Billy Graham[30] and Martyn Lloyd-Jones[31] actually prefer as more biblical the view that as we move closer to the end time, when the forces of evil are expected to rage more fiercely in last-ditch desperation, the Lord may give more and greater gifts of the Spirit to his suffering church. But that does not change the important observation that revival outpourings of the Spirit have more to do with love and conversion than with many extraordinary phenomena. Martyn Lloyd-Jones' view, based on his wide reading in the literature of revivals, was not that extraordinary phenomena have rarely been observed in times of revival, but that they in fact been rarely experienced:

> During those great periods of revival which have come periodically in the history of the church, the phenomena consisted not so much in the working of miracles or healings as in extraordinary power of preaching and extraordinary depth of conviction and an unusual element of joy and exultation.[32]

So, extraordinary gifts are still granted to the church in this post-apostolic era. But, when the recipients focus on them for their own sake and detach them from a concern for the gospel, they have very little to do with revival – no matter how spectacular they are or how beneficial they might be to suffering or depressed humanity.

---

[29] Edwards, *Ethical Writings*, p. 171.
[30] Billy Graham, *The Holy Spirit*, pp. 166f. On the basis of Hosea and Joel, he says we may expect miracles to increase as we approach the end time. God will do more signs and wonders in response to Satan's own increased activity.
[31] Sargent, *Sacred Anointing*, p. 70.
[32] D. Martyn Lloyd-Jones, *The Doctor Himself and the Human Condition*, p. 88.

But none of this can be used to dismiss the need for gifts in the church. Until heaven dictates to the contrary, fruit without gifts is not as useful as it would be with gifts. True maturity is gifts plus fruit, not one or the other: 'Follow the way of love and eagerly desire spiritual gifts, especially the gift of prophecy' (1 Cor. 14:1). It is surely Satan's work to make us take sides in this debate and make us feel that we must choose between gifts and fruit when God clearly wants us to have both. Asked what would happen if the Holy Spirit were to be poured out on us in spiritual revival, Billy Graham replied that, among other things,

> *There will be increased evidence of both the gifts and the fruit of the Spirit* . . . Believers will learn what it means to minister to one another and build each other up through the gifts the Holy Spirit has given. They will be given a new measure of love for each other and for a lost and dying world. No longer will the world say that the church is powerless and silent . . . Our lives will be marked by the gifts only the Holy Spirit can give. Our lives will be marked by the fruit only He can bring.[33]

Conclusion

Gifts and fruit, not gifts or fruit – that is what genuine revival gives. If that is observable historically, as this chapter has demonstrated, it must be true theologically, biblically and experientially. The next chapter deals with each of these areas in turn with a view to reflecting further on the interdependence of fruit and gifts in revival.

---

[33] Graham, *Holy Spirit*, p. 217.

6

Revival and the Work of the Spirit

We have established on historical grounds that, while revivals can produce fruit without evidence of spiritual gifts, both gifts and fruit will more commonly characterize them. The work of the Holy Spirit in a revival usually includes giving gifts to his people in abundance, and those gifts are best understood as the tools or instruments by which God's people produce abundant fruit. The sovereign Spirit does not need such instruments to produce revival fruit, and in the greatest of revivals the focus is on God himself in his glory and holiness rather than on the conspicuous gifts of his people. But integral to most firestorms of the Lord, as the Spirit exalts Jesus and accosts sinful humanity with the reality of the holiness of God, will be the fruit resulting from them and the gifts contributing to them. We will explore below the interdependence of fruit and spiritual gifts in revival theologically, biblically and experientially.

A theology of the work of the Spirit in revival

It is through the study of Martyn Lloyd-Jones' understanding of the 'baptism' of the Holy Spirit and its relationship to revival that a way ahead may be found theologically. It is not an easy path to find, because Martyn Lloyd-Jones was not a systematic theologian, and he sometimes appears to contradict himself. Yet his is an understanding which challenges evangelicals to re-examine the biblical evidence for their beliefs concerning the gifts of the Spirit and revival. Equally, his view challenges charismatics to refocus on the Lord and his word. Here is an understanding that can lay the foundation of unity between evangelicals and charismatics without which we cannot hope to see revival: division within God's family is a great inhibitor of revival.

Martyn Lloyd-Jones understood revival as a mighty outpouring or baptism of the Spirit upon large numbers of people all at the same time. He was far more interested in the experience of Spirit baptism than in the term itself. Sometimes he calls it an 'afflatus' of the Spirit, or an 'effusion' or 'infusion' or 'accession' or 'fullness'.[1] When *an individual* experiences this baptism, it is known as an anointing or unction. When it is experienced by *large numbers* all at the same time, it is known as a revival.[2]

The baptism of the Spirit, he believed, is not the same as regeneration by the Spirit,[3] and it is frequently experienced subsequent to conversion. It is not necessary to be baptized in the Spirit to be a Christian: some Christians never experience it. It can be experienced more than once: some Christians have experienced it repeatedly. It is a definite, felt experience, and hence it will be manifest in some physical observable way, in a changed countenance, in bold speech, in spiritual gifts. These manifestations attract the attention of others, but they never remain the focus of attention, for they point unambiguously to Jesus. The purpose of this baptism is to give us the highest possible level of assurance, an assurance which goes beyond the assent we give to the truth of God's word at conversion, and beyond the assurance which comes from the evidence of the fruit of the Spirit in our lives.[4] It is the immediate, sensible experience of God himself assuring us, in our own spirit, that we are the sons and daughters of God.

Paul spoke of this experience in Romans 8:16. It was this baptism which the mighty and accurate Apollos received after instruction from Priscilla and Aquila and which made him mightier and more accurate (Acts 18:24–28).[5] It was this that John Wesley experienced

---

[1] Sargent, *Sacred Anointing*, pp. 50f., 198.

[2] 'The difference between the baptism of the Holy Spirit and a revival is simply one of the number of people affected. I would define a revival as a large number, a group of people, being baptized by the Holy Spirit at the same time.' D.M. Lloyd-Jones, *Joy Unspeakable*, p. 51. See also pp. 189f.

[3] Sargent, *Sacred Anointing*, p. 34. Lloyd-Jones distinguishes between the regeneration and the baptism of the Holy Spirit in Tape DML-J 28, No. 2, 'Great Biblical Doctrines; Baptism of the Holy Spirit'.

[4] Martyn Lloyd-Jones, *Authority*, pp. 76f.; cf. Lloyd-Jones, *Joy*, pp. 91ff.

[5] Martyn Lloyd-Jones, 'What Baptism did you receive?', Sermon 1080.

at 'a quarter before nine' on the evening of 24 May 1738 when his heart was 'strangely warmed' and he felt assured that his own sins had been forgiven. This is what Charles Finney received on the evening of 10 October 1821 and which empowered him for his amazing life of evangelism. This is the experience that enabled D.L. Moody to preach the same sermons as he had previously, but now in demonstration of the Spirit and of power. This is what Lionel Fletcher, possibly the most prominent evangelist Australia has produced, experienced in 1897, the year after his conversion, and about which he testified, 'My life was never the same again and every blessing I have received since, every soul won, and every Church revived in my ministry, is the result of that night.'[6] This is the experience that Billy Graham received in Wales in 1947 and which made a good evangelist into a great one. 'My heart is so flooded with the Holy Spirit,' Billy enthused on that occasion. 'I have it. I'm filled. This is the turning point of my life.'[7] It is an experience that invariably heightens our love for the person and work of Jesus Christ, especially his cross. This incomparable assurance and these clear convictions about the significance of Jesus' death and resurrection are given to believers to make them mighty in witnessing to the truth of the gospel. In revival, supernatural authorization of the truth of the Bible and of the message of the gospel is given again, sufficient to convince an unbelieving world, so that many are converted and entrenched evil is given a bloodied nose.

Seeing revival as the baptism of the Holy Spirit in the way here understood by Martyn Lloyd-Jones has its advantages and disadvantages. The advantages are that it explains why revival is such a conspicuous matter, which has the prominence to attract the attention of unbelievers. It explains why preaching and witnessing in revivals are so exceptionally powerful. It explains why many in revivals receive such an indomitable assurance that Christ has died for their sins.

But insofar as the baptism of the Spirit is not that which regenerates or 'positions for holiness,'[8] then it would be wrong to limit the

---

[6] Lionel B. Fletcher, *Mighty Moments*, p. 16. This book was dedicated to Ross Thomas, 'who introduced me to the Petersham Conference where I made the greatest discovery of my Christian life – that the fullness of the Holy Ghost is for Christians to-day, as much as for the disciples of old'.

[7] William Martin, *A Prophet with Honor: The Billy Graham Story*, pp. 98f.

[8] Sargent, *Sacred Anointing*, p. 140.

Spirit's work in revival to such a baptism. Conspicuousness, power and assurance are all features of revival, but they are not the most important features. In revival many people are regenerated, and every revival has been a revival of holiness. Nothing 'positions for holiness' as much as revival. In a revival the heart is raptured by Jesus: it is Jesus who is acknowledged as Lord and accepted as Saviour, and it is his gospel of grace which is now understood and proclaimed with irresistible clarity and passion.

No one has understood this better than Martyn Lloyd-Jones himself. In his sermon 'The Holy Spirit in Revival',[9] Lloyd-Jones insists that 'in every revival' all is concentrated on Jesus Christ. The chief work of the Holy Spirit is to glorify the Lord Jesus Christ (Jn. 16:14; cf. Jn. 15:26). Otherwise, it will not be a revival. The one theme of the great revival hymns is Jesus. In every revival there is no dispute about his person: his deity, his eternity, his equality with God, his incarnation and the truth of his two natures in one person.[10] There is never a dispute in revivals about the work of Jesus. You cannot, for example, pray for revival and disbelieve the resurrection, because the Holy Spirit is one of the witnesses of his resurrection (Acts 5:32). Jesus' work of redemption is especially affirmed in revival: his atonement, his death upon the cross, his broken body and his shed blood. In every revival the church glories in his blood. We are given 'boldness to enter into the holiest by the blood of Jesus' (Heb. 10:19). The very nerve, and centre, and heart of the gospel is the crucified Lord 'whom God hath set forth to be a propitiation through faith in his blood, to declare his righteousness for the remission of sins that are past' (Rom. 3:25). It is to testify to that glorious gospel that the Spirit is given in unction to the individual and to the church in revival. It is when charismatic groups lay claim to revival, but speak little of Christ or his cross or the gospel, that they are in most danger of grieving the Spirit who seeks above all to glorify the Lord.

If charismatics are in danger of grieving the Spirit through ignoring in practice the centrality of the doctrine of Christ, then many evangelicals grieve him by holding beliefs at variance with a biblical doctrine of the Holy Spirit. Among these beliefs, Martyn Lloyd-

---

[9]　RV 4, printed as ch. 4 of *Revival*.
[10]　See also Martyn Lloyd-Jones, *The Love of God: Studies in 1 John*, p. 29.

Jones treats the view that revivals are a form of mass hysteria, for the consumption of simple people; that the baptism of the Spirit is 'non-experimental' (not felt subjectively in the experience) – it is just what happens objectively when people are born again;[11] that Pentecost was unique; that all you have to be is filled with the Spirit, which is evidenced by moral obedience rather than emotional response; that revival is impossible because the Spirit has been withdrawn pending the second coming. All these beliefs have in common a tendency to deny the immediate and direct action of the Holy Spirit. But, in the book of Acts, the Holy Spirit does intervene directly. And in all genuine revivals he will do the same.

> The living, powerful, activity of the Spirit; the Spirit coming directly, as it were, and controlling, and leading, and guiding, and giving orders, and indicating what was to be done; the Spirit descending upon them; that is what you always have in revival.[12]

Martyn Lloyd-Jones would have been delighted to hear of an incident from the Aboriginal revival in Australia that illustrates this very point. Arthur Malcolm, a Church Army evangelist and, from 1985, first Anglican Aboriginal Bishop, described the coming of revival to Warburton and Meekatharra in 1981, thus:

> God called all the Christians, and so-called Christians, together in a place called Cement Creek. There God called them to true repentance in heart and soul. The number of people there was 120. It's funny that that was the same number as in the Book of Acts. We wonder was God saying something with a sense of humour; anyway God began to work . . . doing wonders and miracles, and then the rain poured down to fill Cement Creek with water and the whole 120 were baptised. It didn't rain anywhere else – just where God began this work among the people . . .

---

[11] This is the baptism *of* the Holy Spirit referred to in 1 Cor.12:13, which is an action taken by the Holy Spirit at our conversion to incorporate us into the Body of Christ. This is distinct from the baptism *with* the Spirit by Jesus, which is an action taken by Christ to empower us for the ministry of the gospel.

[12] RV 4, printed as ch. 4 of *Revival*, p. 50.

An arrow in the sky told them to go and preach in the town of War-burton. 3,000 people came to the Lord and then 5,000 as they went on towards Meekatharra. So this is a repeat of what happened in the Book of Acts. This is the work of the [underprivileged and powerless] people and the Holy Spirit. It was not a Convention or the Missionary way with people being ordered from here to there. You see, God used peo-ple with an open heart, people who were broken down but open to God, not people who were conformed to some other ways. This is a true story. AMEN.[13]

Revivals will always be 'a repeat of what happens in the Book of Acts'. They will always be characterized by direct and immediate interventions of the Holy Spirit or they will not be genuine revivals. But it will be a direct and immediate intervention of the Spirit that focuses on Jesus and his gospel, which leads to the regeneration of sinners and a new thirst for holiness in believers. If the baptism with the Spirit encompasses that, then revival may be understood as Spirit baptism. But if the meaning of Spirit baptism is confined, as some-times appears to be the position in Martyn Lloyd-Jones, to empow-ering for witness or to the gift of assurance, then revival must be understood as more than Spirit baptism.

Jesus: The baptizer with the Holy Spirit

The centrality of Christ and the immediacy of the Holy Spirit are the two doctrines that are to be recovered if Bible-believing Chris-tians are to unite in the prayerful expectation and longing for revival. We will see the need for this unity more clearly if we understand how it reflects the essential unity of the Son and the Spirit within the triune Godhead. Baptism with the Holy Spirit is the gift of Jesus. He is the one who baptizes with the Holy Spirit and fire (Matt. 3:11). Martyn Lloyd-Jones declared that:

> In every reference to the baptism with the Holy Spirit, the Baptiser is the Lord Jesus Christ . . . The whole object . . . of the baptism *with* the Spirit, is to give us such an assurance and to fill us with such power that

---

[13] Merv Blacklock, et. al., 'Minjung in Australia'.

we become living witnesses and testifiers to the truth as it is in Christ Jesus; we become *his* witnesses. That is the purpose of the baptism with the Spirit and it is a baptism that is done by the Lord Jesus Christ.[14]

All spiritual movements will give the rightful praise to Jesus if he is acknowledged as the baptizer with the Holy Spirit.[15] There will not be this unedifying debate between those who declare that the fruit is what matters and the gifts are irrelevant, and those who insist that the gifts are the key evidence of the divine presence. The gifts will be understood and appreciated as one of the Spirit's means to a great end, namely the fruit of Christlikeness in believers. It is thus understandable why Jesus, the baptizer with the Holy Spirit, is the hero of every revival and why a revival is best understood as a firestorm of the Lord Jesus Christ.

Spiritual gifts in the writings of Paul

In Chapter 5, we reviewed the experience of revival as it presents itself in the book of Acts and in the history of the church. Thus far in this chapter we have reviewed the theology of the Spirit's work in revival, with the help of Martyn Lloyd-Jones. It is now necessary to check this analysis by seeing how consistent it is with that other great source of data about revivals, namely the New Testament letters, where the fruit and gifts of the Spirit and their relationship with the gospel are treated extensively.

In his letters to Christians in Corinth and Rome, Paul wrote to communities who, in their multiculturalism and their very great interest in spiritual phenomena, were not unlike those communities of today who have been so responsive to modern spiritual movements such as the Toronto Blessing. He reminded his readers to use their spiritual gifts in such a way as to become the living sacrifices which God intended every Christian to become (Rom. 12:1). In warning them of the importance of being sober in their judgement (Rom. 12:3), he had in mind that they should avoid either being

---

[14] Lloyd-Jones, *Joy*, pp. 176f.
[15] See the seminal study by Allan Norling, *Jesus: The Baptiser with the Holy Spirit*.

arrogant because they were in possession of the sort of gift which their congregation greatly admired, or being dissatisfied because they did not appear to have one of the highly prized gifts. It is interesting to compare the gifts (*charismata*) which Paul mentions in Romans 12 with those rather more ecstatic gifts listed in 1 Corinthians 12 which he calls not *charismata*, but *pneumatika* (spiritual gifts).

Romans 12 (*Charismata*)	1 Corinthians 12 (*Pneumatika*)
Prophesying	Word of wisdom
Serving	Word of knowledge
Teaching	Faith
Encouraging	Healings
Giving	Miracles
Leadership	Prophecy
Showing mercy	Distinguishing spirits
Tongues	Interpreting tongues

In both letters, Paul gives an all-important principle that is God's word to guide us in our assessment of spiritual movements. The principle is this: It is not the presence of these gifts which signifies God's endorsement of a movement. They can be counterfeited by Satan and imitated by humans. It is their proper use that is the criterion by which we may judge that they are authentically Christian and worthy of incorporation and expression in Christian worship. It is not their presence, but their proper use.

What Paul is doing is really very exciting and highly relevant to the situation in which we currently find ourselves. He wants to put all this religious enthusiasm, which frequently expresses itself in unusual phenomena, and which we see in our day just as he saw in his, at the disposal of Christ and his gospel. In a genuine revival of religion, Christ and his work of salvation are extolled, not the Holy Spirit and his works of wonder. The works of wonder may be used by the Spirit to catch our attention, but our attention is to be quickly and firmly fixed on Christ.

So Paul wants to bring all spiritual excitement into the sphere of the operations of grace. He wants to harness all the interest and energy to the service of the gospel of free grace. For Paul the power of grace, the exercise of grace, the channels through which grace flows, are all constrained by Christ; they are to be controlled by Christ.

Where in Romans 12:6 he says 'we have different gifts, according to the grace given us', the word used for gifts (*charismata*) is the same word he used in 5:17, 'the *gift* of righteousness', and in 6:23, 'The *gift* of God is eternal life in Christ Jesus our Lord.' Paul says in Romans 6:23 that eternal life is *the* charisma, and all the other *charismata* have their point, their origin and their goal in that. All these gifts are for the purpose of promoting and achieving the one big gift – eternal life. In fact, Paul says in Romans 1:11 that he longs to share with the Christians at Rome some spiritual *gift* to strengthen them in the faith. That is what gifts are for.

So, here, and especially in 1 Corinthians 12, Paul confronts a congregation that is expressing remarkable ecstatic gifts all over the place, with reports of miracles, and that is focusing on the supernatural power present in their midst, just as was claimed for the Toronto Blessing. In effect, Paul says, 'Well and good, I've got some of these gifts too. Now I don't want you to become a cult and go in for these things for their own sake.' According to Paul, it is the will of Christ that Christians employ their different and richly variegated gifts – not only or even primarily for the good of the whole, but also and primarily for the sake of the gospel. The gospel is the good news about how we can receive eternal life through Jesus, which is *the* gift, and all the other gifts are given for its sake.

To the spiritual and supernatural, then, which fascinated many in Corinth and in Rome, Paul gives eternal purpose and earthly responsibility. Christians are to use these different spiritual gifts to encourage one another to be living sacrifices in the mission of the church. This will be the purpose of the Holy Spirit in every revival, to give those gifts which promote the gospel by glorifying Jesus and his kingdom and which empower Christians for the work of evangelism and mission.

The witness of personal experience

Finally, I should share with my readers that I am not now writing as an impartial observer, totally unacquainted in my own experience with the subject matter of this chapter. Since delivering the lectures on which this book is based at Regent College, Vancouver in 1995, to my utter astonishment and inexpressible joy, what Martin Lloyd-Jones defines as the baptism of the Spirit, and which he says is second only to the experience of heaven, has been my experience. It was on the evening of 29 February 1996 – an easy day to remember. I had spoken on the subject of revival at the Christian and Missionary Alliance Church in Lindfield, a suburb of Sydney, and afterwards there was prayer for all who wanted to stay. Some moved to the front for prayer, some appointed for the task surrounded them and prayed with them, and some went home. I sat in the congregation and chatted with a couple of its members. Then the minister's wife asked me to join her and others in praying for a couple who were rededicating their relationship to the Lord. It was unusual and rather touching to be with them as they recommitted their marriage to the Lord. It was all very orderly and restrained, and nothing in the way of a 'manifestation' was either evident or expected – at least by me. Then the university professor who had invited me to speak that evening asked if I wanted them to pray for me. I hesitated. I had become so used to being at such gatherings and looking on what happened with an unmoved impartiality, a sort of numb detachment. It really never crossed my mind that the Lord might do anything with me, although I had longed that my own country would be touched by revival. So the group began to pray for me, that I would have the desire of my heart and see revival come to my own heart and land.

The minister's wife read from Psalm 15 and then said to me something like, 'Stuart, are you willing to let the Lord have his way with you?' I actually do not know what she said, but that is what I heard her ask. And I was not sure that I could answer that in the affirmative, for I knew I could not say those things about myself which David said there in that psalm. So I struggled with the answer, and took a long time to get it out, like a mother giving birth to a child. I found myself saying things which surprised me, 'Why do I feel so sad and why is my heart so heavy within me? I long for the water to not only warm up but to boil over, for the rivers not only to rise in their banks but to burst their banks.' Someone said, rather provocatively I thought, 'Why don't you jump into the river?' We all laughed. One of the elders, Russell, asked me if he could anoint me with oil. Up to this point I had no anticipation of what was to come – all I expected was that

I would go home confirmed in my own apathetic acceptance of the appalling fact that there was no greater barrier to revival than myself. Russell reached out to touch my forehead with the oil but, before he actually touched me, I was smitten by the Lord. It happened suddenly, without any warning. I did not see it coming. No one else that night was 'slain in the Spirit'. It was not that I was given any choice in the matter. I just fell backwards immediately, without any resistance, and lay on the floor. The Lord was shining on me like the sun. Psalm 84:11 says, 'The LORD God is a sun and shield.' I was in ecstasy. Tears flowed from my eyes like rivers, and did not stop. The fear and sadness drained out of me with my tears. He was visiting *me*! He was healing *my* spirit. I was just thrilled with him. I was overjoyed. The joy shone through my tears. Such happy tears. Such warm, cleansing, healing tears. He was visiting me. He was not passing me by. He was there to bless and strengthen. Bless the Lord, my strength (Ps. 144:1). I never wanted the experience to end. I wanted to lie and bask in the sunshine of his love and glory for ever.

Eventually, after resting in the Lord, I sat up and couldn't help smiling and laughing and hugging everyone in sight. I had a piece of chocolate cake and a cup of tea and got home at 12:15 a.m. At daybreak, I rang one whom I felt knew the deep things of God to ask him what had happened to me and what I should do about it. He said, 'do nothing, absolutely nothing. Don't try to work it out or systematize it or theologize it – just rest in it and press on. Don't ask for more. If he has given you any of his Spirit, he has given you all of his Spirit. Grace is not a thing. It is the sovereign God and he has visited you in a gracious visitation. He has refreshed you by reminding you that he really has forgiven you, that he dealt with your sin and guilt 2,000 years ago on that cross. He has forgiven you – he really has – he just loves you. So don't get yourself all worked up about what you should be like and what you should be doing. Just be the forgiven, accepted, hugely loved person that you are, and praise him and bless his holy name.'

Such an experience is a firestorm of the Lord, for it confirms in the spirit what I had always professed in my mind, namely that the Lord Jesus had died for me, and that I was a forgiven person. For weeks afterwards I was on holy ground and it seemed that no unworthy, negative or sinful thought had any appeal to me whatsoever. I wondered if this was a step towards sanctification, but since then my old sinful habits have reasserted themselves, and I have come to the conclusion that Martin Lloyd-Jones was so right when he said that the experience of the baptism of the Spirit is not given to us for our sanctification, although it feels like it at first.[16] It is not possible to be so conscious of being near to the holy God and not want to be holy. Yet the experience of baptism and the discipline of sanctification are not the same thing, and many who have received the former have too frequently failed catastrophically in the latter.

Conclusion

But I do not want to end this chapter on a note of warning. I simply want to re-emphasize the point that a revival is about gifts *and* fruit, not gifts *or* fruit. Revival, as defined in Chapter 1, is more than the baptism of the Spirit on a large number of people. It is such a tremendous outpouring of the Spirit that not only are sleepy and enfeebled Christians awakened and strengthened for witness, inundated in love and joy, and utterly assured of the Lord's eternal love for them, but they are also given the grace to fight in the war of their own sanctification, and the silent work of regeneration works in the heart of many unbelievers to bring them to faith. Revival is a firestorm of the Lord, consisting of a powerful intensification of the Holy Spirit's normal activity of testifying to the Saviour, accentuating the doctrines of grace, and convicting, converting, regenerating, sanctifying and empowering large numbers of people at the same time. Revival is the love of God shed abroad in many hearts, and it is a generalized work of regeneration, sanctification and baptizing or filling with the Holy Spirit of love. It is the Holy Spirit testifying to our spirits that, two thousand years ago, Jesus died on a cross to remove all the obstacles to the inexpressible and glorious joy of peace with God. Martin Luther condemned the 'theology of glory', insisting that Christianity is concerned with the 'theology of the cross'. Revival, being a firestorm of the crucified Lord, is a demonstration that glory is found through the cross.

That is why, after much heart-searching, I have shared my experience. In 2 Corinthians 12:4 Paul mentions to a group of Christians

---

[16] Lloyd-Jones, *Joy*, p. 142.

interested only in the 'theology of glory' that he had enjoyed a wonderful vision or revelation and had been caught up to paradise, but that what he then heard was inexpressible and, even if he could express it, he was not permitted to tell it. Does this mean that it is forbidden ever to speak of such experiences? I think reticence is normally appropriate. I have had experiences of God that I have shared with no one. But precisely because this experience was interpreted to me so quickly and convincingly as an outworking of Christ's dying love for me on the cross, I believe it was a manifestation that honours the gospel by accentuating the gift of forgiveness through the cross. Since that night I have only had the sorts of experiences about which the apostle Paul does feel free to speak, namely that God's power is perfected in weakness, and that the normal Christian life is learning to persevere in suffering. When is it right to speak of a manifestation of divine power? When it empowers us to stumble along in the way of the cross.

7

Revival in Anglican and Catholic Churches

Revival and baptism with the Holy Spirit, according to Martyn Lloyd-Jones, have this in common: they need not be the experience of any Christian. Perhaps the vast majority of professing Christians – those in the sacramental churches, Catholics, Anglicans and Orthodox, who make up the great majority of the world's Christians – have experienced neither. But let us first hear from one who has experienced both.

Ian Jagelman, Master of Divinity, Doctor of Ministry, is minister of a city church in Sydney, Australia. At the beginning of 1990 he was in India for a conference. As he was praying for his church back home, he sensed that the Lord put into his mind the strong conviction that his church was self-indulgent and needed to repent. He returned home on a Sunday in February. He was jet-lagged and did not want to deal with the subject on that first Sunday, but, at the conclusion of his sermon, he mentioned his conviction to his congregation. He said that he would return to the matter the following Sunday. At the end of the service, the members of one of the church's intercessory prayer groups came to him in some agitation. They said that while he was away they had received a clear word from the Lord that the church was self-indulgent and needed to repent. God had spoken.

The following Sunday, Dr Jagelman preached on the Good Samaritan. He had been disturbed to learn on his return home that two needy members of the congregation had been neglected in his absence, and that they had stopped coming to church. He managed to get just half way through his sermon, when he could no longer go on. He walked towards the congregation and asked them, 'Why haven't you even asked about these people?' and he broke down.

He felt God was very near, and said, 'Personally, I have to seek the Lord.' And he walked out.

Within a minute, one hundred people came to him, fell on their faces and wept. There were five new families in church. Two entire families were converted on the spot. It was a revival that broke the heart of the church. And it went on for three months. It was a move of the Spirit which Dr Jagelman described as intense and unnerving and too much to live with. But when it passed, the congregation, which had previously plateaued in membership, continued to grow without any programme of outreach or a mission. It was a totally sovereign experience. He knows he could not reproduce it, and he does not particularly want to.

Is Dr Jagelman an Anglican? You will not be at all surprised to learn that he is not. And you will be even less surprised to hear that he is not Catholic or Orthodox. Dr Jagelman is pastor of Christian City Church, Lane Cove, a Pentecostal church in a Sydney suburb.

But he was an Anglican once. He grew up in a nearby prominent Sydney evangelical Anglican Church, under the ministry of a prominent evangelical Anglican minister. He was a fellowship leader there and a leader of the Crusaders, an evangelical fellowship in the private school he attended. In the mid 1960s he was in Papua New Guinea and fellowshipped with the Baptists, since the Anglican Church there was High Church, and he felt more at home with the Baptists. He became dissatisfied with the ineffectiveness of his evangelism. He embarked on a spiritual search that culminated in 1968 in an experience of personal renewal, which he now understands as a baptism of the Holy Spirit for service. It was not, he explains with some difficulty, an experiential experience, but a faith experience. From that day to this he has seen people regularly converted as a result of his evangelism.

It was only later, on his return to Australia, that he first met charismatics. He had no idea before then that there was any such thing as a Pentecostal or charismatic church. The Crusaders Movement, to which he had belonged, excluded him. He also saw that he was an embarrassment at the Anglican church to which he had by now returned. So he withdrew, feeling somewhat rejected by his spiritual roots.

It is a fairly familiar story, but it raises a number of important questions. If Dr Jagelman had been minister of an Anglican parish or priest of a Catholic Church, would revival have come? And can we have a genuine revival of God's Holy Spirit without going down the Pentecostal track?

Martyn Lloyd-Jones, who in 1966 attempted to persuade the evangelicals within the Anglican Church to leave it and establish a new evangelical church in Britain, was of the opinion that revival and Anglicanism do not mix:

> . . . the Anglican Church has not known much about revival. There have been occasions when men in her ministry have undoubtedly been part and parcel of revival, and greatly used . . . but, looking at her history, there has been no such thing as a general revival in the Anglican Church . . . Now why is this? Is it possible that there is something in her form of service that militates against the freedom of the operation of the Spirit? Is it also possible . . . that the whole character of the Church and her view of herself and her parochial system tend to discourage the phenomenon of revival within her ranks?[1]

Unfortunately Martyn Lloyd-Jones did not develop these thoughts, which are tantalizingly suggestive, but unhelpfully vague. We need to unpack them for ourselves. In this chapter we shall attempt to answer four questions: First, is it true historically that Anglicanism has been inhospitable to revival? Second, is it true historically that Catholicism has been inhospitable to revival? Third, what obstacles do sacramental churches in general put in the way of revival? Fourth, what barriers do *evangelical* Anglicans erect against revival?

Revival in the history of the Anglican Church

Martyn Lloyd-Jones is right to concede that some Anglican ministers have been greatly used as instruments in the revival of the church. John Wesley and George Whitefield are, of course, not only the two most famous Anglican ministers who come to mind when one considers revival. They are probably the two most celebrated names in the whole history of revival. Among their contemporaries were other Anglican ministers who witnessed remarkable scenes of

[1] D.M. Lloyd-Jones, *The Puritans: Their Origins and Successors*, p. 3.

revival in their parishes, especially Samuel Walker of Truro, William Grimshaw of Haworth, John Berridge at Everton and William Romaine in London.

Beginning in August 1736, Whitefield preached, in London and surrounding counties, nine times each week for a year. Huge numbers of humble London folk, who rose long before daybreak to attempt to gain entry to the most spacious of London churches, which could not contain the crowds, heard him in wonder.[2] In the Everton Revival in 1759, where Berridge was the minister, wild scenes of crying out and stamping and gasping for breath were all witnessed. People were carried from the church into his vicarage as if the victims of some great disaster. Some also laughed with 'extreme joy'.[3] Grimshaw, who combined indomitable will with startling methods, built up a congregation of a thousand communicants, with 'scarcely a trifler' among them. And, as for Samuel Walker, it was said that during the hours of divine service, the town of Truro appeared deserted as everyone packed into church, and that a cannon could be fired down every street in the town without risk of injury to anyone.

Occasionally the fires of revival burned brightly in a nineteenth-century English parish church. For example, in the Devonshire parish of Fordington, Handley Moule's father, by steadfast gospel life and steadfast gospel teaching, made the hearts of his parishioners tinder dry, until early in 1860 the fires of the 1859 Welsh revival fell.[4]

There have been revivals in Anglican churches outside of Britain. Perhaps the best known is that which began in 1931 in Gahini, in the Rwanda Mission of the Anglican Church Missionary Society.[5] It spread thence to Uganda and, by the late 1930s, had swept much of eastern Africa. It was primarily a revival among blacks, but the openness of such British Anglican CMS missionaries as Joe Church was critical to its success.[6]

So, historically Anglicanism has not been entirely inhospitable towards revival. And the Lambeth Conference of 1988 called Anglicans to pray for 'a fresh movement of the Holy Spirit' in connection

---

[2] *George Whitefield's Journals*, pp. 77, 87–9.

[3] Dixon, *Signs*, pp. 135, 137.

[4] H.C.G. Moule, 'Introduction', p. 10.

[5] Colin Reed, 'Australia and the East Africa Revival'.

[6] Church, *Quest*.

with the decade of evangelism. In other words, Anglicans have been called to pray for revival.

It might be suspected, however, that revivals in Anglican churches are more a tribute to the sovereignty of God than to the suitability of Anglicanism as an instrument. For there is no escaping the fact that the tradition of revival in Anglicanism has been weak. The 1859 revival, so strong in Ulster, Wales and Scotland, managed to ignite only three isolated spotfires in England. Similarly, revivals in twentieth-century Britain have been found only at the geographic peripheral: in Wales, Cornwall, East Anglia, Moray, Firth and the Hebrides. When it comes to the fires of revival, apparently, the Church of England is a wet blanket.

Revival in the history of the Catholic Church

What about revivals and the Catholic Church? Historians have shown that revivals did occur in medieval Catholicism,[7] in eighteenth-century British and European Catholicism,[8] and in nineteenth-century American Catholicism.[9] There has also been a recent revival among Catholics at Wapenamanda in Papua New Guinea.[10]

In the period 950 –1350 AD, missions were largely the work of the monastic orders which were themselves subject to thorough reform stemming from spiritual renewal.[11] Monasticism actually allowed the

---

[7] Augustine Thompson, *Revival Preachers and Politics in Thirteenth-Century Italy: The Great Devotion of 1233*; Carole M. Cusack, 'An Examination of the Process of Conversion among the Germanic Peoples in Late Antiquity and the Early Middle Ages'; M.A. Smith, 'Were there Revivals before 1000 A.D.?'; Davies, *Spirit*, pp. 60–2.

[8] Sheridan Gilley, 'Catholic Revival in the Eighteenth Century', pp. 99–108; Davies, *Spirit*, pp. 106–8; John Kent, 'Have we been there before? A Historian Looks at the Toronto Blessing', p. 97.

[9] Jay P. Nolan, *Catholic Revivalism: The American Experience 1830 –1900*; Gilbert J. Garraghan, *The Jesuits of the Middle United States*; Finke and Stark, *Churching*, pp. 117–23.

[10] R. Seton Arndell, 'The Revival among the Kyaka Enga People of Papua New Guinea', p. 11.

[11] Smith, 'Revivals?'; Davies, *Spirit*, pp. 60–2.

constant renewal of religious life because it attracted ardent souls and honoured the development of the spiritual life. Genuine mass movements of repentance were associated with the preaching of Francis of Assisi, and even more with the preaching of his follower, Anthony of Padua. Spiritually, vital monastic orders possessed all the men and women and machinery to conduct missions, and, when the Reformation came, outflanked the missionary efforts of the Protestants who had no such machinery. But the machinery was not enough on its own. Spiritual vitality was also required – and was apparently forthcoming.

In a class essay, one of my Regent College students, Darrel Bargen, made a very interesting comparative study of Jonathan Edwards and Bernard of Clairvaux, the most prominent leader in the 'new flowering' of Christian mysticism in the twelfth century. This was a spiritual movement which was directed in Bernard's understanding to the 'interior renewal of every monk',[12] but which became a mass movement resulting in a revival of preaching, pastoral care, missionary work, the conversion of large numbers of people and the development of an understanding of the spiritual vocation of the laity,[13] including an increased role for women in the church. It also energized a systematic application of Christian principles to society, resulting in an improved lot for the poor and sick, and a heightened respect for the institution of marriage.[14]

Bargen demonstrated that Bernard's own religious experience satisfied every one of Jonathan Edwards' five distinguishing marks of a work of the Spirit of God.[15] A Protestant might surmise that Bernard would have been unlikely to pass the fourth test, namely that his mind was established in the great central truths of the gospel. But Bernard insisted that his 'philosophy' was 'to know Jesus and him crucified'.[16] He anticipated Calvin in his understanding of the

---

[12] Jean Leclercq, 'The Intentions of the Founders of the Cistercian Order', p. 103.
[13] Colin Morris, *The Papal Monarchy: The Western Church from 1050 to 1250*, p. 288.
[14] Morris, *Papal Monarchy*, pp. 323–9.
[15] See Ch. 3, above.
[16] Bernard of Clairvaux, 'Sermon 67', *The Works of Bernard of Clairvaux*, III, p. 14.

imputed righteousness of Christ,[17] declaring: 'Whatever you impute to merit you steal from grace. I want nothing to do with the sort of merit which excludes grace.'[18]

Bargen wondered if the Protestant revival tradition should be rethought in the light of the Catholic mystical tradition, and that revival might be well understood as a visitation from God such as the mystics enjoyed. Many Protestants balk at the word 'mystical', and it requires careful definition. But A.W. Tozer and Martyn Lloyd-Jones have been among the Protestants who have themselves been described as mystics because of their appreciation of the writings of Catholic mystics.[19] In commenting on my observation that the biblical theology of revival seems to be in an undeveloped state, Bargen wondered if the vast literature of spiritual theology might be drawn upon to fill the gap. The fact that many Protestants have been so nervous about this literature may explain why revivals usually seem to die so quickly. They produce exotic spiritual plants that no one knows how to nurture because of the lack of familiarity with this literature. To become familiar with it might result in the nurture and preservation of much revival fruit.

Historians of the sixteenth century have long argued that the Counter-Reformation is better labelled the Catholic Reformation, because it owes more to new spiritual movements within the Catholic Church than to reaction to the Protestant movement. Both the Catholic and Protestant movements have more in common with each other than their theologians and historians have hitherto allowed. Now, in the remarkable study *The Protestant Evangelical Awakening*,[20] Reg Ward traces the spirituality of the Great Awakening back through the Pietists and the Puritans to the mystics of the Catholic Reformation. That Reformation doctrine combined with Counter-Reformation spirituality is the potent mixture out of which revival grew is now an entirely defensible thesis.

Protestants may be equally surprised to discover that Catholics may have used nineteenth-century revivalism highly successfully.

---

[17] A.N.S. Lane, 'Bernard of Clairvaux: A Forerunner of John Calvin?', p. 534.
[18] Bernard of Clairvaux, 'Sermon 43', *On the Song of Songs*, IV, p. 223.
[19] Sargent, *Sacred Anointing*, p. 182.
[20] Ward, *Protestant*.

Sociologists Roger Finke and Rodney Stark have recently asserted the impact of revival on the growth of the American Catholic Church. They tell us that American Catholics numbered just over one million in 1850 and rose to 7.3 million in 1890, or 12 per cent of the population, to 14 million by 1906, or 16 per cent of the population. True, most of them were immigrants and most came from Catholic countries, but the important point is that a significant percentage of them had not been practising Catholics before they came to America. Something happened to them after immigration that encouraged them to choose their ancestral faith rather than one of the many Protestant options available in the American religious market. That something was Catholic missions which, led by the religious orders, especially the Jesuits, Passionists, Paulists and Redemptorists, spread revivalism and devotionalism throughout America. Catholic parishes were renewed, nominalism was reduced, and the Catholic population was mobilized. Finke and Stark have written:

> At the centre of this new evangelical surge was the Catholic revival campaign. American Catholics didn't call these revivals, nor did they label those who led them evangelists. These events were referred to as Catholic parish missions, and their origins were traced to the Jesuits in the sixteenth century. But revival meetings is what they were, and they occurred about as frequently and regularly in Catholic parishes as in Baptist and Methodist congregations.[21]

Similarly, there have been revivals in Australian Catholic churches.[22] The Redemptorists, introduced to Australia in 1882, were experts in 'Catholic revivalism'.[23] So too were the Vincentians. The Passionists, Jesuits, Paulists and Franciscans were also active in this work. Catholic missions consisted of 'long and impassioned sermons, strong in emphasis on hell-fire, church authority and strict moral laws'.[24] At Flinders University in South Australia, I recently

---

[21] Finke and Stark, *Churching*, pp. 117f.

[22] Hugh Jackson, *Churches and People in Australia and New Zealand, 1860–1930*, pp. 65–76.

[23] John Sharp, *Reapers of the Harvest: The Redemptorists in England and Ireland, 1843–1898*.

[24] P. O'Farrell, *The Catholic Church and Community in Australia*, p. 212; Stuart Piggin, *Faith of Steel*, p. 127.

met a Catholic historian who recalls weeping under conviction at Redemptorist missions in his youth. There was the equivalent of coming forward to receive Christ: in Catholic missions those under conviction went to the confessional. There they received the sacrament of penance, and then they met with others at the altar to receive Holy Communion. At a mission held in the mining town of Thirroul in NSW in 1928, for example, 286 made the journey to the confessional, 675 made the journey to the altar, 168 joined the Sacred Heart Sodality, and one marriage, hitherto invalid by church standards, was 'rectified'. An essential element in religious revival, namely the felt presence of the Lord, is understood and exploited by Catholics in their Marian and Eucharistic processions, such as attracted enormous crowds in the 1950s.

It is tantalizing to speculate on whether the Catholic procedure was more effective long-term than those of the Protestant revivalists. If it is true that every revival is a movement of repentance, then it is difficult to deny that many of these Catholic missions were accompanied by genuine revival. In a typical mission, the missioner priest might spend up to ten hours daily in the confessional, hearing confessions of a kind that the resident parish priest would not have heard. The missioners aimed at 'complete cleansing', not just 'a little tidying'.[25] Maybe many a Catholic mission produced 'fruits meet for repentance'.[26] It has been suggested that these missions were very successful in getting Catholics to attend mass and to observe other religious duties. They reduced the pool of nominal Catholics and became the instrument of maintenance rather than evangelism.[27] Revivals have often been understood as the chief weapon by which the church wages war on nominalism. The study of Catholic revivalism is arguably the best proof of that claim, because Catholics have been one of the most successful of all churches in minimizing this problem. Nominalism is becoming a growing concern in the Catholic Church today, but it may be significant that its re-emergence coincides with the decline of Catholic revivalism.

As far as the late twentieth century was concerned, there was little doubt that the bloodless revolution in the Philippines that

---

[25] Jackson, *Churches and People*, p. 71.

[26] Matt. 3:8.

[27] Jackson, *Churches and People*, p. 75.

ousted the Marcos regime owed everything to Catholic religious revival. Charles Colson, chairman of the board of Prison Fellowship Ministries, put it like this:

> Cardinal Sin of the Philippines, a leader in the Catholic renewal movement worldwide, tells the story of the Philippine revolution against Marcos from his own perspective. After Cardinal Sin heard that Aquino had been assassinated, he began to search the Scriptures. He found in 2 Chronicles that God may punish a people by giving them an unjust ruler. He believed God was punishing the Philippine people. In response, he began to preach a message of repentance and personal commitment to Christ throughout the country. As he pleaded with people to surrender their lives to Christ, renewal began to break out all over the Philippine Islands.
>
> When the election was rigged and the revolution broke out, Cardinal Sin announced over the radio that he wanted all Christians to go into the streets to pray and protect the soldiers. Within thirty minutes, three million people had poured out onto the streets. Every tank was stopped dead in its tracks before millions of people down on their knees praying to God. Not a single drop of blood was shed. The church in the Philippines became the instrument of holding that government to moral account, the instrument of righteousness in that culture. That's what happens when the church is truly the church.[28]

So from the Middle Ages to the present day, the Catholic Church has enjoyed seasons of renewal and revival. But, as with the Anglican Church, the revival tradition has been weak and more frequently reviled than revered. Ronald Knox wrote a comparative study of revival in Catholic and Protestant churches in which his thesis was that the periods of enthusiasm in the history of the church were aberrations much to be deplored.[29] Yet, after thirty years spent studying the subject, he conceded that the enthusiasms he reviewed were 'not exactly heresies, and I have not refuted them'.[30]

---

[28] C. Colson, 'The Secularization of America'.

[29] R.A. Knox, *Enthusiasm*; Lloyd-Jones, *Revival*, p. 73.

[30] Knox, *Enthusiasm*, p. v.

Obstacles that sacramental churches put in the way of revival

In reviewing the obstacles which churches in the tradition of Catholic sacramentalism are perceived as putting in the way of revival, let us begin with the opinions of Lloyd-Jones and J.I. Packer, two evangelical writers outside the Anglo-Catholic tradition. We will then seek a response from those within the tradition.

'There is something in her form of service,' wrote Dr Lloyd-Jones describing the Church of England, 'that militates against the freedom of the operation of the Spirit.' What this might be we can only conjecture. It has been suggested that formalism, the Prayer Book, clericalism, traditionalism, sacramentalism and nominalism have all shielded the church from the fires of the Spirit. J.I. Packer, the evangelical Anglican scholar, has identified formalism in worship style as a Spirit-quencher:

> . . . many churches seem to view worship in a way that can only be called formalistic for their interest is limited to performing set routines with suitable correctness, and there is no apparent desire on anyone's part actually to meet God.[31]

Revival is all about actually meeting the living God. Is formalism a way of avoiding that meeting while creating the appearance of seeking it?

There are those who claim that the Prayer Book has never worked as an instrument to bring people into an actual meeting with the actual God. The Prayer Book has always been an effective instrument of worship only for a small minority. It requires a reading age of twenty-one before it can be understood. Its expression is far more complicated than it needs to be. Pre-written prayers presuppose that one learns by repetition, but repetition breeds contempt. It takes a lot of self-discipline to concentrate on repeated prayers in order to get anything out of them, and is that the most constructive use one can make of concentration in a service of worship? Pre-written prayers actually stop some people from learning how to pray.

---

[31] Packer, *God in our Midst*, p. 42.

Packer identifies clericalism, too, as a Spirit-quencher:

> *Clericalism* as a leadership style is Spirit-quenching. Clericalism, which
> . . . involves more persons than the ordained, is a sort of conspiracy
> beween leaders and those led: the one party . . . says 'all spiritual
> ministry should be left to the leader', and the other party says, 'yes,
> that's right'. Some leaders embrace clericalism because it gives them
> power; others, running scared, embrace it because they fear lest folk
> ministering alongside them should overshadow them, or because they
> feel incapable of handling an every-member ministry situation. But
> every-member-ministry in the body of Christ is the New Testament
> pattern, and anything which obstructs or restricts it is an obstacle to a
> renewing visitation from God.[32]

Sacramentalism, an exclusive reliance on sacraments as the means of receiving God's grace, would inhibit revival. But, while all Anglicans attach importance to the sacraments, not all are sacramentalists in that exclusive sense. In fact, it was the evangelical clergy who were the products of the eighteenth-century evangelical revival who were responsible for a revival in the use of sacraments in the Church of England. In evangelical parishes there were more – sometimes dramatically more – baptisms and numbers of people attending communion than in non-evangelical parishes. There are certainly greater obstacles to revival than the use of sacraments.

Perhaps a greater danger is Anglicanism's inclination to live off its tradition. It is, of course, a great tradition, but after all it is only a tradition based on the memory of God. It will only come to life when the Holy Spirit is there to vivify, heal, convict and convert.

Nominalism is a problem in Anglicanism. But it is interesting that in all revivals, bar none, one of the most conspicuous features is that many who before were nominal Christians are awakened for the first time to such a concern for their soul's welfare that they see the reality of the narrow gate and they know that they must strive to press through it. It is good to have 'nominals' in church: come the revival they are usually the first to be revived.

---

[32] Packer, *God in our Midst*, p. 41.

Anglo–Catholicism and the experience of revival

Having dealt with all these problems advanced by our two evangelical critics outside the Catholic tradition – formalism, the Prayer
Book, clericalism, sacramentalism, traditionalism and nominalism –
we must ask if we have really come to the heart of the matter. Those
things are surely largely external issues, and they do not establish
that, done properly, in the presence of those who have Jesus in their
hearts and the Spirit in their lives, Anglican liturgy and worship is
incompatible with revival. Equally, of course, such externals are no
substitute for 'true, spiritual religion'. Anglo–Catholics have been
quite capable of acknowledging that. The prominent nineteenth-
century mission preacher, Joseph Lyne, more popularly known as
Father Ignatius, to whom is attributed the revival of the Benedictine
Order within Anglicanism, insisted that:

> Unless I have first obtained the blessings of the Evangelical movement,
> the Tractarian [Anglo–Catholic] movement will be to me a curse in-
> stead of a blessing. I do not believe in Sacraments unless the person
> who participates in them has a personal belief in a personal Saviour.[33]

But most Anglo–Catholics would want to say more about Lloyd-
Jones' and Packer's dismissal of sacramentalism. John Moses, a
committed Anglo–Catholic professor of history at an Australian
university, sees a vast cultural divide between the aspirations of most
in the Catholic tradition and evangelicals in the revival tradition. He
finds the longing for revival to be culturally and intellectually alien.
It is the hope of those living in 'another intellectual universe', constituted out of biblical literalism which he calls 'revelation positiv-
ism', a false expectation of 'instant spiritual maturity', and the
downgrading of learning and reverence for tradition.[34] This is a very
important way of perceiving the problem. The divide between
evangelicals and charismatics, reviewed in Chapters 5 and 6 above,
has much to do with cultural differences. How much greater, then, is
the cultural divide between evangelicalism and Catholicism.

---

[33] Quoted in Geoffrey Rowell, *The Vision Glorious: Themes and Personalities of the Catholic Revival in Anglicanism*, p. 138.
[34] John Moses, letter to the author, 22 Oct. 1997.

But church history is not only about differences resulting from different times and different places, it is also about the continuities, the endless line of splendour, the things in common in the great tradition of theological thought and spiritual practice. God's reviving Spirit has been pleased to work in many different ways, in different traditions and cultures. The externals of those cultures need not be Spirit-quenching. It is not so surprising that many with a deep interest in revival and church history develop an interest in Catholic devotional practice and mysticism.

God's Spirit has been known to visit congregations in the Anglo-Catholic tradition with revival. Consider, for example, a movement of the Spirit of God that took place in the small Australian rural township of Balranald in the Anglo-Catholic Diocese of Riverina. The priest-in-charge of St Barnabas' Anglican Church from 1974 to 1979 was Gary Priest. In those years he baptized more than half the total population of the town and immediate district. His is an amazing story. Gary, born in 1941, was converted in Sydney at St James' King Street, a middle to high Anglican parish. There he had a deep experience of God's Spirit at communion, calling him at first to Christ and then to the priesthood. The bishop to whom he applied turned him down because he could not read. An elderly woman living in Sydney spotted this unusual young man and arranged with the Bishop of Riverina for him to be trained at her expense. When he arrived in Balranald, only four people went regularly to church, and the annual income was only $600. For about a year things stayed like that, until a woman was converted and added to the church with her two sons. Another woman took a dislike to her; people took sides and there was major discord in the congregation. Gary pleaded with his congregation to work out their differences, but they would not. Then, tragically, the newly converted woman was killed in a road accident. She had stopped to help a stranded motorist and was hit by a truck herself.

As we shall see in the next chapter, the God who brings life out of death often gives revival to those suffering disaster. That was the case here. As a result of her death, a spirit of brokenness and repentance swept the congregation. There was a great surge in the congregation's growth, both numerically and spiritually. The following Christmas, three hundred people came to church. Many were baptized or had their children, whom they had hitherto left in unchurched paganism, baptized. The bishop observed that Gary seemed to be baptizing the rabbits. Confirmations were huge. Providentially, a group of six evangelical Christian teachers just happened to be posted to the local schools, and they brought a freshness and a biblical rigour needed by the expanding congregation.[35] The church community began to pull together as one. They looked to the mission of the church instead of being a mission. They not only met all their own expenses, but they paid for the training of another priest and gave generously to a bishop in another diocese to facilitate ministry there.

As for traditional Anglican worship, that it need not quench the Spirit was brought home to me by an experience I had while on leave in America. My uncle, then the headmaster of an Australian Anglican Church school, visited me at Yale Divinity School, New Haven. He had been to a number of 'successful' American churches, but he said to me, 'How I long for some good Anglican liturgy – do you know of any nearby Episcopalian churches where we would receive blessing and be able to enjoy the liturgy at the same time?' I did not, so we wandered into the Divinity School quadrangle in quest of an Episcopalian student who could advise us. The first one to whom we put the question replied, without hesitation, 'You must go to St Paul's Church in Darien.'[36]

Darien is about halfway between New Haven and New York, and we not only left it too late to get there on time, but we got hopelessly lost as well. So I went into a bar and asked directions, thinking that, if this church really were alive, members of the local community would know about it – even those who drank in bars during the hour of divine worship. Sure enough, the first person I asked did know where it was, even though we had strayed a long way from the school in which the church met.

We arrived late, and the first thing we saw as we entered the school auditorium were arms waving, and we looked at each other with raised eyebrows and concluded that we had come to some sort of 'Penty show'. The next thing that struck us was that on the stage was an altar draped in a cloth of a colour appropriate to the season.

---

[35] Letter from G.C. Davis, 30 Aug. 1991; discussion with Gary Priest, 31 March 1997.
[36] On Darien, see Bob Slosser, *Miracle in Darien*.

There were half a dozen priests all dressed in vestments. Our eyebrows were raised even higher as we clearly signalled each other that this was a 'High Church Penty show'.

We had not long to wait for the sermon. This was Holy Communion, and the sermon comes early in the Anglican communion liturgy. When the Revd Terry Fullam began his sermon, we were transfixed. Here was an exposition of the divine word so authoritative that we had never heard more biblical preaching anywhere. So this was an evangelical, High Church Penty show. It was all those things at once – a glorious and undivided trinity. After the sermon, people moved forward to take the sacrament and some spent time with elders at the front discussing and praying over their problems. The atmosphere was wonderfully healthy: it was full of warmth and love. The unselfconscious combination, without apology or even explanation, of the great traditions of the church – Catholic, Evangelical and Pentecostal – clearly signalled that the Spirit of God was happy to be there.

Barriers erected by evangelical Anglicans against revival

That it is a side-track to imagine that our worship is not revived because of the deadening effect of such external matters as sacramentalism, traditionalism and formalism is also evident from the fact that the expression of Anglicanism which rejects them is itself often impervious to revival. I refer to evangelical Anglicanism. Evangelical Anglicans commonly have other habits of the heart that shield them from the Spirit's fire. Their clergy are overly academic, and they have a fear of emotion, a horror of error, and a spirit of criticism.

Evangelical Anglican clergy are trained to have an academic relationship with God rather than a personal one. J.I.Packer has warned:

Renewal in all its aspects is not a theme for dilettante debate, but for humble, penitent, prayerful, faith-full exploration before the Lord, with a willingness to change and to be changed, and if necessary to be the first to be changed, if that is what the truth proves to require. To absorb ideas about renewal ordinarily costs nothing, but to enter into renewal could cost us everything we have, and we shall be very guilty if, having come to understand renewal, we then decline it. We need to be clear about that. John Calvin once declared that it would be better for a preacher to break his neck while mounting the pulpit if he did not himself intend to be the first to follow God.[37]

The evangelical revival completely changed the whole tone of preaching, which in the early eighteenth century tended to be learned and moralizing rather than relevant and applied. Teaching, rather than preaching, is an occupational hazard of all learned ministers.

Another reason why revival is not revered in conservative evangelical circles is that there seems to be so much doctrinal error compounded in the theology of those who speak much of revival. But as Edwards said, the presence of doctrinal error in the thinking of those who promote revival, and even the falling of some into gross errors and scandalous practices, is no guarantee that the work in general is not the work of the Spirit of God. There never has been a revival free of error and scandal: it is unrealistic to expect it. Martyn Lloyd-Jones agrees: 'It is sheer Arminianism to insist upon a true and correct understanding as being [an] essential' prerequisite to the pouring out of the Spirit.[38]

Evangelical Anglicans are also commonly afraid of emotionalism. Ever since Wesley and the Methodists were charged with 'enthusiasm' in the eighteenth century, the Anglicans have sought to avoid association with excessive religious excitement. Eugene Stock, historian of CMS, sagely concluded that 'if our clergy had more heartily welcomed the [1857–60] Revival, its effects within the Church of England would have been much greater.'[39]

Evangelical Anglicans also too often have a negative spirit: they do a lot of condemning. They seem to be known for what they condemn. Jonathan Edwards expressed exasperation with ministers who seemed determined to find fault with every aspect of the Great Awakening. He would probably want to make a similar point if he visited some reformed Anglican churches today.

---

[37] Packer, *God in our Midst*, pp. 6f.
[38] Lloyd-Jones, *Puritans*, p. 297.
[39] Eugene Stock, *My Recollections*, p. 83.

Does Anglicanism inhibit revival? And if so, how? I asked Dr Jagelman. He replied that in his opinion it does inhibit revival, and the chief reason is not the Prayer Book, or the cultural inappropriateness of Anglicanism, or its structures. The chief reason is that our leaders, both clerical and lay, are afraid. They are afraid of not being accepted by the club. They have been more concerned about their identity as evangelical Anglicans than with their identity as Christ's soldiers. To be identified with the club, one must work within certain parameters. Lines are drawn which are not to be crossed. Boundaries are set; they are not to be transgressed. This situation is the result of the fear of human beings and not of God.

We evangelical Anglicans pray that the word will be our rule, but it is often the word interpreted in conformity with a particular hermeneutic. The African evangelical Michael Cassidy has spoken angrily of this refined and acceptable way of muzzling the word of God, thus putting ourselves 'on the path either to personal powerlessness or national perdition':

> The old-time liberals were more honest and said simply that they did not believe everything the Bible said. Modern evangelicals fight such people tooth and nail, and cast them to miscellaneous quarters of ecclesiastical or theological outer darkness – but in love, of course! Then we go on to excuse ourselves of huge sections of the Bible by affirming that those things were written for other places and other times. Or else we pull huge hermeneutical tricks on ourselves and by sleight of hand subvert the text by subordinating it either to an alien set of naturalistic presuppositions or an alien set of human ideologies . . . What happens is that we all maintain a surface appearance of respect and obedience to the Bible, and below the surface we have respectfully torpedoed it, even while fighting vigorously for its 'plenarily inspired nature and authority'.[40]

Finally, important as boundaries are to the fruit of any movement, we must not impose limits on God and draw lines across which we do not want him to come. By all means test all things, but do not be judgemental. To return to a question with which I began this chapter: does one have to be Pentecostal to experience revival? 'No,'

---

[40] Michael Cassidy, *The Prophetic Word in the Crisis Context*, p. 14.

replied Dr Jagelman, 'but you do have to be completely open to God and not set boundaries to his work. Having a closed mind about the way God's Holy Spirit works is a quencher of the Spirit.' Is having a biblical understanding of the way the Holy Spirit works in the world to have a closed mind? Of course not. But one must be so very careful that one's understanding is biblical rather than fashioned by a hermeneutic that is not in itself or in its entirety biblical.

Conclusion

Is Anglicanism incompatible with revival? Not primarily or necessarily in its traditions, liturgy, sacraments, prayer book or structures. Christ and the Holy Spirit are happy to work through them. But whenever it puts the fear of human beings before the fear of God or sets boundaries to the way in which the sovereign God can act, Anglicanism is frustrating revival.

8

God's Sovereignty and Human Responsibility in Revival

A revival among German settlers at Evans' Mills in the United States in 1824 commenced when Charles Finney preached on the text 'Without holiness no man can see the Lord'.

> I began by showing what holiness is not. Under this head I took every-thing that they considered to be religion, and showed that it was not holiness at all. In the second place I showed what holiness is. I then showed, thirdly, what is intended by seeing the Lord; and then, why those that had no holiness could never see the Lord – why they could never be admitted to his presence, and be accepted of him. I then con-cluded with such pointed remarks as were intended to make the sub-ject go home. And it did go home by the power of the Holy Ghost. The sword of the Lord slew them on the right hand and on the left. In a very few days it was found that the whole settlement was under con-viction.[1]

Finney's account illustrates the respective roles of the human and the divine in revival. There are a lot of 'I's' in this account. The successful outcome owed much to the preacher who used his intelligence and experience to make 'such pointed remarks as were intended to make the subject go home'. On the other hand, it went 'home' by the Holy Spirit. Success would have been impossible without 'the power of the Holy Ghost'.

Finney has been categorized as a 'New School Calvinist'. Theologically, 'New School Calvinism' looked very like 'Old

---

[1] Charles G. Finney, *An Autobiography*, pp. 73f.

School Arminianism' as it shifted revival away from the Holy Spirit and moved it to the 'I'. The next generation of revivalists got perilously close to speaking of revival as if it were all up to the 'I'. Reuben Torrey, for example, declared:

> [Revivals] are awakened by men who are cocksure of their ground, and who speak with authority . . . Revival preaching must be directed towards the heart and not the head . . . Get hold of the heart and the head yields easily.[2]

Revival in Jonathan Edwards' understanding happens when *God* gets hold of the heart. Revivalism is when the preacher gets hold of the heart.

The opposite extreme – to be unconcerned about revival on the grounds that it is all up to God – is equally wrong. That is fatalism, not Calvinism, and fatalism is never good theology. It is just fatal. The sovereign God will not bring revival without your help or mine. In his sovereignty, God chooses you and me to be his instrument in his revival work.

In this chapter we will redress the view, prominent in Reformed circles, that a due respect for the sovereignty of God is incompatible with an eager longing for revival. We will also seek to correct the Arminian notion that revival is purely a matter of getting the human instrument perfectly tuned to play the revival song. Consideration of the emphasis on God's sovereignty in the thought of Jonathan Edwards and a review of the 'new measures' of Charles Finney that put the emphasis on human responsibility will lay the foundation here. We shall then be in a position to understand how a robust belief in the sovereignty of God intensifies longing for revival. Then, returning to the idea that revival is always a community experience, we will analyze the relationship between revival and disaster in order to illustrate that God's providence is the chief factor in bringing national and community awakening and that revival is concerned not only with personal happiness, but also with the avoidance of community calamity.

---

[2] R.A. Torrey, *How to Promote and Conduct a Successful Revival.*

The Spirit and human initiative in the thought of Jonathan Edwards

The great preachers whom God used to initiate revival in the United States, from Jonathan Edwards in the first Great Awakening to Asahel Nettleton in the second, regarded the doctrine of the sovereignty of God as foundational to their preaching. They were convinced Calvinists. They believed that sinners stand helpless before a sovereign God. The sinner often feels an obligation to repent, but he is so in love with sin that he cannot, and so full of pride that he will not. Therefore God has to subdue the rebellious heart or knit together the divided heart – otherwise he would never be converted. Calvinist preachers did not make appeals and altar calls, for such were appeals to the human will. They counselled those who were under conviction to wait upon God until he visited them with his salvation, thus quieting the distressed conscience.

Such an approach seems remarkably passive in the light of subsequent more aggressive evangelistic methods. But the 'Calvinist approach' was remarkably successful in the sense that the first two great awakenings saw a vast number of converts. In fact, the Calvinists were so excited about the great revivals of the 1740s and 1790s that they taught that God was beginning to bring in the millennium when the Holy Spirit would be poured out in unprecedented abundance. The revivals, they believed, were the early rain of this promised divine deluge of blessing.

The belief that God would pour out his Spirit in a thousand years of unprecedented blessing for the church before the Lord returned was known as postmillennialism. It was a belief calculated to encourage the faithful 'to come to the aid of the Lord'. The Calvinists argued that all history was on the side of the elect. And they used history as an incitement to human initiative. At first sight this appears strange in a Calvinist context. Why bother to exert yourself if you are going to win anyway? But few Calvinists have ever seen it that way. Instead, with shrewd psychological insight, they have argued that people come the more willingly to help a cause when it is a winning cause. 'Labouring beyond the power of mortality' became the ambition of the sanctified soul. In all this, we have a major conviction of Edwards. Divine determinism and human free will are not in conflict. Divine sovereignty excites human determination.

The corollary was plain. It was necessary to understand God's plan of redemption so that one could co-operate with it. Edwards therefore concluded his treatise *Some Thoughts Concerning the Revival* (1742) with Part V, 'Showing Positively what ought to be done to Promote this Work'. Among those human initiatives which believers could and should make were: removing stumbling blocks; affirming orthodox doctrine; nurturing true religion in students for the ministry; and using wealth for religious purposes. Inspired by such reasoning, the evangelicals developed their characteristic stress on *means* for the conversion of souls: prayer, union, preaching, Bible and tract distribution and missions. A great flowering of evangelical voluntary societies, dedicated to the improvement of society and the conversion of the nations, ensued at the beginning of the nineteenth century.

If Edwards devised one way out of the straitjacket of determinism and complacency, Charles Finney devised another. He challenged Edwards' Calvinism, insisting that sinners were not helpless before God. They were quite capable of turning from their sins and therefore had the responsibility of doing just that. Finney also extended Edwards' range of legitimate 'means' to promote the extension of the kingdom, ushering in a new era of pragmatism: if it works, use it.

Charles Grandison Finney: From the divinely appointed means to human techniques

Finney has been castigated by Calvinists both during his own lifetime and since for his reliance on human means in the promotion of revival, thus commencing the erosion of the church's reliance on God's sovereignty. It must be said in Finney's defence that he had no desire to undermine reliance on God's sovereignty. But he was driven to undermine the abuse of that doctrine, especially when it was used as an excuse to do nothing for the salvation of sinners. On the teaching of one Revd Gilbert of Wilmington, Finney wrote:

> I soon found that his teaching had placed the church in a position that rendered it impossible to promote a revival among them, till their

views could be corrected. They seemed to be afraid to make any effort, lest they should take the work out of the hands of God . . . their theory was that God would convert sinners in his own time; and that therefore to urge them to immediate repentance, and in short to attempt to promote a revival, was to attempt to make men Christians by human agency, and human strength, and thus to dishonour God by taking the work out of his hands. I observed also, that in their prayers there was no urgency for an immediate outpouring of the Spirit, and that this was all in accordance with the views in which they had been educated.[3]

If his harvest is anything to go by, Finney cannot have been completely wrong. He is said to have won over half a million people to Christ and to have brought renewal to countless more. Even his opponents concede that while many of Finney's converts fell away, some were 'truly converted to Christ'.[4] It is probably the readiness to be impressed by Finney's numerical 'success' that has resulted in over-toleration of his heterodoxies. Nevertheless, it is important to learn from his own pen what his practice and beliefs were before passing sentence. So, before we take sides, let's set out the ten tenets of 'Finneyism' so that we can ponder and learn from this instrument so honoured of the Lord.

First, as to doctrine, Finney insisted on 'the atonement of Jesus Christ, his divinity, his divine mission, his perfect life, his vicarious death, his resurrection'.[5] He taught the need for 'repentance, faith, and justification by faith, and all the kindred doctrines'.[6] Finney taught 'the total moral depravity of the unregenerate' and 'the unalterable necessity of a radical change of heart by the Holy Ghost'.[7]

Second, he 'laid great stress upon prayer as an indispensable condition of promoting the revival'.[8]

Third, as to means, he employed 'preaching, prayer and conference meetings, much private prayer, much personal conversation, and meetings for the instruction of earnest enquirers'.[9]

---

[3] Finney, *Autobiography*, p. 234.
[4] Bennet Tyler and Andrew A. Bonar, *Nettleton and his Labours*, p. 340.
[5] Finney, *Autobiography*, p. 77.
[6] Finney, *Autobiography*, p. 77.
[7] Finney, *Autobiography*, p. 77.
[8] Finney, *Autobiography*, p. 77.
[9] Finney, *Autobiography*, p. 77.

Fourth, he changed current understanding of the role of God in conversion. This practice assumed that anxious sinners were willing to be Christians, and that their responsibility was 'to persuade God to convert them'.[10] Finney sought to persuade them that 'God was willing, and they were unwilling; that God was ready and they were not ready'.[11] He told them that God required of them faith and repentance, submission to his will, and acceptance of Christ. And he argued that God required these things *now*. All delay was an evasion of responsibility and duty. All attempts to do anything good for God before this was settled were hypocritical and delusive. It was unhelpful to encourage sinners to remain for a long period of time under the conviction of sin, as the older evangelists had done, since that only encourages self-righteousness in those who feel they have laboured long in earnest praying for their own conversion.[12] Sinners were not to be pitied so much as blamed for persevering in their refusal to accept Christ. 'We expect to get a verdict,' he wrote, 'and to get it upon the spot.'[13] Most preaching does not aim for a verdict and does not expect to get one. But almost all of Finney's preaching resulted in the conviction and conversion of sinners within a few hours.[14] The day of sudden conversions had arrived.

Fifth, Finney used simple, everyday language. He was determined when preaching the gospel to be 'thoroughly understood'.[15] He refused to follow the current practice of using ornate language or striking illustrations. He proved that even educated sinners are converted not through being entertained or impressed by oratorical refinements, but by being persuaded by argument. 'We are set on getting a verdict. Hence we are set upon being understood.'[16]

Sixth, he was always ready and willing to preach, as his heart was full of the gospel message. He did not insist that every message had to be painstakingly prepared beforehand.[17]

---

[10] Finney, *Autobiography*, p. 79.

[11] Finney, *Autobiography*, p. 80.

[12] Finney, *Autobiography*, p. 189.

[13] Finney, *Autobiography*, p. 86.

[14] Finney, *Autobiography*, p. 190.

[15] Finney, *Autobiography*, p. 81.

[16] Finney, *Autobiography*, p. 86.

[17] Finney, *Autobiography*, p. 82.

Seventh, he was quite prepared to abandon the pulpit and roam around the aisles, like a lawyer before a jury.[18]

Eighth, he was prepared to jettison a number of pulpit conventions in order to make his point. He addressed people directly, saying 'you' instead of preaching impersonally about sin and sinners by using 'they'.[19] He would resort to vehemence, not always maintaining a calm and rational demeanour. He did not mind offending people:

> Now you resent this, and you will go away and say that you will not come again; but you will. Your own convictions are on my side. You know that what I tell you is true; and that I tell it for your own good; and that you cannot continue to resent it.[20]

Ninth, he believed that the validity of preaching was to be measured by its results in the conversion of sinners. He constantly strove to improve his preaching, but he would never model it on the preaching of one whose preaching bore no fruit in soul winning.[21]

Tenth, Finney is the barrister, the advocate as preacher. He would use much repetition until he was confident that his hearers had understood and affirmed his contentions. He would take one point and 'turn it over, and illustrate it in various ways'.[22]

Now, none of this sounds terribly erroneous, and indeed much of it sounds helpful to those who long to be used of God in reviving his church. But one must have a look at what Finney does not say, as well as what he does.

Although Finney insisted that he did teach the total moral depravity of the unregenerate, he did not teach either inherited depravity or that sinners were in their very nature sinful. That total moral depravity which he taught he described as 'voluntary'. Sinners are totally depraved because they decide so to be, not because, in their own strength, they are incapable of being anything else. They are not depraved by nature, but by choice. Therefore, sin is

---

[18] Finney, *Autobiography*, p. 82.

[19] Finney, *Autobiography*, p. 83.

[20] Finney, *Autobiography*, p. 93.

[21] Finney, *Autobiography*, p. 83.

[22] Finney, *Autobiography*, p. 83.

humankind's selfish choice in the exercise of our free will. We sin because we choose to. Sin is a deliberate choice to do evil, a wilful refusal to do our plain duty.

Similarly, Finney insisted that it is we who deliberately choose whether or not to repent. We are all perfectly able to repent, but we choose not to. So our problem is not a natural inability but a moral unwillingness. We do not need any special divine agency to convert us; we just need to resolve to do the right thing. Therefore the role of the Holy Spirit is not to breathe life into or to revive a dead soul, but to persuade the will to do what is best for the soul. The role of the Holy Spirit is limited to 'moral suasion', or persuasion based on an appeal to the conscience. And the Holy Spirit does this through the divine word, which is spoken by the preacher. So the preacher is critical. A revival is not a miracle, Finney insisted. It is the result of *the right use of the constituted means.*

These means were now subtly translated into the techniques of persuasion: powerful denunciatory preaching; harsh accusations; 'crushing' and 'breaking down' techniques; protracted meetings; naming sinners in public prayer (a habit modified after someone prayed earnestly in Finney's presence that the great man might be given the spirit of meekness); the anxious bench, where those under conviction could move for counselling; prayers and exhortations by women during the appeal for conversions after the preaching. Revival meetings grew longer and longer, not as the hearers waited on God, but as they waited on the sinner to make up his mind to repent. Even prayer was reduced to technique: the prayer of faith *must* be answered (whereas Edwards always taught that prayer must remain submissive).

Finney's techniques were known as the 'new measures' and were justified on the grounds that anything that persuaded a sinner to repent must be legitimate. This is 'revivalism', and it is ultimately a work of the flesh. True revival will always be a surprising work of the sovereign Spirit of God, never an anticipated outcome of the application of human techniques. On witnessing the effects of the 'new measures' in the town of Troy, New York, in the United States, some godly ministers of the gospel declared, 'We do not want such a revival as they have in Troy.'[23]

---

[23] Tyler and Bonar, *Nettleton*, p. 343.

Finney came to dominate the religious scene in America. In joining him, Lyman Beecher, the influential Boston theologian, removed much of the opposition from the conservative east. Both he and Finney became presidents of colleges that energetically peddled the new theology. Oberlin Theology, emanating from Finney's Oberlin College, was based on sinless perfection, a concept that would divide the evangelical world for the next century and beyond.

The controversy quickly provoked the writing of a classic work from the conservative side. William B. Sprague, a New York Presbyterian and graduate of Princeton, published his *Lectures on Revival* in 1832. It was republished in 1958 by Martyn Lloyd-Jones for the Banner of Truth Trust to celebrate the centenary of the 1859 revival. It is a masterful statement of the nature of true revival. As to the agency of the Spirit in the work of conversion, Sprague insists not only that it is essential, but that 'more of his omnipotence is exerted here than in any other part of his work'. Far from being an expression of human volition, conversion is an act of 'the almighty energies of God's Spirit'.[24]

Revival, we must conclude, is the work of the omnipotent sovereignty of God – of God the Father, who sends the Son, who pours out the Spirit, whose almighty energies convert the soul. The implications of this insistence on the indispensable role of the sovereign Spirit of God in revival should be made quite explicit.

Four corollaries of the sovereignty of God in revival

First of all, a robust belief in the sovereignty of God will greatly strengthen the expectation of and longing for revival. If this is not true in your case, then you either do not really believe in the sovereignty of God or you are illogical . . . or both.

Many who pride themselves on their Reformed orthodoxy have a particular understanding of Calvinism which encourages them to be faithful in the ordinary, but not expectant of the extraordinary activity of the Holy Spirit. The argument goes something like this: Revivals are out-of-the ordinary manifestations of the sovereign

---

[24] W.B. Sprague, *Lectures on Revival*, p. 102 of the 1958 edn.

Spirit. They are not man-made, and therefore we might as well leave it all up to God. He will bring revival in his own time without any help from you or me, so let's talk about something else.

It is not a very logical position to adopt. It is precisely in those areas where the sovereignty is critical that we should work hardest and wait the more expectantly on God, for there we are most likely to enjoy the greatest success. Broughton Knox, one-time principal of Moore Theological College in Sydney, Australia, was fond of saying, 'If God is not sovereign over everything what is the point of praying?' But if he is sovereign over everything, then why not pray expectantly for revival? Martyn Lloyd-Jones does not have any difficulty understanding why Arminians should give up on hoping for revival. What perplexes him far more is that Calvinists give up on it.[25]

'Ah!' you object, 'it is where God's sovereign Spirit works in an ordinary, regular way, such as conversion following evangelism, that we should pray expectantly, but not where he works in an exceptional way such as revival. For we might be labouring for something that will never happen.' That is nonsense – the ordinary might never happen either – still we evangelize.

'Still,' you say, 'conversions are more frequent than revivals. I prefer to work and pray for the more frequent.' That, I suggest, is a very arbitrary preference.

'Well,' you say, 'I work and pray for conversion, because human agency is the normal instrument of conversion used by our sovereign God.' I dare say the same is true of revival. Revivals begin when God puts a bomb under preachers to get them really preaching, or he puts a bomb under pray-ers to get them really praying. In both the ordinary and the exceptional activity of the Holy Spirit humans need not be used as instruments, but normally they are. The activities of the Holy Spirit are not dissimilar in that respect. A robust belief in the sovereignty of God should encourage us to expect revival. It has been well observed that the 'permanent elements in revival are the Word, prayer, the Holy Spirit, and a sovereign God who uses man as his instrument.'[26]

---

[25] Perhaps the explanation one might offer the good doctor is that to be an Arminian one must not give up on working for the salvation of others. To be a Calvinist one must not give up on praying for their salvation. We humans find it easier to give up on praying than on working.

[26] Cairns, *Endless Line*, p. 22.

A second corollary of our insistence on the sovereignty of the Spirit of God in revival is that God can, and frequently does, use very humble people as his instruments in revival. He delights to use the humble, for humility is a far more precious quality to God than it is to most of us. And God also uses the humble to demonstrate that his strength is perfected in weakness. Josiah, who has been described as an amoral vegetable amoeba turned into a nuclear reactor, is a biblical example of this. The best known biblical examples are Moses and Isaiah, both of whom had serious reservations about their suitability for their calling – but they became mighty spokesmen for God. Another of the scriptural archetypes is Ezekiel who felt totally unsuited when called, but the Spirit gave him the gift of the gab. God gave him his message: 'Then,' said Ezekiel, 'I was no more dumb' (Ezek. 33:22).

Occasionally in revivals, the sovereign God comes upon one of his humble servants to endow them with an extraordinary gift. For example, in the Welsh revival of 1859, David Morgan was given a prodigious memory. He awoke one morning at 4 a.m., aware of a marvellous illumination of his mental faculties, especially his memory, with which he was able to recall in intercessory prayer the names and spiritual history of hundreds of converts and their needy relatives. One night, less than two years later, the Lord dispossessed him of this extraordinary gift.

We should all aspire to be mighty warriors in the Lord's revival army. We should commit and dedicate and train ourselves for the service of the Lord. That is no guarantee that the sovereign Lord will come upon us as he came upon Ezekiel or David Evans, but he will probably not come upon us if we do not so consecrate ourselves. And, after we have given ourselves to him as instruments of his sovereign will, then no matter how humble we may seem in the eyes of the world, he can choose us for his glory's sake.

A third corollary of the sovereignty of God in revival is concerned with what may be called 'God's cooling-off period'. A fascinating, sobering fact of much church life, even in keen evangelical churches, is that there are so many would-be, near-miss revivals.[27]

---

[27] On the related interesting question of why some revivals continue for a long time while others are short-lived, see Albert C. Outler, *The Works of John Wesley*, I, Sermons I, 1–33, p. 46, n. 67.

The temperature rises. The water nears boiling point. But it never boils. The saints get discouraged, asking 'How long, Lord?', and they disperse, perhaps in some confusion and doubt. 'Maybe,' they think, 'it was all manufactured excitement and not Godufactured.'

But maybe the delay itself is 'Godufactured'. The human instrument may thereby be tested and tempered for the greater heat of real revival. For, if revival were to break out, Satan would aggressively attack the human instrument – better for the human agent of revival to learn in advance how to persevere. And many well-meaning Christians would praise the human instrument – better for the honoured instrument to learn in advance humble dependence. So the point is clear: when the temperature cools, redouble your prayer effort. For the cooling is God's way of preparing the human instrument for the greater heat which is to follow. Do not despair that he tarries. It may be that you are not ready. But, if you realize that you are not ready, do not give up on prayer for revival. God's cooling-off period is to discourage immature zeal, not ardent prayer.

A final corollary is that we should expect the sovereign God to bring revival out of extreme community adversity. The relationship between revival and disaster raises two of the most problematic issues of Christian theology, namely theodicy, God's purpose in allowing suffering, and providence, God's purpose in history. Revivals often follow quickly on community catastrophes, apparently giving people the spiritual resources to cope with the calamity that has overcome them. More intriguingly, however, revivals have often come *before* disasters, and have the effect of preparing people in advance for their suffering. Most intriguing of all, however, is that revivals may be sent by the Lord *instead of* disaster. Each possible scenario illuminates the sovereign Lord's purpose in sending his firestorms precisely when he does within the course of human history.

Revival: A response to disaster

It is sometimes suggested that religious revival is a response to social trauma such as a plague or earthquake or war in the face of which the individual feels powerless and turns to religion as a last resort. There is a definite correlation between revivals and church growth in nineteenth-century Britain, and a definite correlation between some of those revivals and outbreaks of cholera. The Azusa Street revival of 1905 followed closely on the San Francisco earthquake, which took ten thousand lives on 18 April 1905.

In so far as it is true that there is often a close connection between a community disaster and revival within that community, it is only sensible to use such events as an opportunity for revival preaching. John Fletcher of Madeley, Wesley's associate, used a flood which took many lives to preach a powerful sermon in which he dwelt on that tragedy and which was used of God to awaken many souls. Wesley himself preached a thumping sermon on the Lisbon earthquake of 1751. Martyn Lloyd-Jones comments:

> 'Because thine heart was tender' is the favourable comment on King Josiah . . . and we remember the words of the hymn, 'Saviour, while my heart is tender, I would yield my heart to Thee'. There are times when our hearts are tender, and we are more likely to respond. It is the essence of wisdom, it is but common sense, if we should take advantage of all these things. Though you may have planned out the greatest series of sermons the world has ever known, break into it if there is an earthquake! If you cannot be shaken out of a mechanical routine by an earthquake you are beyond hope.[28]

If only I had known that passage when the Ash Wednesday fires in Victoria and South Australia took 80 lives in 1983. Even this could not divert us from our preaching schedule. The minister of another nearby church did not make the same mistake in 1979 when a local mine disaster plunged the whole community into mourning. He preached a sermon that moved and challenged many. Similarly, after a storm tore through the northern suburbs of Sydney in February 1991, causing hundreds of millions of dollars worth of damage to some of Sydney's most opulent houses, the Christian churches combined with the local Council to hold a service of prayer and thanksgiving for the amazing fact that not one life was lost. About four hundred grateful residents turned up and shared stories of the many surprising providences of God. Wise Christian leaders spoke to the tender heart and in turn allowed residents to speak from the tender heart.

---

[28] D.M. Lloyd-Jones, *Preaching and Preachers*, p. 194.

Talk of mine disasters calls to mind the Creswick, Victoria, gold mine disaster of 12 December 1882, which took 22 lives. Entombed men sang hymns and prayed as they waited to be rescued. The Wesleyan preacher A.R. Edgar, instrumental in other revivals on the gold field, preached at the mine itself to the multitudes who converged on the site. Then, in nearby Ballarat, he preached on the text, 'For here we have no continuing city' to four thousand mourning people who identified with the miners and their families in their grief.[29] Edgar was one who took advantage of the tender heart to preach the gospel.

Disasters heighten religious awareness in a number of ways. There is a new reverence for the forces of nature and of God. Teenagers are quietened by this novel experience and by emotions that they have never felt before. The godless use language that they do not habitually employ, such as 'May it please God' and 'we pray'. During the emergency phase created by a disaster people are not after elaborate theological explanations, but they do need grace to cope. Thus disasters more frequently strengthen faith than weaken it, precisely because people feel their need of it. In a survey after a hurricane which took many lives, some affected American citizens were asked if the experience weakened or strengthened their faith. Of those who replied that their faith had been altered by the suffering, all said that it had strengthened their faith.[30] Disasters reinforce solidarity as people come together to expel the disaster agent that has so cruelly violated their community. Thus disaster victims at first have the *esprit de corps* of a nation in wartime.

Following disasters, individuals are conscious of a brush with mortality, and they are sobered by the clear discovery of their vulnerability. All people tend to believe in their own immortality until something like this interrupts their normal lives. Disasters always give a solemn warning of our own death. '*Memento mori*' is the chief lesson to be learned from disasters. Disasters may even be understood as a vivid anticipation of judgement, and can be used to urge

---

[29] W.J. Palamountain, *A.R. Edgar: A Methodist Greatheart*; I.H. Murray, *Australian Christian Life from 1788*, p. 316.
[30] Stuart Piggin, 'Religion and Disaster: Popular Religious Attitudes to Disaster and Death with special reference to the Mt. Kembla and Appin Coal Mine Disasters'.

those affected to flee to Christ and to make their salvation sure. Australia's worst peacetime land disaster, the Mount Kembla mine disaster, took 96 lives in 1902.[31] A headstone of a victim reads:

Death little warning to me gave
And quickly called me to my grave.
Make haste to Christ make no delay
For no one knows their dying day.

Take advantage of the tender heart.

Revivals preceding disaster

Still, the relationship between disaster and revival is more complex than that of a grateful or frightened response to a threat to life on a large scale. For revivals do not always follow human trauma and tragedy; sometimes they precede it. I was first alerted to this when, on making a study of the Mount Kembla mine disaster, I discovered that just three months earlier a genuine revival had added 131 people to the village churches.

Dr Edward Hindson[32] made the observation that every major revival came in a time of peace and was followed by war. The Great Awakening preceded the American Revolution, the Second Great Awakening preceded the War of 1812, and the revival of 1857–59 preceded the American Civil War.

From a human point of view, it is perhaps easy to explain why a revival might have broken out among Confederate forces in the second year of the American Civil War. It is not so easy to explain the widespread revival that preceded the war, nor that which preceded the First World War.[33] Revival was experienced in Eastern Europe in the 1930s just before World War II. Norway enjoyed an awakening that lasted from 1934 to 1941, when that country's

---

[31] Stuart Piggin and Henry Lee, *The Mount Kembla Disaster*.

[32] Edward Hindson, *Glory in the Church*, p. 24.

[33] Orr, *Evangelical Awakenings*, p. 98. Orr cites a biographer of evangelist J. Wilbur Chapman: 'In the history of revivals, it has often been that such restoral periods are a warning of, and synchronize with, impending judgment. The harvest is gathered before the field is doomed to death.'

sufferings began. Revival came to China immediately before the Communist takeover in 1949. It came to Korea just before the beginning of the Korean War. It came to the Congo (Zaire) in 1953, just before the bloodbath which followed independence. It is as if showers of the sovereign Spirit are sometimes poured out on whole communities or nations to prepare them for disaster. Not that God sends the disaster. Most disasters and all wars are the products of human sinfulness, not divine vengeance. But the revivals which frequently precede mass suffering are always initiatives of the divine mercy.

This takes our focus off the human response to disaster and puts it squarely on God's purposes in history. In other words, revivals preceding community disasters raise for us the question of God's providence. One would not wish to affirm that God is the agent of disaster, but we can affirm that he not only can overrule all such tragedies for his own purposes, but he does so partly by preparing people in strengthening them with his grace for future suffering.

Should we, therefore, fear revival as the harbinger of disaster and suffering?

Revivals instead of disaster

No. The commonest pattern seems to be that revival comes not so much in the wake of a disaster, nor before a disaster, but instead of a disaster. It is as if the sovereign God allows people to choose between revival and catastrophe – they can have one or the other. The great flood in the time of Noah was a disaster that overwhelmed a sinful generation because they did not heed the call to revival. The Scriptures tell us (2 Pet. 2:5) that Noah was a 'preacher of righteousness'. Through that preaching God called the people to repentance, but they would not heed the call, and they were destroyed (Gen. 6, 7). Similarly, God visited his people with salvation in the person of Jesus, but the people rejected him, and as a result Jerusalem was destroyed (Lk. 19:41–44). In the latter case, it is interesting to speculate on how, by accepting Jesus, the people would have saved their nation. They would have rejected violent revolution and war as a means of liberation, and they would therefore have avoided inviting disaster upon their heads. Often disaster is not a direct 'act of God' as in the case of Noah's flood, but is rather the natural outworking of destructive behaviour. God is long-suffering, but we must pray for our regional and national communities – for ultimately it is either revival or disaster.

The most chilling example of this in recent history is Rwanda. The World Evangelization Crusade prayer diary lists countries to be prayed for around the world a day at a time. In the entry on Rwanda that was published before the recent horrific genocide began, readers were exhorted to pray for revival for Rwanda as the only solution to the country's terrible racial tensions. Fifty years earlier, the East African Revival had made significant inroads on tribal hatreds, and the entry's author exhorted his readers to plead with God to do it again. Rwanda, we were warned, would either enjoy revival or experience calamity.[34]

We are not just playing religious games when we encourage one another to pray for revival in our needy communities or nations. For we are praying for revival rather than disaster, social as well as spiritual.

Conclusion

In 1906, a participant in the Welsh revival penned a profound and reflective study of the movement of God's Spirit that had just ended. He was nowhere more sensitive and profound than on the relationship between human responsibility and divine sovereignty in revival:

> Are these seasons of refreshing, in whole or in part, beyond control of the Church? Can we compel their coming? Or are they to be placed among the predestinate things, unconditional blessings of God's sovereign will? One is tempted to answer the second part of the question affirmatively, when considering it in this light: no amount, no form of organized effort could produce in 1906 what seemed as natural as a breath of air in the early months of 1905. I have seen, occasionally, an elaborate attempt to make it come; nothing was produced but disaster

---

[34] Patrick Johnstone, *Operation World*, p. 472. 'Pray for revival that will truly nail tribalism and carnal living to the Cross of Christ.'

. . . We must settle down patiently to wait – work and wait – for another such season; but we know little whether we can 'haste the coming' of the day. Of one thing, however, we are sure, that our waiting, our soul's thirst, our instant and constant prayer, our whole life of walking with God, create and supply a reservoir of spiritual influences which the Spirit can use at the right hour. If there is something absolute in the coming of the Spirit, there is also something conditioned. Predestination does not make human action of less value, but of more. We are of worth enough to have been taken into account in God's eternal counsels.[35]

Waiting, working, thirsting, praying, walking with God: these are the duties of the Christian which longing for revival helps the Christian to see more clearly than if he or she had no such longing. If revival is all of God and we can do nothing to produce it, or be certain that we can do anything at all to hasten it, what can we do? We can wait, work, thirst, pray and walk with God. And:

- We can take heart. If revival is a work of God, it is a work that will get done. It is a spiritual work; therefore one looks entirely to the Spirit for success in the work and to human beings not at all. 1 Corinthians 2:14 says, 'The man without the Spirit does not accept the things that come from the Spirit of God, for they are foolishness to him, and he cannot understand them, because they are spiritually discerned.'
- We must pray. If someone without the Spirit can discern nothing spiritual, we must pray that they be given the Spirit. That is why extraordinarily fervent prayer for the lost usually precedes revival.
- We can remove blockages to the coming of the Spirit, especially our habitual sins. But there are perceived barriers which it is illegitimate to attempt to remove. Finney sought to make faith and regeneration simpler by removing the notion of humankind's inability consequent upon his sinful nature.[36]
- We can expand our vision to embrace a broader understanding of the way God works, because he never works in

---

[35] H. Elvet Lewis, 'With Christ among the Miners', pp. 6f.
[36] Murray, *Revival*, p. 365.

precisely the same way twice. No two revivals, in spite of the frequent presence of the six elements in our definition, are ever entirely the same. Revivals always take everybody by surprise. Even those who long and pray for them most never quite anticipate the form that they take.

- We can work harder than ever. Martyn Lloyd-Jones said that 'the Spirit uses a man's best preparation'.[37]
- Fervently we can invite sinners to repent – not because of any conviction that they have within them the power to repent simply by virtue of their humanity, but in the surer confidence that the sovereign God is calling these sinners to repentance, and because the very fact that they are under conviction means that they may be of the elect.
- We can trust that God in his sovereign mercy will send us revival in response to human suffering. He will revive us again if we suffer, revive us before we suffer, and revive us instead of letting us suffer.

---

[37] Murray, *Lloyd-Jones: Fight*, p. 758.

9

Preaching for Revival:
The Power of the Gospel Proclaimed in the Power of the Spirit

The centrality of the cross in revival

In our definition of revival (Ch. 1), we emphasized that a revival is a supernatural work – a work of God. A revival is an outbreak in the present world of the great victory over Satanic and demonic forces that took place in the past on the cross. Therefore revivals are always associated with the preaching of the gospel, which is the message of the cross.

The cross is the power of God for revival because that is where God chose to focus his power to save. He has not decreed that human strategies, intellect, church growth principles or being loving are to be the avenues of his power to save. The only avenue is the cross. The cross is all about what God did for us. Everything else is about what we can do for ourselves. There is nothing of supernatural power in any of that. In a revival, people are converted in great numbers through the preaching of the cross. Whatever happens to them after the preaching of any other message might be a great experience, but it will not be heaven-sent revival.

Genuine revivals always challenge modern culture because culture is a human construct. Culture is what we do for ourselves. Revival, however, acknowledges that God is the construction worker. In revival God is central, not humanity. Revival is waking up to the reality that God is the centre of the universe, not us, and that we are created for his glory – we have not created God for our comfort. Revival brings home to us that we must be like God – holy. We must not make a god after our own image – that is idolatry.

Revival challenges many aspects of our modern culture, especially the cult of achievement or the cult of the self-made person. 'You are what you achieve' is the motto of many in western materialistic cultures based on commercial prosperity. It is therefore understandable that the central Reformation doctrine of justification by faith alone without works is also the central revival doctrine. Those achievements, on which so many of us base our self-esteem, are of no help in getting us right with God. True religion is not concerned with giving us assistance in our quest for self-achievement. The living God is no respecter of persons or of their achievements. Revival preaching insists that, in the end, it is not the prevailing social ideas of morality which count, but what God makes of us. The important thing is not to be a self-made person, but to be a person made righteous. And we are made righteous not on account of our achievements, but on account of what Jesus achieved on the cross. So justification by faith in a crucified Saviour is the first essential of revival preaching.

Integral, secondly, to the revival message's challenge to modern culture is the insistence on original sin. If sin is understood merely in social terms, then redemption is only about what it takes to become acceptable and accepted in our society. God is really left out. Society and its values come to take the place of God. So, the recovery of a sense of sin may be one of the most urgent tasks on the agenda of the preacher who seeks to confront modern culture with the truth of the gospel.

The third plank in the revival message's challenge to modern culture is that faith is a matter of the heart as well as the head. In fact, the unconverted can have a rational view of God. But it is not head knowledge of the doctrines of Christianity that is critical, but heartfelt appropriation and assimilation of these doctrines. The converted has a new heart, and the doctrines of the faith become a matter of life and death. The unconverted do not grasp the power and life-changing implications of these doctrines and therefore they regard them as, at best, aspects of our culture to be tolerated.

Justification, original sin and heartfelt faith and conversion – those are the ingredients of the revival message by which our modern culture so needs to be challenged.[1]

Revival, then, is a recovery of the doctrines of grace. It occurs when preachers give pride of place once more to those doctrines: the sinfulness and corruption of the human heart and the forgiveness and cleansing which comes only through faith in the shed blood of Jesus. Christ's death for sinners is the principal doctrine of the New Testament. It has been the hope and glory of the faithful in every age. When it goes underground, either because we obscure its simplicity with a more elaborate means of salvation or deny its reality by substituting salvation through human effort, the church goes to sleep. When it resurfaces, the church springs again into the new life of revival.

Geoffrey Bingham, who was instrumental in bringing revival to Pakistan, where he served in the 1950s with the Church Missionary Society, analyzed the success of his labours in terms of his preaching the gospel of grace:

> The ministry we had in Pakistan was that of preaching the Scriptures, and especially the great themes. That seemed to raise the spiritual 'water-table' – so to speak – until eventually there was a great outflowing of grace and the Spirit in the truth of Christ. That is how I see what happened with Edwards and his ministry, and no less the Wesleys, Whitefield and the somewhat later English Evangelicals. I think the rise of Pentecostalism has thinned out the substantial proclamation of the gospel because there has been a down-hill slide in the telling out of the gospel – 'the whole counsel of God' . . . My thinking is not in terms of revival, but in the power of the gospel proclaimed in the power of the Spirit.[2]

Revival in the church, then, often involves a recovery of the pure gospel and its clear proclamation in anointed preaching. Let us look at the anatomy of this gospel message, the manner of its delivery and the demeanour of the preacher. Such dissection obscures the fact, of

---

[1] This analysis of the relevance of revival for modern culture is based on Alister McGrath's brilliant chapter on Jonathan Edwards in his *A Cloud of Witnesses: Ten Great Christian Thinkers*, pp. 100–110.
[2] Geoffrey Bingham to the author, undated letter c. Sept. 1997.

course, that it is the combination that accounts for the effectiveness. Effective preaching for revival is a combination of clear understanding of the gospel, giftedness as a communicator and passion in the delivery.

The anatomy of the revival sermon

Sin and the law

Effective gospel preaching often begins with the proclamation of God's law. This is known as 'law work', and it was a conspicuous feature of the preaching of the Great Awakening. Nearly all those truly converted in revivals have had to pass through a period of wounding before the gospel balm could be applied. It is a mistake for a preacher to be too hasty in pronouncing forgiveness before the conviction has been allowed to do its work. Feeble faith grows out of soil where the nutrients of conviction have not been supplied with sufficient intensity or duration. Hence preachers in the Great Awakening in America in the 1740s looked for 'bitter mourning' as well as 'sweet melting'.

Asahel Nettleton, perhaps the greatest preacher of the Second Great Awakening in America at the beginning of the nineteenth century, had strong views on this subject. These views are best expressed in his published sermon, 'Slain by the Law'. As biblical precedents for these experiences, he cites the converts on the day of Pentecost who were cut to the quick (Acts 2), the Philippian jailer who trembled before his conversion (Acts 16), and Paul who, in Romans 7, speaks of being 'slain by the law'.[3] The preacher, then, is the doctor who lays bare the malignancy of sin with the scalpel of the law and heals the wound with the medicine of the gospel.

George Whitefield was an effective preacher for revival – not because of his acting ability and his thundering voice, but because he was so searching in his application of the law and his diagnosis of sin, so clear in his understanding of the remedy, and so tender and persuasive in his appeal, which he called the 'exhortation', to people to

---

[3] J.F. Thornbury, *God Sent Revival: The Story of Asahel Nettleton and the Second Great Awakening*, p. 96.

accept the remedy. Reading his sermons is the best prescription for revival preaching.

In his sermon on 'The Method of Grace' preached in Glasgow on 13 September 1741, Whitefield's text was Jeremiah 6:14, 'They have healed also the hurt of the daughter of my people slightly, saying, Peace, peace; when there is no peace.' Here he seeks to persuade his hearers to see, feel, weep over and bewail, not only their actual transgressions against the law of God, but also the inward disposition to sin, the sinfulness of their best achievements, and the sin of unbelief. 'Before you can speak peace to your hearts,' he advised, 'you must not only be troubled for the sins of your life, the sin of your nature, but likewise for the sins of your best duties and performances.'[4] He argues the doctrine of sin strongly – but experimentally, not controversially: 'If you have never felt the weight of original sin, do not call yourselves Christians.'[5]

The truth that revives, then, is the truth that is felt in the conscience. Revival sermons are searching applications of gospel truth to the conscience. It follows that preaching for revival probably has to be far more searching than it normally is, and possibly more dramatic. Our sense of reality is such a defence against true self-awareness that it must be attacked with a sharp sword if it is to be pierced. Piercing the conscience with the sword of the law is the foundation of preaching for revival.

The Lord Jesus Christ and his cross

Having done his law work faithfully, the preacher then offers Christ to the needy sinner. In his famous *Lectures on Revival*, W.B. Sprague wrote:

> It is not only of the incorruptible seed of the word of God that men are born to newness of life, but it is by the gospel, in distinction from the law, that this work is effected. It was the law that made the jailer tremble; it was the gospel that brought peace and gladness to his soul. It was the law that caused the three thousand to be pricked in the heart;

---

[4] G. Whitefield, 'The Method of Grace', p. 22.

[5] Whitefield, 'Method', p. 22.

it was the gospel – Christ crucified – that melted them into contrition, and transformed them into disciples. And you see the reason of it – the law speaks terror, and nothing else; it points to a most eventful trial; and anticipates the eternal wrath of God. The gospel proclaims good news. It tells the sinner that his case though deplorable, is not desperate; and hope encourages exertion. It holds up the glorious truth, that through the merits of Christ's atoning blood, there is eternal life; and the sinner, through the agency of the Holy Ghost seizes hold of this truth as of life from the dead; and in view of it, he melts down, in humble submission at the foot of the cross.[6]

Since the power of God is the gospel (Rom. 1:16), the faithful evangelist is determined that nothing be elevated above the gospel, which is the message of the cross (Gal. 6:14). In his preaching, George Whitefield does not offer the cross in the abstract. He speaks of the cross of the Lord Jesus Christ, the Saviour, the intimate, personal friend of the sinner:

Jesus Christ feels every sigh, every pang, every throe of your poor soul; Jesus feels the load with you, and he will take the load off from you. Jesus Christ has got a sovereign remedy to heal you. What is that? It is his precious blood – it is a soul-saving remedy. Here is a healing remedy; and, therefore, if your hearts are broken with a sense of sin, come away to the blood of Christ. There is the remedy the poor creature shall have for the accepting of. No one came to Jesus Christ, and went away uncured. And when the Lord undertakes to cure you, he will do it to purpose. Come to Jesus Christ – look at him – do not look to yourselves too much; look out of yourselves, and look up to Christ. The more you will look to yourselves, the more you will fall into unbelief; but look out of yourselves to Christ by a direct act of faith, and one look of faith will heal your hearts. You will feel the power of Christ's blood – it is omnipotent! It is almighty! It can cure all broken hearts! Come to the Lord Jesus Christ, and he will heal you. He can speak the word, and it is done; and the more you come the more welcome you are to Jesus Christ.[7]

---

[6] Sprague, *Lectures*, p. 103.
[7] G. Whitefield, 'The Duty of a Gospel Minister', p. 11.

Jonathan Edwards preached on justification by faith alone at Northampton, Massachusetts, when revival broke out in that town in 1734. But again the emphasis was not on justification understood in an abstract, forensic manner. It was on that faith which unites our heart with Christ's. In that famous new language, which was one with experience, which appealed to the senses, and which was addressed to the affections, Edwards explained that 'justifying faith . . . is that by which the soul, which before was separate and alienated from Christ, unites itself to him . . . it is that by which the soul comes to Christ, and receives him'.[8]

That does not sound like any verdict in a law court. It sounds more like a love story. It is the means by which lonely and broken hearts are brought into a relationship so intimate that it can only be described in marital terms. Edwards dared to suggest that the loving relationship that we inadequately describe as the Trinity would be squared by the inclusion of the elect. Father, Son and Holy Spirit would bring into itself holy church, the bride of the Son, whom the Son will present to the Father as the radiant beauty redeemed by his own blood.

If the clarity of Edwards' understanding owed much to his keen intellect and brilliant mind, the warmth of his love for Christ was the expression of a deep personal encounter with the risen Lord, which he described in a famous passage:

> Once, as I rode out into the woods for my health, in 1737, having alighted from my horse in a retired place, as my manner commonly has been, to walk for divine contemplation and prayer, I had a view that for me was extraordinary, of the glory of the Son of God, as Mediator between God and man, and his wonderful, great, full, pure and sweet grace and love, and meek and gentle condescension. This grace that appeared so calm and sweet, appeared also great above the heavens. The person of Christ appeared ineffably excellent, with an excellency great enough to swallow up all thought and conception – which continued, as near as I can judge, about an hour; which kept me the greater part of the time in a flood of tears, and weeping aloud. I felt an ardency of soul to be, what I know not otherwise how to express, emptied and annihilated;

---

[8] Edwards, *Works*, I, pp. 625f.

to lie in the dust, and to be full of Christ alone; to love him with a holy and pure love; to trust in him; to live upon him; to serve and follow him; and to be perfectly sanctified and made pure, with a divine and heavenly purity.[9]

This must be one of the most remarkable visions of the Chalcedonian Christ recorded in history. It is a vision of personified doctrine. Soteriology (the mediatorship of Christ) is based on Christology (meek and gentle condescension). The writer was so gripped by the great doctrines of redemption that they gave him ecstatic visions of the author of those doctrines. No one can preach for revival who is not gripped by the doctrines of grace and the unsurpassed perfection of the Saviour's love.

The appeal

Preaching for revival does not merely end with an appeal. It makes its appeal throughout. It is clear from Whitefield's sermons how tender, affecting and prolonged were his appeals. His sermons were really extended appeals or exhortations. The doctrine of salvation by a crucified redeemer was expounded and applied at the one time.[10] To persuade sinners to come to Christ, Whitefield not only reasoned vigorously, and taught the principal doctrines of redemption fully as well as clearly, but he adhered to his scriptural text closely, and appealed from it to all people in all situations. For example, a major aspect of most revivals is the restoration of lapsed or backslidden Christians. Whitefield included them in his appeal:

My dear friends, you must keep up a tender, close walk with the Lord Jesus Christ. There are many of us who lose our peace by our untender walk; something or other gets in betwixt Christ and us, and we fall into darkness; something or other steals our hearts from God, and this grieves the Holy Ghost, and the Holy Ghost leaves us to ourselves. Let me, therefore, exhort you that have got peace with God, to take care

---

[9] Edwards, *Works*, I, p. xlvii. The wording has been modernized. The earliest extant version is the first printed version of 1765. It is reproduced in Edwards, *Letters and Personal Writings*, p. 801.

[10] Murray, *Lloyd-Jones: Fight*, p. 724.

that you do not lose this peace. It is true, if you are once in Christ, you cannot finally fall from God: 'There is no condemnation to them that are in Christ Jesus;' but if you cannot fall finally, you may fall foully, and may go with broken bones all your days. Take care of backslidings; for Jesus Christ's sake, do not grieve the Holy Ghost – you may never recover your comfort while you live. O take care of going a gadding and wandering from God, after you have closed with Jesus Christ.[11]

Whitefield urged hearers in his appeals not only to believe. It is not believing which saves, but regeneration. This is because the whole person is involved in conversion, not just the mind. Whitefield was not just preaching for some mere intellectual assent or grudging submission to his powerful oratory. He was after the deep, spiritual work of the Holy Spirit in the soul which commonly follows sincere repentance of the heart and will:

Come away, my dear brethren – fly, fly, fly, for your lives to Jesus Christ, fly to a bleeding God, fly to a throne of grace; and beg of God to break your hearts, beg of God to convince you of your actual sins, beg of God to convince you of your original sin, beg of God to convince you of your self-righteousness – beg of God to give you faith, and to enable you to close with Jesus Christ.[12]

The single most important thing any preacher can do to preach for revival is to focus on the appeal or the exhortation. It is missing from preaching today and must become an art again.

The delivery of the revival sermon

In a revival, preaching is more powerful and authoritative than the customary fare.[13] Preaching for revival is not lecturing. It is not only addressing the mind. The essence of the gospel is the cross, but this must move the heart. The truths of the gospel are to touch us deeply and affect us greatly. A faith that does not touch the heart is no faith

---

[11] Whitefield, 'Method', p. 27.
[12] Whitefield, 'Method', p. 29.
[13] On the impact of revival on preaching, see F.R. Webber, *A History of Preaching in Britain and America.*

at all. If it is to touch the heart, one whose own heart is touched must preach it. 'The sense I had of divine things,' writes Edwards, 'would often of a sudden kindle up, as it were, a sweet burning in my heart; an ardour of soul that I know not how to express.'[14] It is out of that sweet burning in the preacher's heart, that ardour of soul, that the fires of revival are kindled.

Accurate exposition is not the only goal. The word of God leads to the God of the word. It is arguable that theophany is the goal of theology. The preacher is not a scribe dealing with textual concerns alone. He desires the 'bush' to burn. He wants people to draw near to God. A successful 'preaching' leaves the worshipper with the echo of God's voice and with the recall of God's presence.[15]

Revival preaching should also aim at greater immediacy, for, as Edwards insisted, the main benefit for the hearer comes from the impression made on the mind while the sermon is being preached – not later as it is recalled.

Revival preaching has to be far more searching than the normal run of preaching, and possibly more dramatic. Our sense of reality is so at variance with God's that it probably has to be hit hard before it will disintegrate. The occasion when the sermon is preached is the battlefield where the preacher has to capture, then conquer, the heart for the service of God.

Preaching which is effective in revival, which is 'a word in season', which is 'understanding of the present time' (Rom. 13:11) is preaching where the tongue has been instructed by the Lord (Isa. 50:4). The Puritans called it 'anointed' preaching. They used to say that one must be not only a teacher, but also a *preacher*, and not only a teacher and preacher, but an *anointed* teacher and preacher. The charismatics distinguish between *logos* and *rhema* and insist that every preacher of the *logos* (the general reason and will of God) should have the special *rhema* (the specific, personalized word) given him by the Lord for his hearers. Bultmann says that the New Testament is formed by such preaching: the *kerygma*, or proclamation, is situational. So preaching to a congregation is addressing the people where they are. The preaching must be applied to the real situation and not be just a hit-or-miss exegesis.

---

[14] Edwards, *Letters*, p. 793.
[15] Sargent, *Sacred Anointing*, pp. 181f.

Jonathan Edwards agreed. He maintained that all preaching was 'occasional' – it was addressed to a particular occasion and made it an occasion. It is always a response to a particular situation. Some of his sermons were preached six or seven times. The revisions show how he adapted the examples to each occasion. For example, when he left the farming community of Northampton for the Indian mission of Stockbridge, he replaced references to local farming and business affairs with allusions to nature, hunting and tribal customs. So, whatever the abstract theology which he designed every sermon to convey, he changed the packaging for the occasion. Every sermon must be an occasion.

It is sobering to realize that our typical good-humoured, positive sermons probably do not often contain the gospel. The gospel is different from our best and kindest thoughts. It has the power of God about it. 'You were not yourself tonight,' someone said after a sermon I preached which was more powerful than usual. Another said to me, 'I sat there thinking, where is he coming from?' To preach for revival you have to be not yourself; and your thoughts have to come not from you. It is no wonder that revival preaching is so rare.

The deliverer of the revival sermon

In a revival, a preacher who is being used of God will sometimes report that his whole frame is electrified by spiritual energies; his hearers say that his voice pierces each heart like a knife and his face is radiant: he is to them an angel of God. Psalm 104:4 says, 'He makes his ministers a flame of fire.' Of the preacher John Blair Smith in the 1860 revival in America, one observer wrote: 'I still see him stand the accredited ambassador of the Great "King of kings and Lord of lords," while every feature and every muscle of his face, every word and action, as well as the lightning of his eyes seem to bespeak a soul on fire.'[16]

There is nothing new in his message. The only difference is in his spirit. Now he is an anointed preacher of the word. Now he preaches with indomitable earnestness. As Thomas Edwards wrote of preaching in the 1859 Welsh revival:

---

[16] Murray, *Revival*, p. 108.

It would appear that the object is, more than ever, to preach the substantial truths of the gospel, so earnestly, closely, and personally, that the hearers may feel that the preacher's aim is to save their souls, and that God, by *his* means, desires to bring them to himself. The people are compelled to believe this. The preacher comes near them . . . It is not a fight at arm's length, but the preacher advances immediately to the people, lays hold of them, and they feel the sermon has entered into them, and that the preacher has taken possession of the throne of their hearts in the name of Jesus.[17]

In the church in Northampton is a plaque applying the words of Malachi 2:6 to Jonathan Edwards: 'True instruction was in his mouth, and no wrong was found on his lips. He walked with me in peace and uprightness, and he turned many from iniquity.' I stood in front of that plaque and I felt convicted. That is the sort of preacher whom God honours and uses to bring revival. And it is revival that produces ministers like that. From revival they catch fire and they are the means by which others are ignited. Behind all great preaching, somewhere in the background, will be someone's experience of revival. God will have inflamed one to set the rest on fire.

Iain Murray has reflected much on the qualities required in preachers if we are to see revival again:

It may be that a generation of freshly-anointed preachers is already being prepared . . . They will be hard students of Scripture. They will prize a great spiritual heritage. They will see the danger of 'unsanctified learning'. While they will not be afraid of controversy, nor of being called hyper-orthodox, they will fear to spend their days in controversy. They will believe with John Rice that 'the church is not purified by controversy, but by holy love'. They will not forget that the wise, who will shine 'as the stars for ever and ever' are those who 'turn many to righteousness' (Dan. 12:3). They will covet the wisdom which Scripture attributes to the one 'that winneth souls' (Prov. 11:30). But their cheerfulness will have a higher source than their work. To know God himself will be their supreme concern and joy.[18]

---

[17] Evans, *Revival Comes to Wales*, p. 113.
[18] Murray, *Revival*, p. 387.

In the penultimate paragraph of his monumental life of Martyn Lloyd-Jones, Iain Murray writes thus of the relationship between revival and preaching:

> He was a preacher. He believed in preaching which was unadorned, unstudied (so far as mere sentences were concerned) but alive, a union of truth and fire . . . With John Knox and his successors, he knew that the 'tongue and lively voice' are *the* chief means to which God has promised his power to the recovery of lost mankind . . . His prayer for revival was accordingly associated with the profound conviction that every great movement of the Spirit will be found to be bound up with the giving of men who *preach* 'with the Holy Ghost sent down from heaven'.[19]

Conclusion

To make sinners see God's reality, which alone is reality, one must preach awakening sermons. The most distinctive and commanding part of God's truth is the gospel: that is the power of God for salvation. The focus of the gospel is the cross: evangelicals have always been crucicentric (cross-centred). In the cross is power and wisdom and truth and reality.

It is a commonplace to say that revival must begin with the individual. I think it must begin with the individual preacher. It has been said of Luther that what went on in that man's private soul determined the fate of Europe. Christians in the pew or the plastic chairs, if they are to be revived and the instruments of revival, must first witness revival in someone. Our hearers are witnesses of what God is doing in our souls and of how *he* has enlightened our minds. This means that in a sense my every sermon will have to be a testimony, a testimony to what I know to be reality. Revival, then, will begin in our devotional life, with the sweet burning in our heart and with the ardour in our soul, as we first experience and then testify to what we know of the intimate relationship made possible with our God, himself an intimate relationship in his plural oneness in the Trinity.

---

[19] Murray, *Lloyd-Jones: Fight*, p. 777.

In revival, then, one of the first things to be revived is the preaching. It is now understood as a manifestation of the great things of God, and never a demonstration of the ability of the preacher. It is urgent, focused on the essentials, anointed and delivered with plainness and power. It is searching on the reality of sin, tender and Christ-centred in the offer of the remedy, and, in the appeal, aiming not just for belief but for heartfelt repentance as the surest foundation for regeneration. The task of preaching is to be so gripped by the doctrines of redemption that one preaches primarily out of the experience of redemption rather than out of any need to defend those doctrines. The grace of God displaces the wisdom of man; the cross of Christ displaces the philosophy of the schools; the presence of God displaces the awareness of men. So it was with Luther, who preached *coram Deo* – in the presence of God – so it must ever be with revival preaching. Whom God chooses he makes a flame of fire to turn many from iniquity.

10

Praying for Revival

Revival, as we have said, is a sovereign work of God consisting of a powerful intensification of the ordinary work of the Holy Spirit, which is usually preceded by extraordinary prayerfulness among Christians. This prayerfulness is itself an aspect of revival as the Lord himself gives his hitherto prayerless people a new spirit of prayer.

The following discussion of praying for revival is largely descriptive. An examination of scriptural data on the relationship between prayer and revival will lay the basis for a review of prayer movements in Asia, Australia and America and an examination of the prayer offensive which accompanies every Billy Graham Crusade. Billy Graham speaks so freely in his crusades not only because he has the confidence of experience, but also because he knows that he has prayer warriors all over the world wrestling in prayer for the anointing of his preaching.

The disciplined prayer that characterizes reviving churches is a costly exercise. Hence in the next chapter, on paying for revival, we will return to the subject of prayer and analyze the very important concept of *prevailing prayer*, which has received so much attention in connection with revival. Suffice it to say for the moment that if we are not praying fervently and regularly for revival, we should not expect to witness it. George Strachan, who experienced the long-lasting revival in the Solomon Islands, beginning in 1970, answered the question 'why do revivals not start?' thus:

Lack of real prayer is a major hindrance. For many of us prayer is of no great importance. It is just an 'extra' to a busy life. But prayer that brings power takes precedence over all else. Nothing should be allowed to steal away time spent with God in prayer.[1]

Samuel Chadwick said:

> The one concern of the devil is to keep Christians from praying. He fears nothing from prayerless studies, prayerless work, and prayerless religion. He laughs at our toil, mocks at our wisdom, but trembles when we pray.[2]

The relationship between revival and prayer in the Scriptures

The principles governing the relationship between revival and prayer may and must be deduced from the Scriptures.

- Prayerlessness is sin (1 Sam. 12:23): 'As for me, far be it from me that I should sin against the LORD by failing to pray for you.'
- We are never to give up on prayer (Lk. 18:1): 'Then Jesus told his disciples a parable to show them that they should always pray and never give up.'
- God has decreed that his work of redemption will be effected through the prayers of his people. Only the Lamb *can* open the seals, only through the prayers of the saints *will* he open the seals (Rev. 5:8; 8:1–5).
- The fire of the Spirit comes in answer to prayer (Acts 1:4,14; 2:1–8). Prayer releases the Holy Spirit, arms angels, and these result in the forcing back of Satan.
- The Saviour longs to hear our prayers and kindle that fire (Lk. 12:49). The firestorms of the Lord have always come in answer to prayer. The dedication of the temple in Jerusalem, built by Solomon, was accompanied by prayer. 2 Chronicles 7:1–3 vividly portrays what happened next:

> When Solomon finished praying, fire came down from heaven … and the glory of the Lord filled the temple. The priests could

---

[1] Strachan, *Revival*, p. 55.
[2] Quoted in Vernon Brewer, 'Prayer: The Keystone of Revival'.

not enter the temple of the Lord because the glory of the Lord filled it. When all the Israelites saw the fire coming down and the glory of the Lord above the temple, they knelt on the pavement with their faces to the ground, and they worshipped and gave thanks to the Lord, saying, 'He is good; his love endures for ever.'

- God expects us to pray for revivals. Jonathan Edwards wrote, 'For though God has appointed the time of these things in his own counsels, yet he will be enquired of for them by his peo ple before he accomplishes them: Ezekiel 36:37–38, "Thus saith the Lord God, I will yet for this be enquired of by the house of Israel, to do it for them; I will increase them with men like a flock".'[3]
- Divine outpourings in the Scriptures can be either for blessing or for judgement. In the book of Revelation, God pours out judgement on his enemies in response to the prayers of his people.[4] Similarly, God will pour out the divine blessing of re vival ('times of refreshing' – Acts 3:19) from the throne of grace in response to the prayers of his people.

According to the Scriptures, then, prayer is the anointed means by which the divine blessing is brought down from heaven – it is not worked up from men. Well has it been said, 'We do not just pray *for* the work, prayer *is* the work.' And 'When man works, man works; when man prays, God works.'

American prayer movements for revival

The inextricable connection between united prayer and revival has been recognized at least since 1748, when Jonathan Edwards pub lished *An Humble Attempt to Promote . . . Extraordinary Prayer for the Revival of Religion.*[5] He recommended that Christians gather in monthly concerts of prayer, that is to pray for revival in a concerted

---

[3] Jonathan Edwards, *Sermons and Discourses 1720 –1723*, p. 336.
[4] See Rev. 8:4,5; 9:13; 11:6 and Paul Barnett, *Apocalypse Now and Then*, pp. 87, 91, 96.
[5] The best edition is found in *Apocalyptic Writings*, pp. 307–436.

way, for seven years. Only after seven years should they pause to evaluate what had been achieved and if they should continue.

In the next century, Charles Finney developed Edwards' contention that the Lord had put himself at the disposal of his praying people into a 'law of revival'.[6] A constant feature of Finney's preaching which led to endemic revival was much praying, but it was prayer with a difference. Finney habitually wrestled with God for hours until he was confident that he had prevailed.[7]

The 1859 revivals in Wales and Ulster were caught from the revival in North America, which was ignited by prayer. In 1857, Jeremiah Lanphier had started a prayer meeting in New York that grew from six in the first week to 40 in the second week to ten thousand within six months. This is known as the 1859 Prayer Revival.

Edwards' call for concerts of prayer has been taken up in recent years by David Bryant of the American InterVarsity Christian Fellowship and member of the Lausanne Committee for World Evangelization. His prayer gatherings for fullness (that is, revival) and fulfilment (that is, world evangelization) aim to reflect not only the earnestness implied in the adjective 'concerted', but the joyful celebration implied in the noun 'concert'. They are to 'involve the dynamics of a harmonious celebration – like a grand symphony – as pray-ers blend their hearts, minds and voices by faith in God's Word'.[8]

Revival and prayer in Australia

The first revival on Australian soil of which I am aware was a prayer revival at Hobart, Tasmania in June 1834, during the ministry of the Revd Nathaniel Turner, a Wesleyan.[9] It stemmed from a prayer meeting started by a few eminent Christians posted to Tasmania in the 48th Regiment.[10] Turner reported:

---

[6] Murray, *Revival*, p. 377.
[7] We will return to the matter of prevailing prayer in Ch. 11.
[8] David Bryant, *Concerts of Prayer*, p. 14.
[9] Turner later became a missionary and took revival to Samoa.
[10] Murray, *Australian Christian Life*, p. 130; Murray, 'Lessons'.

At our quarterly fast the power of the Spirit came down so that many were led to cry aloud for mercy. Several souls found peace with God. The spirit of prayer was given in an extraordinary degree. Such wrestling and pleading with God I never beheld in these regions. Our people seem all on fire. At most of our prayer meetings, which are numerously attended, souls are crying out for mercy. At one meeting a man and his wife were kneeling side by side. The man was made happy, and immediately prayed aloud for his wife. She too found the Saviour.[11]

A revival in Parramatta, NSW in 1840, associated with John Watsford, the first Australian-born Methodist clergyman, had its roots in a prayer meeting convened by two local preachers. Together with John Watsford, they resolved to pray three times a day for the outpouring of the Holy Spirit. Watsford explained what happened:

At the end of the fourth week, on Sunday evening, the Rev. William Walker preached a powerful sermon. After the service the people flocked to the prayer-meeting, till the schoolroom was filled. My two friends were there, one on each side of me, and I knew they had hold of God. We could hear sighs and suppressed sobs all around us. The old minister of the Circuit, who had conducted the meeting, was concluding with the benediction, 'The grace of our Lord Jesus Christ, and the love of God' – here he stopped, and sobbed aloud. When he could speak he called out, 'Brother Watsford, pray'. I prayed, and then my two friends prayed, and oh! the power of God that came upon the people, who were overwhelmed by it in every part of the room! And what a cry for mercy! It was heard by the passers-by in the street, some of whom came running in to see what was the matter, and were smitten down at the door in great distress. The clock of a neighbouring church struck twelve before we could leave the meeting. How many were saved I cannot tell. Day after day and week after week the work went on, and many were converted.[12]

---

[11] Quoted in Murray, *Australian Christian Life*, p. 130, from J.G. Turner, *The Pioneer Missionary: Life of the Rev. Nathaniel Turner.*

[12] Quoted in Murray, *Australian Christian Life*, p. 153, from Watsford, *Glorious Gospel.*

Indeed, the conclusion we must draw from the early history of Methodism in Australia is that its remarkable record of revival is due to the prayerfulness of its people. As one of them wrote in 1858:

> Our church started into being and was fostered and enlarged in the midst of amazing difficulties. Fasting and prayer were constantly used by the early Methodists and followed by outpourings of the Holy Spirit.[13]

When news of the 1859 revivals in Wales, Ulster and America reached Australia, a general call to prayer was issued. Right across the country, concerned Christians met in halls and churches to pray for a share in the revival. The showers of revival blessing began to fall on 22 May 1859 at Brighton in Victoria, and for seven years, throughout Australia and the islands of the Pacific, the drought did not return.

Moody's and Sankey's campaign in Britain in 1874 unleashed a second wave of prayer in Australia. From the beginning of that campaign, prayer meetings were held in Sydney each Monday over which the leaders of the Protestant churches presided in rotation.

The 1902 revival in Australia, which was characterized by contemporaries as a 'remarkable religious awakening' and 'the big revival', was the culmination of a third wave of prayer for revival in Australia. It had a long gestation period. In 1889 John MacNeil and three other ministers formed 'The Band of Prayer', which continued to meet every Saturday afternoon for two hours, and sometimes for whole nights, praying for the 'Great Revival' until, in 1902, it came. On the impact of the prayer band, Helen Dyer was to write:

> But we must go further back . . . to realise fully what God has done in answer to prayer; to reach the hidden springs that have welled up from burdened souls agonising for the Kingdom of God to come in power. The outpouring in Australia which commenced the days of grace of this present era, was traced to a band of four who 'agreed to pray' thirteen years before the blessing came into its fulness. One of the four, the sainted John MacNeil, was translated to heaven before the answer was

---

[13] *The Christian Advocate and Wesleyan Record*, 21 Dec. 1858, quoted in Murray, *Australian Christian Life*, p. 343.

given, but the band constantly augmented its numbers and continued to pray, till the wave of blessing flooded the land.[14]

So behind the 1902 Melbourne mission is a story of one of the most concerted prayer efforts known in Australian evangelical history. We are fortunate that Reuben Torrey himself left an account of this prayer movement. It is found in his classic work, *The Power of Prayer and the Prayer of Power*, 1924:

When Mr Alexander and I reached Australia we found that there was a group of about ten or twelve men who had been praying for years for a great revival in Australia. They had banded together to pray for 'the big revival,' as they called it in their prayers, to pray for the revival no matter how long it took. The group was led by the Rev. John MacNeil, the author of *The Spirit-Filled Life*, but he had died before we reached Australia. A second member of the group, Rev. Allan Webb, died the first week of our meetings in Melbourne. He had come to Melbourne to assist in the meetings, and died on his knees in prayer. A third member of the group, even before we had been invited to Australia, had been given a vision of great crowds flocking to the Exhibition Hall, people hanging on to the loaded street cars wherever they could; and when that vision was fulfilled he came a long distance to Melbourne just to see with his own eyes what God had revealed to him before.

We also found that a lady in Melbourne had read a book on Prayer and had been very deeply impressed by one short sentence in the book, 'pray through,' and that she had organised prayer-meetings all over the city before we reached the place; indeed, we found when we reached Melbourne that there were 1,700 neighbourhood prayer-meetings being held every week in Melbourne . . . In the four weeks, 8,642 persons made a definite profession of having accepted the Lord Jesus Christ as their Saviour . . . The report of what God had done in Melbourne spread not only all over Australia, but to India, and England and Scotland and Ireland, and resulted in a wonderful work of God . . . the outcome of the prayer-meetings held in Chicago, and of the prayers of the little group of men in Australia.[15]

---

[14] Helen S. Dyer, *Revival in India*, pp. 17f.
[15] R.A. Torrey, *The Power of Prayer and the Prayer of Power*, pp. 48f.

Prayer and revival in China and Korea

In that same book, *The Power of Prayer and the Prayer of Power* (1924), Torrey observed that 'there have been revivals without much preaching, but there has never been a mighty revival without mighty praying'. Many of the accounts of heroic prayer today come from the new churches of Asia. Chinese Christians, currently enjoying possibly the most sweeping revival in the church's history, have a motto similar to Torrey's: 'Much prayer, much power; little prayer, little power; no prayer, no power.' Like the church in the book of Acts, the Chinese church is a praying church. Where we in the apathetic west rationalize our failure to pray, Chinese Christians pray that obstacles to prayer will be removed:

> It appears that the distinguishing feature of the present-day church growth in China is the disciplined prayer life of every believer. Chinese Christians pray to the Lord for (1) a watchful and praying spirit; (2) a burden to pray for others; (3) a time and place to pray; (4) energy to pray with fellow workers; (5) the right words to use in prayer.[16]

Indeed, the very fact that there is a revival in China at the moment owes much to the power of intercessory prayer. When the Communists forced missionaries to leave China in 1951, they did not eliminate the influence of those missionaries. One of the last to leave, Mary Andrews, declared, 'We can no longer help with personnel or finance. But we can work for China mightily by our prayers.'[17] Many missionaries agreed, refusing to accept that it was all over for Christianity in China. For decades they prayed, remembering by name those Chinese known to them and whom they had left behind, and praying for the defeat of the powers of darkness. Similarly, the collapse of atheistic Communism in Russia may be attributed to the hand of the Lord acting in response to the persistent, prevailing prayer of the faithful in the church during the last 70 years. Perhaps few had the faith to believe that a system so powerful and so entrenched could fall so quickly – but God is the Lord of history, and evil powers cannot forever hold sway in his world.

---

[16] Quoted by Lawrence in *Against All Odds*, p. 69.
[17] Margaret Yarwood Lamb, *Going it Alone: Mary Andrews – Missionary to China*, p. 206.

Prayer is also the most pronounced feature of the Korean revival. In a chapter entitled 'The Miracle of a Praying People', Colin Whittaker gives the following breathtaking account of prayer, Korea-style:

While the prayer life of the churches in the West has declined, in Korea it has not only been sustained throughout the century but has actually increased. The sudden emergence of the feature of thousands praying aloud simultaneously, which marked the revival of 1907, is a mark of the continuing revival. That is one form of intercession which can be witnessed regularly in thousands of churches in Korea today. But it is not the only type of praying they do; the secret of the Korean church is that they practise every kind. It is surely what Paul is talking about when he refers to 'praying always with all prayer and supplication in the Spirit, and watching thereunto with all perseverance and supplication for all saints' (Eph. 6:18). In the West, we believe in prayer; in Korea they believe in praying! There the level of praying is inspiring. They all pray, they are always doing so, and they intercede in every way possible. They pray alone and in twos; they pray in small groups and in their homes; they pray in their churches and on their mountains; they pray in their own language and they 'pray in the Spirit' in other tongues; they pray silently and loudly (sometimes very loudly); they pray with tears and with holy laughter; they sing their prayers and sometimes they groan their prayers as they intercede and get under burdens which the Holy Spirit lays upon them; they pray in the morning and in the evening; they pray at midday and at midnight; they pray with fasting and they pray over their meals; they pray for their friends and for their enemies; they pray for their neighbour and for their nation; they pray for the church and for the world; they pray for everyone and about everything.[18]

Billy Graham crusades and prayer

There is little doubt that the Billy Graham Evangelistic Association has been serious about prayer. There is more than lip service in the Standard Operational Procedures directive: 'The most vital of all is the Prayer Committee. Please give your prayerful thought to the

---

[18] Whittaker, *Korea Miracle*, pp. 49f.

selection of personnel for this committee. They should be your most spiritual people.' Hence, in Melbourne, Australia in 1959, Leonard Buck, a leading evangelical businessman, was chosen as the Chairman of the Melbourne Crusade Prayer Committee. Buck took as the key verse for the united prayer programme the great revival text 2 Chronicles 7:14:

> If my people, which are called by my name, shall humble themselves, and pray, and seek my face, and turn from their wicked ways; then will I hear from heaven, and forgive their sin, and will heal their land.

Among the stated objectives of the prayer programme was:

> To have the people of the Melbourne Area become 'revival conscious'. Only as God's people become concerned and burdened for conditions around them; and only as people become aware of their spiritual need, can the Holy Spirit come in mighty convicting and converting power.

The prayer meetings were to pray 'for a heaven-sent revival'.[19]

This 'vital National Prayer Offensive' was launched at an all-night prayer meeting in five centres in Melbourne on 21 September 1958. The first hour focused on the need for 'heart searching and revival among the people of God, beginning with we who pray'. Subsequent hours were devoted to praying for the country areas of Victoria, 'that revival may come there', and for 'a mighty awakening among college and school children, high school and university students'. One leader commented, 'I have attended many prayer meetings before, but never have I seen such spontaneity in prayer. I noticed through the night that there was never any lagging in the praying. There was a very evident leading of the Spirit of God throughout.'

Under Buck's generalship, the churches went on to a war footing, alerted to the task and to the fact that this was the Lord's appointed time to bless Australia. Buoyed by the news that 1,400 home prayer meetings were now praying for the Crusade, Buck wrote to the leaders of the All Night of Prayer set for 6 February 1959:

---

[19] Crusade Prayer Bulletin (CPB), Melbourne.

It is impossible to express to you the importance which the Committee sets on this most Scriptural of all holy exercises, or the strength of its conviction that this further night of united intercession may well determine the character of the Melbourne Crusade, and the calibre of the spiritual impact made on the life of this city and the souls of its people.

In view of the stupendous promises given to us by our Lord regarding prayer, and the teaching of the Word of God on its vital relationship to the work of the Spirit of God, we enter this warfare . . . with solemnity and reverent trust. We must afresh lead the Lord's people to see that organisation, meticulous though it has been in preparation for the Crusade, does not and cannot endue Divine power and unction. We are dependent on his Sovereign Spirit, and we humbly submit our plans and ourselves to Him, who alone can do wonders, and honour the work and witness of His servants. 'It is time, oh Lord, for *Thee* to work.'[20]

To inspire his prayer warriors to relish the battle, he encouraged them to repent at length for the years of timidity and unbelief, and for the 'bewildering prayerlessness in the light of God's promises and provisions for those who pray'. He urged them 'corporately and individually' to accept the blame for the powerlessness of Christ's church. We should be 'terrible as an army with banners' (Song 6:4), he wrote, 'the gates of hell (not prevailing) against us' (Matt. 16:18). We have been 'at ease in Zion' (Amos 6:1), thus perpetuating our spiritual flabbiness. We have been content with our flabbiness 'while the world is on the edge of a nuclear and spiritual volcano'. Unlike our Lord who was eaten up by zeal for the Lord's house, we have been complacent in 'our vain shew of formality'.

Petitions were to be for revival: for a 'mighty awakening among all of us who know Christ'; for 'an awakening among the unconverted; awakened to their need of Christ, of the reality of sin; and of judgment'; 'above all for a Heaven sent revival among the people of God in our Commonwealth'.[21]

Billy Graham's 1959 crusades, then, were saturated in prayer, and never has Australia come closer to a great awakening.

---

[20] CPB, Melbourne, Prayer Committee, 29 Jan. 1959.
[21] CPB, Melbourne, Prayer Committee, 29 Jan. 1959.

The Wheaton Revival, 1995

It is easy to be dispirited by accounts of massively organized prayer movements. We all know what hard work they are, of the many hours we have prayed for revival, but the heavens have seemed like brass (Dt. 28:23). Why do some Christians persevere with such an exhausting prayer programme, while others give up discouraged? Doggedness can be the work of human stubbornness or it can be that perseverance which is the gift of the Holy Spirit. Maybe it is both, since the Holy Spirit can galvanize human determination for his own purposes.

But we should observe the motivation of those we have studied in this chapter. These prayer movements arose not only from a human desire to organize, but also, as Helen Dyer observed about the Melbourne prayer movement at the beginning of the twentieth century, it was the welling up 'from burdened souls agonising for the Kingdom of God to come in power'. This burden, this agonizing, is itself the work of the Holy Spirit, which creates a determination to go on praying no matter how long it takes, to pray through to victory, to prevail in prayer, to take hold of God, and to wrestle with him until he blesses. 'When God intends great mercy for his people,' declared the Bible commentator Matthew Henry, 'the first thing he does is to set them to prayer.'[22]

In mid-1993 a member of my own congregation, John Lillyman, went to Wheaton College to spend 18 months doing a Master's degree in evangelism. He wrote to me regularly of the prayer movement on campus. He was personally involved in organizing it. He reported that the tide of blessing was rising, that first the undergraduates were praying for a visitation of the Spirit, then that graduate students had joined the undergraduates, then that staff had joined the movement. He returned to us in December 1994, satisfied that he had been involved in a movement which had raised the spiritual temperature, but aware that boiling point had not been reached. Imagine his joy when, on Saturday 25 March 1995, he received a phone call from Wheaton with the news that the previous Sunday, 19 March, the rising tide had burst the banks and that the river of the Spirit was flowing freely through Wheaton.

---

[22] Brian H. Edwards, *Revival! A People Saturated with God*, p. 84.

I have received a copy of the official history of the Wheaton Revival – so quickly published after the event. How moving it is to read the record of my friend's involvement, which has blessed tens of thousands of American university students. In an analysis of the 'immediate causes' of the Wheaton revival, John Lillyman's commitment to praying for revival is mentioned first:

> For three semesters previous to the March revival, God sent an Australian evangelist, John Lillyman, to study at Wheaton College Graduate School . . . Lillyman and his wife, alumna Rebecca Rupprecht, are an unusual couple. Everyone who made their acquaintance recognized their radical commitment to following Christ whatever He called them to do. Their love for Jesus was nurtured by a contagiously dynamic prayer life. They had a remarkable impact on the student community.
>
> John Lillyman was especially burdened for revival. He spent as much time as possible with Dr Robert Coleman, reading his books, attending his prayer meetings, and generally absorbing all that he could on revival, evangelism, and histories of great visitations of the Holy Spirit. John was particularly inspired to pray for revival at Wheaton College. He took the lead organizing a day of prayer in the autumn of 1994, and everyone who worked with this energetic Australian felt certain revival would break forth on the campus soon. Both of the Lillymans prayed with unusual urgency for revival, and they left behind a hard core team of prayer warriors whom they had mentored along the way.[23]

Conclusion: Mobilize for prayer

Learning how to mobilize the church to pray in response to the Spirit's leading is one of the lessons church leaders must learn if we are to see revival. The lesson from these mobilizations for prayer which have led to revival is clear, but it needs to be spelt out. Revival will not come without prayer. The Lord will not come down unless we besiege heaven. Of course, we should not look to the power of our siege for results. We look to God for revival, not prayer.[24] But we

---

[23] Beougher and Dorsett, *Campus Revival*, p. 87.
[24] Murray, *Lloyd-Jones: Fight*, pp. 763f.

look to God through prayer. The prayer of faith is the eye with which we look to and see God.[25] So mobilize.

> Blow the trumpet in Zion, declare a holy fast, call a sacred assembly. Gather the people, consecrate the assembly; bring together the elders, gather the children, those nursing at the breast. Let the bridegroom leave his room and the bride her chamber. Let the priests, who minister before the LORD, weep between the temple porch and the altar. Let them say, 'Spare your people, O LORD. Do not make your inheritance an object of scorn, a byword among the nations. Why should they say among the peoples, "Where is their God?" ' (Joel 2:15–17)

---

[25] Andrew Murray, *With Christ in the School of Prayer*, p. 90.

11

Paying for Revival

Not as many are praying for revival as should be. But more are 'praying' for revival than are prepared to pay the cost of revival. The price is high, but the cost of doing without revival is higher. Remember (Ch. 8) that God, in his mercy, normally sends revival as the divine alternative to disaster, which is too often the outcome of coping with reality with only human resources. We must know what the cost is, and we must pay it.

What is the cost? 2 Chronicles 7:14 spells out the fourfold cost of revival. This, the most famous of Old Testament verses on revival, speaks of the Lord's coming to his people, forgiving their sins, and healing their land on condition that they humble themselves and pray and seek the Lord's face and forsake their wicked ways. The community aspect of revival is strong here. 'If my people . . .' The Chronicler stresses especially the dependence of blessing on humility. Scholars[1] call this famous verse a programmatic addition to the corresponding account in the book of Kings, and they draw our attention to the fact that the humility of the people of God is the repeated means by which the disaster of judgement is averted and the blessing of revival achieved.[2]

Everyone who gets on the revival bandwagon cites this verse so often that Old Testament scholar Bill Dumbrell was asked if the text could be taken validly as a basis for praying for a spiritual awakening in the church today. Dr Dumbrell saw the passage as part of a prophetic concern for the renewal of Israel. John the Baptist and the ministry of Jesus expressed this concern in the New Testament. It culminated in Pentecost, which, said Dr Dumbrell:

---

[1] H.G.M. Williamson, *Israel in the Book of Chronicles*, p. 113.
[2] See also 2 Chron. 12:7; 15:2–7; 30:6–9,18f., 33:12.

denoted spiritual renewal for Israel and then for the Gentiles . . . Paul's
letters . . . contain fine examples of pastoral concern for spiritual renewal within established congregations. The call to spiritual renewal is
so totally biblically prominent as to convince us that renewal and reformation is an ongoing need of the church.

And on the specific verses, 2 Chronicles 7:13,14, Dr Dumbrell
concluded:

> . . . the final meaning for Christians is clear biblically. If we have vio-
> lated the new covenant erected by the death of Jesus and promised by
> Jeremiah, but genuinely repent, as individuals or confessional bodies,
> or congregations or groups, then God will grant forgiveness appropri-
> ate to our personal or corporate circumstances.[3]

It is valid, then, to encourage Christians to long for revival and to use
this passage of Scripture as a description of the fourfold price upon
which the Lord makes revival conditional: humbling ourselves,
praying, seeking the Lord's face and forsaking our wicked ways.

Condition 1: Be a gospel-conveyor

'If my people, who are called by my name, *will humble themselves . . .*'
The Lord clearly attaches far greater importance to humility than
we do.

> I live in a high and holy place,
> but also with him who is contrite and lowly in spirit,
> to revive the spirit of the lowly
> and to revive the heart of the contrite. (Isa. 57:15)

In the New Testament, this biblical condition of humility is put
positively. There we are told to bear the shame of the cross of Christ,
to take up our cross and follow him, to die to self-serving and
commit ourselves to a life of service (Lk. 14:26,27). The chief

---

[3] Bill Dumbrell, 'Should Christians be Praying for a Spiritual Awakening
and the Spread of the Gospel?'

service that the Christian owes to others is to evangelize them. This is the labour of bringing all, by all means, to know Jesus. One of the conditions of revival, then, is being prepared to accept the persecution that comes when one fearlessly witnesses to the cross of shame.

We all long to see a myriad brought to Christ, rejoicing in sins forgiven and prayers answered. But it cannot happen unless some Christians somewhere are prepared to pay the price:

> Whenever you ripe fields behold,
> Waving to God their sheaves of gold,
> Be sure some corn of wheat has died,
> Some saintly soul was crucified,
> Someone has wrestled, wept and prayed,
> And fought hell's legions undismayed.[4]

'Blessed,' said Jesus, 'are those who are persecuted because of righteousness' (Matt. 5:10). He did not say that this experience would evaporate with the triumph of the gospel. There is a high price to pay for humbling oneself in any age and in any culture. Have we realistically counted that cost, and having counted it are we still prepared to pay the price? Unless we are, we need not fantasize about being used as instruments of revival (Matt. 10:38).

Another sobering thought is that the Lord may ask someone to suffer in this way so that another might see the fruit of revival. Samuel Leigh, the first Methodist minister in New South Wales, wore himself out in the service of his Lord without seeing revival. He saw that to be a witness for Christ in this harsh new land, Christians had to be 'full of faith and the Holy Spirit'.[5] But though he was full of both, he did not see the infant colony refreshed with revival showers. We might not see revival in this generation in our own nation, but we must pay the price for that future revival now, by falling like seeds into the ground and dying. It has been well observed: 'If you suffer without reaping, it is that others may reap after you. And if you reap without suffering, it is because others have suffered before you.'[6]

---

[4] Samuel Zwemer, quoted in Wallis, *China Miracle*, pp. 112f.
[5] Murray, *Australian Christian Life*, pp. 49f.
[6] Quoted in Wallis, *China Miracle*, p. 114.

Martyn Lloyd-Jones did not see big revival. In the last year of his life he compared himself with the little-known Griffith Jones of Llanddowror, the 'morning star' or forerunner of the eighteenth-century Welsh revival, who did not himself see the revival. Martyn Lloyd-Jones confided to his biographer, 'I never thought it was going to take so long. I thought I was going to see great revival but I am not complaining. It wasn't God's time and this preparatory work had to be done.' Iain Murray comments: 'If he could die believing that he had been permitted to do something to prepare the way for better men and greater days, that was enough.'[7] Will it be enough for you?

Humbling oneself for the task of evangelism and bearing the shame of the cross is not something any old Christian can do any old time when it takes his or her fancy. It rather necessitates training in the spiritual disciplines. The first condition of revival is readiness to be an evangelist no matter what the cost. It is to be a *gospel-conveyor*.

Condition 2: Be a prevailing pray-er

'If my people, who are called by my name, will humble themselves and *pray* ...' Revival will cost you much prayer. A revival will not just happen. It will not come by chance or accident. It comes in response to the importunate prayer, 'Will you not revive us again?' (Ps. 85:6). Note the 'you' – God is the author of revivals. They are brought *down* from God by prayer; they are not worked *up* from men by excitement. 'Oh, that you would rend the heavens *and come down*, that the mountains would tremble before you!' (Isa. 64:1).

Again, the prayer that brings the holy and glorious Lord down from his lofty throne to revive his needy people will not be any old prayer. Roger Ellsworth, in his study on the theme of revival in Isaiah, argues that God does not count all that we call prayer as prayer.[8] True prayer has at least three elements: intensity of desire, humility of heart and tenacity of purpose. Revival will not happen unless you believe God and can pray 'the prayer of faith' or 'believing prayer' or 'true, intercessory prayer' or 'prevailing prayer'.

---

[7] Murray, *Lloyd-Jones: Fight*, p. 773.
[8] Roger Ellsworth, *Come Down Lord!*.

Revival is the flooding down of the waters from heaven drawn from the fountain of life by prevailing prayer.

What is prevailing prayer, and how can one pray prevailingly?

Prevailing prayer is based first on a biblical understanding of the purposes of God for his church throughout history. This is an under-standing of the church not confined to the present or to the relatively trivial preoccupation with the local church's programmes and concerns. Prevailing prayer elevates the concerns of Christians to the level of God's concern for the mission of his church. It is the quality of a church's prayer life which determines whether or not it will be able to rise above the preoccupation with the seen and the pressure of institutional demands to share in God's great plan of redemption. When prayer for the true mission of the church rises to a passion, the storm clouds gather and the land is destined for that holy inundation which we call revival. One who prays prevailingly has a large vision of the purpose of God instead of a small focus on the concerns of the local church.

So the first characteristic of prevailing prayer is that it is prayer based on our complete identification with the purpose and charac-ter of God. The ultimate prayer is 'not my will, but thine'. Jesus' prayer is not mere passive submission to the Father, but a determined plea that God's will would prevail over all else. Prevailing prayer is active conformity to the will of God. This sort of prayer is never easy. It is hard work. It made Jesus sweat. Through it, Jesus prevailed at Calvary. Through it, we too shall prevail. Sidlow Baxter said, 'Men may spurn our appeals, reject our message, oppose our arguments, despise our person – but they are helpless against our prayers.'[9]

Second, prevailing prayer is that true, intercessory prayer which results when the believing heart has been sanctified by the blood of Christ, thus making a clean channel for the Spirit.

The cleansing which we receive through the blood of Christ enables us to assume the role of a priest before God, and our ministry in this capacity finds its highest expression in prayer for others. Hence the whole purpose of redemption while we live on this earth culminates in intercession. As Dr Chafer puts it:

---

[9] Robert E. Coleman, *Dry Bones Can Live Again: A Study Manual on Re-vival in the Local Church*, p. 38.

The personal element in true soul-winning work is more a work of pleading for souls than a service of pleading with souls. It is talking with God about men from a clean heart and in the power of the Spirit, rather than talking to men about God.[10]

Paul (now David) Yonggi Cho attaches great importance to this understanding of prayer. It is through his blood on the cross that Christ disarmed Satan. Christ has not only witnessed the fall of Satan (Lk. 10:18), but he has also blocked his access to the Father's throne of grace (Rev. 12:10,11). So prayer which prevails against the deceits and discouragements of Satan has as its sure foundation the blood covenant of Jesus Christ. Cho brings out well the practical implications of this:

> Satan no longer has access to God, accusing his people continually. However, Satan still accuses us to ourselves in our own minds. He tells us that we are not worthy to pray. He continually puts thoughts in our minds that we don't have the right of access to the Throne of Grace from which we can find strength in time of need. Therefore it is extremely important, particularly when we are battling the devil in prayer, that we realise that the effectiveness of our prayers is based on the blood covenant in the shed blood of Jesus Christ . . . We can overcome every thought that is not of God. We can bind every negative, accusing and self-depleting word that comes into our minds, trying to destroy our self-image. This we can do because the legal right to access has been purchased.[11]

Prevailing prayer, then, is interceding with God for souls from a heart cleansed by the blood of Christ.

The third characteristic of prevailing prayer is that it comes from a heart which is completely satisfied by the love of Jesus and does not hanker after other loves. In prevailing prayer, the heart that belongs to Jesus alone experiences Jesus alone:

> Saint Paul said, 'To me, to live is Christ' (Phil. 1:21). So it is in revival. It is not reaching an intellectual decision after thinking about things,

---

[10] Coleman, *Dry Bones*, p. 36, n. 8.
[11] Paul Y. Cho, *Prayer: Key to Revival*, p. 155.

but rather experiencing fullness of life through being brought into touch with the Lord.

Then we don't just know about Jesus. We see Him, and our spirit is quickened to understand and receive His Word. He breaks into our lives and becomes the living – resurrected Christ – God's provision and only answer for our every heart hunger and need.

He truly is the Way, the Truth and the *Life*.[12]

But most of us cannot just decide after years of bad prayer habits that, whenever we want, we can have hearts which rejoice in Jesus alone and which in prayer experience Jesus alone. Prayer is a discipline, and like all disciplines, mastery of it is progressive. In her *Autobiography*, St Theresa of Avila (1515–82) likens the soul to a garden, the watering of which requires four stages of prayer. This suggests the stages we Protestants might go through in our longing for revival:

> To water these flowers the beginners at prayer have no option but to draw water wearily from a well. In the second state, watering is easier because there is a windlass. In the third state, water flows in abundance; it comes from a river or stream which is very much easier, because the soil is soon saturated and the gardener has much less work. Finally, in the last state, it rains a lot, the Lord himself watering the garden without our having to take any trouble over it.[13]

In Cho's chapter on 'The Prayer of Faith', he makes the point, on the basis of Romans 10:9 'That if you confess with your mouth, "Jesus is Lord," and believe in your heart that God raised him from the dead, you will be saved', that confession is linked with faith. He also makes the very practical observation that our confession should not be a negative one in an attempt to manipulate God, such as 'Here I am Lord praying, but I don't really think you will answer'. Cho says that God responds to faith, not self-pity. An essential step to prevailing prayer is to clear out all the self-pity.[14]

A fourth characteristic of prevailing prayer is that the one who does the praying never gives up. It is very easy to give up on praying

---

[12] Strachan, *Revival*, p. 3.

[13] J. Delumeau, *Catholicism between Luther and Voltaire*, p. 51.

[14] Cho, *Prayer*, p. 136.

for revival because it often takes so long to come. Paul says in Galatians 6:9 that at the proper time we will reap a harvest if we obey the Lord's teaching (Lk. 18:1) and do not give up. The opposite of giving up is 'praying through'. Most of us give up far too easily in our prayers, but 'praying through' is needed. Daniel's prayer, though heard, was not answered for 21 days (Dan. 10). It is just as well that he 'prayed through'. So 'set your mind to gain understanding and to humble yourself before God' (Dan. 10:12) and never give up: 'pray through'.

Believing, persistent, determined prayer is the way to victory and to revival. We can do more than pray after we have prayed, but we cannot do more than pray until we have prayed. But it must be prayer which is undertaken in faith for the long-term spread of the gospel and the triumph of the kingdom – whether that comes in your lifetime or not. One of the harbingers of the East African Revival of 1933 was Jack Warren, who was appointed to Rwanda in 1925 and died in 1929 – but not before calling down on that region a great prayer offensive. 'Pray until it hurts,' he pleaded in 1926, 'that the mighty, indwelling, keeping power of the Holy Spirit may be experienced by the Christians.'[15]

Cho is convinced that if you want to see revival you have to organize a massive prayer offensive.[16] Some would object that this is to put too much emphasis on the quantity of prayer. But quantity is not an irrelevant guide to the intensity of desire and the commitment which Jesus taught were essential to answered prayer (Lk. 11:5–10).

Prevailing prayer is out of the experience of most of us, but revival will only come after God has given us a hunger for victory in prayer. The scriptural model to be followed here is Jacob, who literally wrestled with the Lord (Hos. 12; Gen. 32:22–30) until the Lord blessed him. When the spirit of prayer had come powerfully upon him, Charles Finney always knew that God was about to revive his hearers:

The praying power so manifestly spreading and increasing, the work soon took on a very powerful type; so much so that the word of the

---

[15] Cited in Jocelyn Murray, *Proclaim the Good News, A Short History of the Church Missionary Society,* p. 188.

[16] Whittaker, *Korea Miracle,* p. 50.

Lord would cut the strongest men down, and render them entirely helpless.[17]

So the second condition of revival is to be a *prevailing pray-er.*

Condition 3: Be a Bible-obeyer

'If my people, who are called by my name, will humble themselves and pray and *seek my face* ...' When the Lord hides his face, there is despair and deadness (Ps. 30:7). When his face shines upon us there is joy and new life (Ps. 4:6,7). It is best, then, to seek his face (Ps. 27:8).

In some ways this is the costliest of all the conditions of revival, because it takes great humility to discern what the Lord wants of us in our day. The churches have their own media, and they are bombarding us with numerous appeals to do it their way: charismatic renewal; liberation theology for the intellectual and socially-committed; entertainment evangelism with its beguiling music, explosive dance and searching drama; church growth through the application of managerial wisdom; or relevance through counselling at the point of need. Zeal for the church might legitimately commit us to one or more of these. But the hunger for revival dictates a different path – the deepening of our experience of Christ. The Lord's face is to be sought through humble prayer. The Lord's face is seen in worship when our pastors are feeding us on the finest wheat of the word. Such a diet will develop a spiritual palate that can be satisfied by no other food.

The revived Christian is not content with worship that is need-centred, man-centred or results-centred. All three are doing rather well at the moment in our lively churches because they are a whole lot better than dead services which have no centre of any kind at all. But God-centred worship is what the revived Christian's palate craves.

How does one seek the Lord's face? The answer to that question is not as simple as it should be. This is a crux for the student of revival. In the Bible, the Lord's face signifies the presence or the sight of the Lord. In Christian theology, the presence of the Lord may be

---

[17] Finney, *Autobiography*, p. 229.

understood in three ways. There is the general presence of the Lord, for he is creator of all and present to all, though all are not aware of his nearness (e.g., Acts 17:27,28). There is the particular or saving presence of the Lord whereby he is near to all who call on him for salvation (Ps. 139:7–12). And thirdly there is the manifest presence of the Lord, when, occasionally, he makes his presence palpable to his people (2 Cor. 6:16). Revival is concerned with the second and third of these. He comes palpably in his glory, but he comes to save.

Evangelicals, charismatics and Catholics differ in their understanding of how the Lord's presence is to be found. Evangelicals seek his presence in his word, charismatics in the Spirit and Catholics in the sacraments. The Bible tells us that he is present in all of those and in many other places besides.[18] The experience of revival shows that the presence of the Lord is found in his word by the Spirit. This means that the face of the Lord should be sought primarily in his word, in dependence on the Spirit's guidance rather than our own intellect. This means that the presence of the Lord is not to be found in theories about the word, or in debates about the meaning of the word. Rather, we will find the face of the Lord in the word fed to us as the bread of life and meditated upon as the divine means of challenging the heart, stirring up the affections to hate sin and love righteousness and to live for God's glory alone.

---

[18] The risen Lord is present:
1. In his words spoken to us by prophets.
2. In his words written and interpreted by apostles.
3. In his Holy Spirit (Lk. 24:49; Acts 2,8; 2:33,38,39; 16:6–7).
4. In the assembly of his people (Matt. 18:20).
5. In the hearts of believers.
6. The sacrament: The risen Lord is present when we gather for the Lord's Supper (Lk. 24:31,35).
7. In the rule of his kingdom in the world.
8. Through his powerful name (Acts 2:21,38; 3:6,16; 4:12; 10:43; 16:18).
9. In the presence of witnesses (Acts 3:22–23; 18:5–11; 26:23).
10. Through visions (Acts 7:55–6; 9:1–19).
11. In signs and wonders (Acts 4:22f.).
12. In appearances: epiphanies and christophanies and angelophanies (Matt. 14:27–33; 28:17).
13. 'The whole of every day' (Matt. 28:20).

Preaching, if it is to beget revival, must be based on the word of God, but it must not be the dry, intellectual teaching of the Bible that passes for preaching in many evangelical churches. 'What is the chief end of preaching?' asked Martyn Lloyd-Jones in his book *Preachers and Preaching.* 'I like to think it is this. It is to give men and women a sense of God and His presence.'[19]

In the Korean revival, priority both in preaching and in studying is given to the word.[20] The typical believer is therefore much more biblically literate than the western believer who is exposed to a whole range of Christian literature and teaching, much of it not rooted in biblical truth. Similarly, the essential background to the revival in the Solomon Islands was that from the beginning of missionary activity there the church had been steeped in the word of God, and the vital importance of the Bible in the lives of individual Christians was always stressed. So when revival came, both church and national leaders were able to give strong scriptural leadership, thus keeping the revival going.[21]

How do we seek the Lord's face? We seek him primarily in his word. Do we trust and obey the word of God? It is really the first condition of revival. It defines reality. All the rest is delusion. Revival is waking up to the reality of God – the reality found in his word.

So the third condition of revival is to be a *Bible-obeyer.*

Condition 4: Be a sin-slayer

The fourth and final condition of revival is to turn from our sins. 'If my people, who are called by my name, will humble themselves and pray and seek my face and *turn from their wicked ways* . . .' Dr W. Graham Scroggie said that:

> there never has been a spiritual revival which did not begin with an acute sense of sin. We are never prepared for a spiritual advance until we see the necessity of getting rid of that which has been hindering it, and that, in the sight of God, is sin.[22]

---

[19] Quoted in Murray, *Lloyd-Jones: Fight*, p. 623.
[20] Whittaker, *Korea Miracle*, p. 25.
[21] Strachan, *Revival*, p. 14.
[22] Quoted in Wesley Duewel, *Revival Fire*, p. 10.

Human sinfulness restricts revival like hardened arteries stop blood getting through. There is a blockage. God will not clear the guilty. In revivals, sinners wake up to the reality of their situation. Sin is no longer treated as a matter of indifference. Frivolity seems out of place. There is no place to hide from God. Broken and contrite in heart, we heed any offer of mercy.

Conviction leads to repentance. There can be no revival without confession of sin. My soul, thirsting for revival, knows what it must do. I must turn from my evil way. I must throw myself on the mercy of the Lord. 'If I cherish sin in my heart, the Lord will not hear me' (Ps. 66:18). The impediments must be removed.

God can use a small vessel in a revival, but he cannot use a dirty one. When we wrong God, he hides his face from us: 'You have hidden your face from us and made us waste away because of our sins' (Isa. 64:7). That we lack the Lord's love, power and approval is our own fault, for we have not 'striven to lay hold of him'. We must repent of the sin in our lives and of our prayerlessness. We must wait for the Lord, patiently and expectantly.

In 1949, a great revival came to the New Hebrides. A group of earnest Christians entered into a covenant with God that they would 'give him no rest until he made Jerusalem a praise in the earth' (Isa. 62:7). Months passed, but nothing happened. One night a young man read Psalm 24:3–5:

> Who shall ascend into the hill of the Lord? or who shall stand in his holy place? He that hath clean hands, and a pure heart; who hath not lifted his soul unto vanity, nor sworn deceitfully. He shall receive the blessing from the Lord, and righteousness from the God of his salvation.

The young man closed his Bible and, looking at his companions, said, 'Brethren, it is just so much humbug to be waiting thus night after night, month after month, if we ourselves are not right with God. I must ask myself, "Is my heart pure? Are my hands clean?"'

His friends were smitten and fell on their faces in confession and consecration. That night revival came and quickly spread over the island, sweeping thousands into the kingdom. Are our hands clean? 'Search me, O God, and know my heart; try me, and know my thoughts, and see if there be any wicked way in me' (Ps. 139:23,24).

So, as the greatest and surest test of our desire for revival, we come to the necessity of confession. Are we prepared to face that besetting sin and apply to it that powerful detergent, that deadly antibiotic, the blood of Christ?

One of the reasons why revival came to the Solomon Islands in 1970 was that the missionaries of the South Sea Evangelical Mission taught strongly the necessity of separation from evil:

> Separation from all that encourages fleshly affections and lusts is vital, for the flesh and the Holy Spirit are in conflict until the end of life's journey. To fail in teaching separation would pander to the flesh and open the door to enemy activity.[23]

Why does revival tarry? It tarries primarily because of our sin. And it is merciful that it should. For God would not be kind to bless while we persist in our wilful sin. Eddie Smith has written:

> If the Lord sought to bless us singularly now, in the present state of apostasy, we would wrongly equate His blessing with our bankrupt way of life. We would continue in our sin, while we blithely received His grace. It is better for us to be shown our sin and shame before he blesses us, for only then do we see Him as He truly is: One who is gracious, but one for whom we must reserve reverence and awe.[24]

Should this confession, so essential to revival, be secret and private – or open and public? The thought of openly confessing one's sins seems an appalling prospect to most of us. There is not only the embarrassment and the risk of permanent damage to one's reputation, but there are also spiritual dangers – such as the pride which sometimes motivates us to want our humiliation to be public. Yet there is biblical warrant for the practice. James 5:16 says, 'Confess your sins to each other and pray for each other so that you may be healed.'

It is intriguing that the public confession of sin has been one of the most conspicuous features, even the defining feature, of some revivals: Wales 1904/5; Korea 1907; East Africa 1933; Eastern

---

[23] Strachan, *Revival*, p. 15.
[24] Eddie Smith, 'Prayer Plus'.

Europe in the late 1980s; and American college revivals in 1995. In the Welsh revival, Evan Roberts decreed that, while the confession of Christ was to be open, the confession of sins was to be to God.[25] But those under conviction did not obey his decree, and there was open confession of sins. Many have found that the chances of defeating sin are increased if they are brought into the light and confessed with the mouth. It also helps our war on sin to find so many wrestling with the same difficulties.

The public confession of sin is always a possibility in any revival, for the soul that is under conviction has a different view of reality from that which normally prevails. He or she now sees sin as so serious that one will do anything to jettison it rather than continue to offend a holy God. The revived soul instinctively perceives that it is best to deal with besetting sins now (and drastically) so that we can start to really live and be confident that we will not have to endure far greater embarrassment on the day of judgement.

So the fourth condition of revival is to be a *sin-slayer*.

Conclusion

Do you really, *really* want to see revival?

Then you must humble yourself and do the work of an evangelist, ignoring the shame. You must learn how to prevail in prayer. You must seek the Lord's face by learning the Bible's teachings and obeying them. You must challenge the sin in your life to a duel to the death.

To be a good soldier in Christ's revival army, then, you must be:

- A gospel-conveyer
- A prevailing pray-er
- A Bible-obeyer
- A sin-slayer

Until we have an army made up of men and women who have all four qualifications, we will not see revival.

You might think at first that this is a depressing conclusion. Upon reflection, however, you may agree that this catalogue of things we

---

[25] Lewis, 'With Christ', p. 44.

must be and do surely provides a basis for a syllabus for preaching and teaching, a programme of exercises and activities. Let us not be too quick to despise the intentional pursuit of revival. There is much that we can do to put our house in order. We cannot ignite a spark of life in anyone's soul, but there are numerous obstacles we can remove. Revival is all of God, but he normally uses human instruments. So, let us turn finally to the subject of planning for revival.

12

Planning for Revival

The fact that God is sovereign does not make nonsense of all human strategies to promote revival. It would be nonsense to strategize for revival if we knew nothing of God's sovereign will or if we knew that he had willed that we do nothing to facilitate revival. In fact, we know enough of God's sovereign will to be convinced that revival is part of his sovereign purpose, and that he usually uses human instruments in the fulfilment of his purpose. That is the plain message of Ezekiel 37, the most famous Old Testament passage on revival.

The prophet Ezekiel knew that revival is the work of the sovereign God, but that did not mean that he could not feel excited about the fact that revival was about to come, or that he should not pray for revival or plan for revival or preach for revival.

When he was shown the valley of the dry bones, the Lord asked him (Ezek. 37:3), 'Son of man, can these bones live?' Ezekial replied, 'O *Sovereign* LORD, you alone know.' Ezekiel knew that revival was the work of the sovereign Lord. And he knew that it was the sovereign will of the sovereign God that he was about to revive his people, because the Lord said to him (37:9), 'Prophesy to the breath; prophesy, son of man, and say to it, "This is what the *Sovereign* LORD says: Come from the four winds, O breath, and breathe into these slain, that they may live." '

It is precisely because revival is a sovereign work of God that we can pray most confidently that it will come. If we can with integrity pray that the sovereign Lord will send revival, can we with integrity have a strategy or blueprint for revival? The answer to that must also be 'yes'. We can have a blueprint for revival if the sovereign Lord gives us one, as he gave one to Ezekiel.

The blueprint, if it is indeed from God, will reflect what God has revealed about what revival is in its essence. Revival is essentially a spiritual solution to the spiritual problem that lies at the root of community and individual need. When people confess their sins publicly in revival, one of the most moving features of their confessions is the appalling human need they often reveal. The temptation, then, is always for the compassionate Christian to want to help redress the need rather than the cause. But the joy of those who are revived arises from the conviction that God has given them the ultimate answer to the root cause of their problem. They see the problem in its true light: it is sin against a holy God. And they see God's solution in the death of his Son for the forgiveness of their sin as the only true and ultimate answer.

It follows that a strategy for revival should be based on the greatest of all realities – namely God's glory – rather than on a secondary reality – namely human need. Revival is the glory of God shed abroad in human hearts and it is the ultimate, radical answer to human need. Any strategy for revival should seek first to promote God's glory. This is to be done primarily through the spreading of the gospel, which is the divine instrument for the glorification of God through the relief of the sinner's need, which is fundamentally a spiritual need.

The sovereignty of God, divine glory and the overflowing of God's love to the world

The greatest strategist for revival, Jonathan Edwards, was also one of the church's greatest champions of the sovereignty of God. When he was just twenty-six years of age, Edwards wrote of the time he fell in love with the doctrine of divine sovereignty:

> Absolute sovereignty is what I love to ascribe to God. God's sovereignty has ever appeared to me a great part of his glory. It has often been my delight to approach God and adore him as a sovereign God.[1]

---

[1] 'Personal Narrative', in *Jonathan Edwards, Selections* (New York: Hill and Wang, 1962), pp. 59, 67; see also Jonathan Edwards, *Freedom of the Will*, p. 380.

Sovereignty is a great and glorious part of an infinitely glorious being. Since the supreme aspect of God is his glory, it follows that the goal of all that God does is to display his glory.

Our duty is to delight in that glory. We are to glorify God and enjoy him for ever, but the joy is no more an option than the duty to glorify him. He is to be enjoyed. Delight is an affection and true religion, that is, saving faith, consists of the holy affections – the more vigorous and felt exercises of the inclination or will of the soul, such as joy, delight, hope, faith, perseverance, compassion, zeal.

It is from the heart of that all-sufficient overflowing sovereign God that revival gushes like a fountain. Revival will ever be at the centre of the work of God, whether people are conscious of great need or not. A key verse of Scripture in this connection is Philippians 2:12,13: 'Continue to work out your salvation . . . because it is God who works in you to will and to act according to his good purpose.' His good purpose is to glorify himself through the salvation of sinners. That is why sinners will go on being saved, and that is why whenever we are most aware of the glory of God, which occurs during times of spiritual awakening, we will also have the greatest hunger to share the glorious gospel through evangelism.

The essence of humanity and the essence of revival is an essence which reflects the character of God himself. God is spirit. Man is a spiritual being, and revival is a spiritual movement. In revival we see the reality of man's deepest need from God's perspective.

Jonathan Edwards made an important distinction between two aspects of God's character. For want of better terms, we will label them the natural and the spiritual attributes of God. By the natural attributes of God we mean his power, his knowledge, his being eternal, his greatness and his awesome majesty. By his spiritual attributes we mean his righteousness, truthfulness, faithfulness and goodness. These spiritual attributes of God are what we mean by his holiness.

Just as there are two kinds of perfection in God – the natural and the spiritual – so there is a twofold image of God in human beings. We possess God's natural image, which is expressed in our reason and understanding and ability and our dominion over the rest of nature. There is also God's spiritual image in us, or the image of his holiness. In human beings, this image of God's holiness is represented in our love for God, love towards others, justice, kindness, mercy, humility and gentleness.

If God's grace is working in the human heart for salvation, it will give the heart a great affection or love and appetite for, or a taste or sense of, the beauty and excellence of God's spiritual attributes. The thing which most excites the revived soul and activates its will is the loveliness of God's holy attributes: his righteousness, truthfulness, faithfulness and goodness. And the ruling passion of the revived person will be to see those attributes of God's holiness as the reigning concerns in his or her own life. The thing in which we will be most concerned to make progress is the development of those attributes in our own life: love for God, love to others, justice, kindness, mercy, humility and gentleness. Natural attributes – knowledge, reason, understanding, strength – will only be important in so far as they find their expression and fulfilment in terms of the values arising from those spiritual attributes.

It was the spiritual image of God in human beings which was lost at the fall. God gives this back to us at our conversion, and he gives the love of it back to us when we are revived. Whether or not we are in need of revival depends on whether or not delight in God's holy character is the great love of our life. What is it that directs our living? Are we primarily concerned to develop our intellect? Are we primarily concerned to develop our bank balance? Are we primarily concerned to develop a fit or beautiful body? Are we interested in the attributes of holiness, but only in so far as they will help us to develop into a finer, stronger, more attractive or happier human being? In other words, are we more gripped by the usefulness to ourselves of the divine attributes of holiness than we are by their own intrinsic beauty for the sake of God's glory?

If we have to say 'yes' to any of those questions, we yet know little of the reality of God or the essence of true religion. We are sleeping the sleep of death, and our soul is in desperate need of revival. We are, in truth, little different from the demons or evil angels, for they put the natural attributes first, and are only interested in the spiritual attributes in so far as they strengthen the natural attributes and allow them to be used for the self-aggrandizement of the creature. The glory of the elect angels of God, on the other hand, consists not so much in their staggering beauty, their great power and their awesome intellect. Their glory is to be found in their holiness, in their admiration for and emulation of the holy character of God above all else. They allow the moral or spiritual perfections of God to sanctify the natural attributes that God gave them at their creation.

You can be like an angel in your attitude to the moral or spiritual attributes, or you can be like a devil. The Lord made us a little lower than the angels with the capacity to be like them, not in natural attributes, but in the spiritual. And, indeed, one day through Christ we shall be exalted above them, not in strength and knowledge, but in purity and love – that is, in holiness.

If the grace of God is at work in you and you are fully alive to the work of the Holy Spirit in your life, then the beauty in which you will most delight will be in the beauty of holiness. Psalm 29:2 says, 'Ascribe to the LORD the glory due to his name; worship the LORD in the splendour of his holiness.'

That is what revival is all about. It is the visitation of God's Holy Spirit to the soul, re-establishing and confirming in it the image of the holy perfection of God. We can thus see why all revivals are revivals of holiness. To be holy, as God is holy, is the greatest need of the individual soul made in the image of God.

Three propositions on revival and strategy

A godly and biblical strategy for revival will have to take that understanding of the essence of revival into account. The following are three propositions advanced from Ezekiel 37 that are foundational to a biblical strategy for revival.

Proposition 1: A clear understanding of the deadness of our own nation outside of Christ is essential to developing a biblical blueprint for revival.

Ezekiel's vision was one of death. In 37:1,2 the prophet wrote: 'he brought me out by the Spirit of the LORD and set me in the middle of a valley; it was full of bones. He led me back and forth among them, and I saw a great many bones on the floor of the valley, bones that were very dry.'

God showed his prophet this scene of devastation – probably a massacred army, the victim of one of King Nebuchadnezzar's ruthless campaigns. The mutilated and dismembered bodies were not buried; the hyenas and the vultures had picked the bones clean, exposing them to the sun and wind which had bleached them white.

If the Holy Spirit were to come upon us and revive us, we would see our community and nation as God sees them – full of dry bones – with the corruption of death everywhere. If the Lord has given you a deep understanding of the deadness of your own nation, that is a sign that he purposes revival.

Proposition 2: We must eliminate errors and remove excesses that stand in the way of the coming of the Holy Spirit.

Ezekiel continued (37:4–8):

> Then he said to me, 'Prophesy to these bones and say to them, "Dry bones, hear the word of the LORD! This is what the Sovereign LORD says to these bones: I will make breath enter you, and you will come to life. I will attach tendons to you and make flesh come upon you and cover you with skin; I will put breath in you, and you will come to life. Then you will know that I am the LORD".' So I prophesied as I was commanded. And as I was prophesying, there was a noise, a rattling sound, and the bones came together, bone to bone. I looked, and tendons and flesh appeared on them and skin covered them, but there was no breath in them.

After the noise like distant thunder, bone was joined to bone, and then the tendons and the flesh appeared on the bones, and then the skin covered them.

One of the first concerns of a congregation, when it is impressed with the power of God and wants to respond to the Lord in a way which will honour him, is to put the whole house in order – that is a concern for reformation. This is the desire for everything to be done properly: all the bones put in the right places anatomically; all the theology systematized; and all the procedures and structures worked out. It looks a lot tidier than the scattered bones. So when any revival comes, there is first felt a need for reformation. Our desire will be to reform what we can and to be diligent to avoid all errors and misconduct. Jonathan Edwards, in part III of *Some Thoughts on the Revival*, suggested four things that we are to avoid if we want to see revival: spiritual pride; excesses and extravagances; censuring other Christians; the love of novelty in spiritual things.[2]

Avoid spiritual pride

Pride is the worst viper that there is in the heart. It is the first sin which ever entered the universe, and it is the sin that makes us most like Satan. God has given us all we need to withstand the evil one, but he expects us to take great care and to take great pains to protect ourselves, by daily putting on the whole armour of God. When the great days of revival blessing come upon our churches and our land, it is the humble who will have the largest share of the blessing. When the Lord Jesus, the mighty one, clothes himself with majesty and splendour and girds his sword upon his side and rides forth victoriously, it will be on behalf of truth, humility and justice (Ps. 45:4). It is the meek who will inherit the earth (Matt. 5:5).

Avoid excesses and extravagances and immediate illuminations

It is the devil who loves extremes. He does not care on which side of any issue the pendulum is swinging – he just lends his weight to the momentum and drives the pendulum hard, way beyond its natural point.

Since the extremes are Satan's domain, Edwards looked for balance as evidence of the Spirit of God. Problems arise if the preacher either addresses the affections rather than the understanding, or just fills heads with knowledge instead of touching hearts. Balance is desirable between religious excitement and restraint and between a conviction of the love of Christ and the fear of the Lord. One needs the help of the Spirit to get the balance right.

Those who are experienced doctors of the soul have observed that when someone has a great and high and unusual experience of God, there are commonly four elements in that experience: the Spirit; the emotions; the imagination; and pride. With the passage of time it is very easy for the last three to take over and the Spirit departs from such an unholy place. So Satan sees to it that such high experiences easily degenerate.

---

[2] Edwards, *Great Awakening*, pp. 384–408.

And let us not expect to have revealed to us all we need to know immediately. Let us give ourselves time to study and learn the things of God, for they are not all imparted in a moment. Do not despise human learning. Moses, Solomon and Paul were all very learned men, and the Lord blessed and used their learning. Revival demands that we do not despise others and that we do not belittle learning.

Avoid censuring other Christians
Nothing hinders the work so much as the habit of looking only to find fault. Nor is it helpful to pour scorn upon those who disagree with us about the Holy Spirit's gifts. We must eradicate the bitter root of censoriousness if we are to have revival with integrity. We Protestant Christians have developed the bad habit of emphasizing our Protestantism above anything else. We are better at protesting than growing. We brawl too much in the name of 'contending earnestly for the faith'. We find fault and nit-pick over doctrine. We love to shoot our own troops. Revival, historically, has come when traditionally divided and feuding churches seek to express their essential unity in Christ. Billy Graham, just before his wonderful New York Crusade of 1957, wrote:

> God cannot bless us if there are divisions, fighting and strife within the church. How many churches we hear about today that are filled with divisions, jealousy, revenge, spite, pride. How can God possibly bless a situation like that? Pastors and Christians need to repent of the sins of strife, controversy and fighting. I tell you, this is not of God.
>
> Many people wonder why revival has not come to the evangelicals of America. This is one of the primary reasons. We have had enough name-calling and mud-slinging. Let's repent of our sins, fall on our faces before God and spend the time in prayer that we used to spend in controversy and see what happens. I guarantee that God will send a revival.[3]

Christians of a separatist tradition have castigated Billy for this attitude. But he has withstood their carping, and his crusades have been massively blessed of God.

---

[3] Billy Graham, 'What's the Next Step?', p. 22.

Avoid the love of novelty in spiritual things

Many of us just lust after new teachings and perspectives. We get easily bored with the old. In 2 Timothy 4:3 we read, 'People will not put up with sound doctrines. Instead, to suit their own desires, they gather around them a great number of teachers to say what their itching ears want to hear.' Innovation in teachings gets everybody arguing. It is divisive and diverts some down side-tracks and greatly hinders God's work. Revival with integrity calls for concentration on old truth, not new ideas.

So revival calls for reformation in all those areas of error and mis-conduct. But reformation is not enough. After the bones had come together, bone to bone, and tendons and flesh appeared on them and skin covered them, it looked better – but there was no breath in them. Everything was reformed and in order, but there was still no breath in them. In place of the scattered dead army there was now an ordered dead army. The scene was one of a cemetery rather than of a massacre. So often, after a little reviving, churches are content to put their house in order and to look decent and respectable. But it's still a cemetery. It's still a place of the dead. It is not yet what God wants for his people.

From this I conclude that reformation is never enough. That is only the first step, and being truly revived by God is a two-stage process: first prophesy to the bones (v. 7); then prophesy to the breath (v. 9). Revival is the great twofold divine work of recreation – reformation plus in-breathing.

Proposition 3: To prepare the way for the coming of the Lord in his revival glory, we must start with ourselves, pray up our generals, get a committed nucleus and then train up the troops. For revival creates God's army.

> . . . there was no breath in them. Then he said to me, 'Prophesy to the breath; prophesy, son of man, and say to it, "This is what the Sovereign LORD says: Come from the four winds, O breath, and breathe into these slain, that they may live." ' So I prophesied as he commanded me, and breath entered them; they came to life and stood up on their feet – a vast army. (Ezek. 37:8–10)

Start with yourself

People respond to a demonstration of revival – not an explanation. You must be the man or woman. Revival requires that people not only hear a holy message, but see a holy messenger. Revival comes through personalities, not through techniques. Men and women are God's method.

Most of the books on revival call for full obedience as a prerequisite for revival. For example, Dawson Trotman was fond of saying, 'God can do more through one man who is 100% dedicated to Him than through 100 men 90% dedicated to Him.' What does it mean to be 100% dedicated? Has there ever been such a person since the Lord Jesus? I've always had problems with this demand for complete consecration, suspecting that people, discouraged by the awareness that they are less than perfect, allow themselves to settle for doing very little for the Lord. I've even thought of writing a book called 'My second-best for God', on the grounds that that is better than nothing.

'Full obedience' does not mean to be sinless, but to have an over-riding single-mindedness. It means to have an undivided heart, neither half-hearted nor torn between two loyalties. It means to have crucified the demands of the ego. Samuel Chadwick, a prince of preachers, began his ministry infatuated with his own oratorical powers. He was convinced he would preach up a revival. Nothing happened until God confronted him with his sinful egotism, which sought to displace the power of the cross with the eloquence and wisdom of a man. God had a simple command for him, 'Burn those sermons.' Colin Tilsley, director of the Brethren Literature Outreach Crusade, once observed: 'How mightily God can use for His glory one who has no designs on His glory.'

You must be the person.

Pray up the generals

Though revivals are entirely the work of the sovereign Lord, the sovereign God does choose ministers to be the bearers of the revival message and developers of the revival strategy. The Lord involves Ezekiel himself in the work. The sovereign Lord can do it without Ezekiel, but he chooses not to: 'he said to me, prophesy', that is, preach. And he has been saying that ever since. Preaching is the Lord's normal means of bringing life to the dead. Ezekiel had not felt particularly suited to the job of proclaiming the word of God. He was a priest. He was not a born preacher, but God gave him the message, 'So my mouth was opened and I was no longer silent' (Ezek. 33:22).

Similar experiences of timid people being given the gift of the gab have been reported in subsequent revivals. One of the earliest revivals we know about in the Presbyterian Church of Scotland was in 1630 and involved the Lord laying his hand on a very timid and reluctant minister. John Livingstone was only twenty-seven and not yet ordained when he was asked to preach to thousands of people who had gathered at the Kirk of Shotts in Scotland to partake of the Lord's Supper, which was then only an annual event. Livingstone was consumed by nerves and wanted to run away. But the Holy Spirit came upon him, convincing him of God's power to save, and for two and a half hours he preached with great scriptural eloquence, way beyond his formal preparation. It is said that five hundred were born again during that one sermon.

A burning love for the lost has ever been the hallmark of those whom God has used to revive his people. On 25 May 1735, Howell Harris was converted. If it had ended there we would never have heard of him. But three weeks later, on 18 June 1735, he had a second experience that was critical in making him the impassioned evangelist of the Welsh revival. He was reading and praying in the tower of the church at Llangasty when, to quote him:

> Suddenly I felt my heart melting within me like wax before a fire, and love to God for my Saviour. I felt also not only love and peace, but a longing to die and be with Christ. Then there came a cry into my soul within that I had never known before – Abba, Father! I could do nothing but call God my Father. I knew that I was his child, and He loved me and was listening to me. My mind was satisfied and I cried out, Now I am satisfied! Give me strength and I will follow Thee through water and fire.

Martyn Lloyd-Jones does not hesitate to label this a baptism of fire or of power subsequent to conversion which gave Harris an indomitable compassion for the lost. When he preached, Harris always looked for this unction of the Holy Spirit. He would write in his diaries of 'the authority' when preaching or the coming down of 'a strong gale'. Such anointed preaching also empowered him to withstand extraordinary persecution with that supreme disregard which stamped him as an aristocrat of the Spirit. Such anointed preaching, which Martyn Lloyd-Jones describes as 'prophesying', is a sign that the Lord purposes revival.[4]

Part of any strategy for revival must be to pray that God will give ministers a vision of the dry bones and of his great power to save. For through such a vision, as we read in Psalm 104:4, 'he makes his ministers flames of fire'. The plaque in Northampton Church applying Malachi 2:6 to Jonathan Edwards (referred to in Ch. 9) shows us whom God chooses in his sovereignty, he makes a flame of fire to turn many from iniquity. But to do that, our leaders must have no wrong on their lips and walk with the Lord in peace and uprightness. Pray up the generals.

Get a committed nucleus and develop a group discipline
The lesson of history is that many revivals have begun with a small group dedicated to pray for revival. First they desire revival and then they learn what the cost of revival is and are prepared to pay the price. Examples of this include the home Bible study meetings of the Pietists; Wesley's Holy Club and then the Methodist class meetings; student prayer meetings before the Second Great Awakening in America; the haystack prayer meeting before the launching of the modern missionary movement in America. It is surely significant that Jesus came to focus his ministry on the Twelve. They became the nucleus of the revival that began at Pentecost.

There is, I believe, in every local church a group of disorganized, restless Christians who do not know quite what they want and who are not aware that others feel like they do, who are just waiting to catch fire. In Matthew 12:20 we read that the Messiah would not quench the smoking flax. Jesus was concerned to set the spark of faith ablaze with the fire of revival. Once you have caught the fire of revival yourself, why not start a smoking flax club in your local church and seek to stoke the flames. Seek out those concerned for revival and give them of your best in teaching, prayer and fellowship.

What is church? It is the time the soldiers come together to be trained. The church building is simply the 'drill hall for the

---

[4] Lloyd-Jones, 'Howell Harris and Revival', in *Puritans*, pp. 282–302.

Christian task force'. In 2 Timothy 2, Paul dwells on the importance of training by representing it in four different images: the
Christian needs be a soldier who endures hardship to please his
master; an athlete who seeks to win by strict observance of the rules
of the game; a farmer who works hard; and a workman who knows
how to use the tools of his trade with skill. A church with members
so trained, committed and skilled will have much greater penetra-
tion of the forces of darkness than one where the members are half-
asleep. It has been well observed that it is no easier to pray in Korea
or to win converts in Korea than it is in Australia, but the Christians
are so much more committed. It is not that the territory is easier to
take; it is just that the troops are more effective.[5] The Chinese evangelist Watchman Nee said:

> . . . if you have not yet brought your body under control you had better
> call a halt in the work and gain dominion over it before you try to exer-
> cise authority in any wider realm. You may take great pleasure in the
> work, but it will have little value if you are dominated by your physical
> cravings.[6]

Train the troops
Train them in the costly implications of 2 Chronicles 7:14 as out-
lined in the previous chapter on the cost of revival That is, train your
revival troops as gospel-conveyers, prevailing pray-ers, Bible-
obeyers, and sin-slayers. That will give you a programme, a curriculum, to prepare for revival.

Conclusion

That would be my strategy for revival: start with yourself, pray up
the generals, get a committed nucleus, and then train up the troops.
The following addendum is a catalogue of practical suggestions of
things you can do to help promote revival.

---

[5] Whittaker, *Korea Miracle*, p. 22.
[6] Quoted in Wallis, *China Miracle*, p. 134.

Addendum
Revival: What Can You Do?

1. Catch fire from those who are on fire themselves

A friend wrote to me from China on 19 November 1991:

> Yesterday was the most exciting day in my life. Oh Stuart, what disarmingly charming Christians they are. Not that they are perfect, but they are *revived*. I have seen something of revival in reality. There is an overwhelming sense of God's power and sovereignty as well as the great power of Satan's attack. You have to be in church by 6 a.m. to get a seat for the 6:30 service – 1500 present.

Revival has been endemic in the Solomons since the early 1970s. In 1992, the South Sea Evangelical Mission brought Pastor Michael Maeliau from the Solomons to Australia. He spoke much on walking and talking with God. I just knew I had to get closer to this flame for the Lord so that I, too, might catch the fire. So I joined a few others on a retreat with him, and it was while under his ministry, during a time of repentance, that, with tears, I felt the Spirit of God come upon me, convicting me of my own sinfulness, especially my chronic lack of faith in him. I had always been afraid of that aspect of revival, and I was therefore surprised at how gentle and sweet the Lord was in dealing with me. But my surprise was proof of the authenticity of the experience.

So get close to those who are on fire, and make sure your own heart is combustible.

2. Preach and teach the doctrines of grace

Certain theological emphases are more calculated to promote revival than others – focus on them:

- The glory of God
- Justification by faith in the crucified redeemer
- Holiness
- Spiritual warfare
- The manifest presence of God

3. Practise the spiritual disciplines

Certain spiritual disciplines promote revival – focus on them:

- Walking and talking with God
- Entering into the presence of God
- Prevailing prayer
- Time and quietness to commune with God
- Knowing how to evangelize

4. Make worship work

Make sure you hear God speak and do not sing too much. The Revd Christopher Idle, Rector of Oakley in Suffolk, and author of many hymns in *Hymns for Today's Church*, writes:

> More than one true revival has trickled away somehow in the songs that flowed from it. Endless singing is neither edifying nor true praise, but self-indulgence. 'Take away the noise of your songs' says the Lord when other things are left undone . . . Come and sing . . . then stop singing; bow down and listen . . . God can live without our words; we cannot live without his. Never let our singing drown the music of the gospel![1]

5. Study the history of revivals

Read the histories of revivals; catch fire from them; have your expectation raised by them; and your desire to pray for revival excited by

---

[1] Quoted in *ACL News* (July 1990), p. 6.

them. One might do a course on revival: they are increasingly on offer. You might even become a historian of revival, and if you have the great privilege of experiencing one, record it meticulously and circularize news about it conscientiously. It pays to speculate on why, for example, the 'Toronto Blessing' has been called the 'Internet Revival'.

6. Study the theology of revival

Read everything written by Jonathan Edwards you can lay your hands on. Among modern authors, Martyn Lloyd-Jones and J.I. Packer will repay close study. The serious study of the theology of revival has scarcely begun. It is much needed, particularly in the area of pneumatology. J.I. Packer says that there are three things that those who long for revival should do:

- Preach and teach God's truth
- Prepare Christ's way by removing obvious obstacles such as habitual sins, neglect of prayer and fellowship, worldly-mindedness, etc.
- Pray for the Spirit's outpouring

7. Read and study Paul's letter to the Romans

It is because Romans is the finest exposition of the key doctrine of justification by faith alone that it has had, historically speaking, such a time-honoured role in the history of revivals. Justification is not a doctrine that has had its day. It is the eternal gospel. As Bishop Gore, who was no evangelical, wrote:

> . . . it remains true that no revival of religion can ever attain to any ripeness or richness unless this central doctrine of St Paul's gospel resumes its central place with us also.[2]

Godet concurs:

> The Reformation was undoubtedly the work of the Epistle to the Romans . . . and the probability is that every great spiritual revival in

---

[2] Charles Gore, *St Paul's Epistle to the Romans*, I, p. 44.

the Church will be connected as cause and effect with a deeper understanding of this book.[3]

If Romans is a key to revival, why is it so relevant to church growth?
Because, as E. Käsemann has said in his wonderful commentary on
Romans, 'God's grace wants the world. If not, we end up with a
Christian mystery religion.'[4] Only the grace that wants the world is
sufficient to confront and defeat the secularism and demonism of
our world.

8. Remember the definition and deliberately work towards it

Revival is occasionally preceded by an expectation that God is
about to do something exceptional; it is usually preceded by an
extraordinary unity and prayerfulness among Christians; and it is
always accompanied by the revitalization of the church, the conversion of large numbers of unbelievers, and the diminution of sinful
practices in the community.

- Seek to create expectation. Make people long for revival:
    remind people of the need
    tell them what God has done – he can do it again
    create a vision of a community which is revived
    imagine taking a city for Christ – a school for Christ –
    a university for Christ

- Pursue unity:
    co-operate on the basic doctrines of grace – not over-
    systematizing of doctrines
    address the male/female divide
    address the charismatic/evangelical divide

- Promote prayerfulness:
    join a prayer movement for revival
    be diligent in your own prayer – people need to see a holy
    messenger as well as hear the message of holiness

---

[3] Frédéric Godet, *Commentary on St Paul's Epistle to the Romans*, I, p. 1.
[4] Ernst Käsemann, *Commentary on Romans*, p. 255.

- Seek the revitalization of the church:
  encourage balanced biblical teaching
  address the heart as well as the head – preaching should be
      heart to heart
  foster the move from orthodoxy to vital Christianity
  inculcate a positive biblical theology (don't major on
      criticism)
  promote holiness
  emphasize spirituality
  be focused on the things which should be our priorities –
      the glory of God and the primacy of evangelism,
      appropriate worship
  understand preaching as mass counselling from the Bible

- Promote evangelism:
  pre-evangelism
  evangelism – confidence that the gospel can change
      people's lives
  incarnation – live the truth as well as speaking it

- Ask: will this help the community?

9. Pray that the spotfires will come together into one mighty firestorm of the Lord

Or, to change the metaphor, pray that the tributaries of renewal will flow into the river of revival. Revival is the river of God's love flowing freely and fully through the church, and it may come when the existing tributaries start to flow together.

There is an enormous amount of revival activity going on in the world today. With modern communication methods, including the Internet, more people will get to know more quickly about more revivals. One of the most amazing and interesting things about the Toronto Blessing is how influential it has been. Modern cheap transport has enabled thousands of Christian leaders to visit Toronto. Modern communication systems, including computers and videos, have spread the experience all over the globe. In future, revivals will spread along such channels among such networks. Networking for Jesus will be a major way of using revival to promote worldwide evangelization.

Epilogue
The Next Great Awakening: What Will It Look Like?

In 1995, I had the privilege of delivering the lectures on which this book is based at the Regent College Summer School in Vancouver. My 27 students made this an unforgettable course. At the end of the course I asked them what the next great awakening would look like. What would it achieve in the world? I had emphasized that revivals are always the surprising work of the sovereign God, and that God never sends a revival identical in every respect to revivals which the church has already enjoyed. One student had taken this point to heart and insisted that: 'The next great awakening won't fit any of our categories. We won't know what to do with it. What we need is fire, but we cannot control the divine fire.'

No student dissented from this, but, for the next two hours, roles were reversed as they plied me with their hopes and aspirations for a revived church and nation, while I took copious notes. They also wrote many fascinating essays from which I learned much, as we have already seen in Chapter 7. Their thoughts covered their longings for revival at the individual, church fellowship, and community and national levels. At the end of the two hours, they invited me to sit while they gathered round and laid hands on me and prayed for me. We had become part of each other's pilgrimages as we bonded quickly during that course, and I want to conclude this book by weaving their thoughts into mine with the prayer that the Holy Spirit is directing the whole exercise.

Three strong emphases had come through in the course, as I hope they have in this book. First, revival is waking up to reality, which is

God's perspective on the world. This perspective we begin to apprehend with awe as God comes down from heaven in his glory, which is what he does in all revivals. Revival results in radical reprioritizing of aspirations in the light of the glory of God, now manifest. Second, Jesus is the hero of all genuine revivals, and not the Holy Spirit whose gifts are given to adorn the great gift of eternal life. Revival is Jesus' firestorm. Third, the object of all revivals is not the individual or the church, but the community or nation – as God, in the power of his Spirit, rescues and regenerates his suffering creation in anticipation of the radical recreation of the last day. Revival jolts Christians out of their self-absorption and their plausible side-tracks and refocuses their ministries on the community.

In reflecting on those three always-present characteristics of all genuine revivals, I dare to suggest, with the help of my students, that the next great awakening will lead to revival in the following areas.

1. A revived concentration by the church on the centrality of Christ and his gospel

Much of this book addresses the problems which large sections of the church have with the whole idea of revival. The liturgical churches – the Catholics, Orthodox and Anglicans – largely ignore revival, perhaps because they believe that in the sacraments they have the divinely given instrument for experiencing the presence of the living God. If revival is God's glory manifest, then they believe that in the sacraments they have this glory as manifest as God intends it to be in this age. For their part, many Reformed evangelicals have jettisoned revival from their agendas on the grounds that it seems to owe more to history than to the Bible. They also dismiss it because it has become an unhelpful obsession with charismatic Christians. And, as for the charismatics, they speak of it all the time – but they do not mean by it what Wesley and Edwards meant by it. So, depending on one's tradition, revival is: 1) never talked about, 2) rejected on theological grounds, or 3) much spoken of but never understood.

We have not argued that all such objections are absurd and merely a sad reflection on the objectors. All these objections do point to a major and objective problem. Revivals have been so much more evident in some periods than in others in the experience of the church that it is very easy to understand those who look for a more common manifestation of the grace of God as the chief vehicle of his blessing – such as the sacraments, or pure gospel preaching, or even extraordinary spiritual gifts.

The next great awakening will sweep aside that easy understanding in favour of a different assessment of the evidence. Revival will be seen again, as it was in the days of Wesley and Whitefield and Edwards, as the fullest flowering of the gospel plant. It is the most abundant harvest of the doctrines of grace. It is the most gracious manifestation of biblical Christianity. In the past, revival has been expressed most vigorously in evangelical churches because they embodied the gospel, the doctrines of grace and the truth of the Bible most clearly. All three are different ways of characterizing the essence and purpose of real Christianity, namely salvation.

It is therefore not at all surprising that revival has been most conspicuous in those periods when the church was most concerned with soteriology, or salvation. That is why it is wrong for Reformed evangelicals to dismiss revival as a limited, finite period of church history, coinciding with the flowering of Puritanism in the seventeenth century and of evangelicalism in the eighteenth and nineteenth centuries. That was a period in church history when the main thrust of the Bible was better understood in the general population than in any period before or since. God will do it again when this understanding of his word (namely, as having as its grand and pre-eminent theme the glory of God in the salvation of sinners through the death of God's Son preached in the power of God's Spirit) is recovered.

In the next great awakening that understanding will grip the imagination and fire the soul as well as convince the mind. When awakenings correct the false view of reality of those who are revived, it is not a merely intellectual activity. Revivals restore orthodoxy to the church as the doctrines of grace are recovered. But it is not rational orthodoxy that reforms the church – it is, rather, vital orthodoxy. The doctrines of grace are felt most in the affections, as Edwards felt them in his great vision of Christ the redeemer. In the next great awakening the recovered understanding of the centrality of the gospel as Christ dying for sinners will become a matter of the heart as well as the head. Because this is an understanding that does reach to the affections, it will result primarily in greater openness to the largeness of God's mercy across denominations of Christians, rather than in a determination to defend one's own theological tradition. If the current state of the church is that it is divided between rational orthodoxy and vital heterodoxy, then the next great awakening will restore vital orthodoxy to the church.

The next great awakening will result in undreamed-of unity among Christians of many different traditions. Recovery of the centrality of the gospel will be seen as primary and essential, but not exclusive. The unconvincing compromises of the ecumenical movement and the scornful denunciations of the fundamentalists will both be subsumed by a new passion for the doctrines of grace and a new apprehension that those doctrines are divinely intended more for the comprehensive salvation of the creation and not for the exposure of heretics. In fact, the narrow employment of the doctrines of grace for sectarian purposes will be exposed in the next great awakening as a damnable refusal to give water to Christ's needy ones.

This means that the next great awakening will result in:

2. A revived Trinitarian theology

While Christ and salvation will be seen as central, the place of the work of Christ within the Father's cosmic purpose for the recreation of the universe and the Spirit's ministry to broken-hearted individuals will become luminous. While every one of the 66 books of the Bible has salvation as its ultimate aim, biblical theology is concerned also with the creation and with holy living. It is concerned, in other words, with those areas that have attracted the attention and devotion of Catholics and charismatics as well as evangelicals. It is concerned with the incarnation and with sanctification, as well as with justification. The next great awakening will give Christians a heart for all those things rather than an exclusive and primarily intellectual interest in any one of them.

Elements in a revived, biblical theology

Father	creation	incarnation
Son	salvation	justification
Holy Spirit	godly living	sanctification

We have argued that genuine revivals are marked not so much by amazing manifestations the likes of which no one could prophesy, but by the accentuation of the doctrines of grace as revealed in the word of God. Jesus and his gospel will be the twin foci of the next great awakening, just as they have been of all genuine revivals hitherto in the history of the church. But Jesus will deepen our understanding of the love of the Father and heighten our vision of the power of the Spirit. The next great awakening will reawaken the church to the glory of the Holy Trinity. And it will thereby revitalize the church with its threefold mission of caring for the Father's creation, propagating the Son's gospel and reflecting the Spirit's nature in holiness of life. Regent College students are particularly well versed in Trinitarian theology thanks to the quality of the world-class theologians who instruct them. It is logical for them to understand and discipline their own natural and strong desire for intimacy in the light of the intimacy between the three Persons of the Trinity. It was also logical for them to instruct me on how the next great awakening, in making manifest Christ's great love for us in our salvation, would simultaneously manifest the Father's love and the Spirit's. Among their teachers at Regent College is Gordon Fee, who has written thus about recapturing, and re-integrating into today's church, the apostle Paul's perspective on the Holy Spirit:

> This will mean not the exaltation of the Spirit, but the exaltation of God; and it will mean not focus on the Spirit as such, but on the Son, crucified and risen, Saviour and Lord of all. Ethical life will be neither narrowly, individualistically conceived nor legalistically expressed, but will be joyously communal and decidedly over against the world's present trinity of relativism, secularism, and materialism, with their thoroughly dehumanizing affects. And the proper Trinitarian aim of such ethics will be the Pauline one – to the glory of God, through being conformed to the image of the Son, by the empowering of the Spirit.[1]

---

[1] Fee, *God's Empowering Presence*, p. 902.

3. A revived spiritual agenda within the church fellowship

One Regent student waxed lyrical about how wonderful it would be to be transformed into the sort of person who can be an instrument of revival. 'Surely,' she said, 'this is a great way to be: namely one who has a clean heart and who walks closely with God and who prevails in prayer. This is what I would like to see in the next great awakening.' She put her finger on the great appeal of revival to Christians from the point of view of one's own individual walk with God. As the Puritan forerunners of the great revivals taught, it is never wrong to long to be as holy as a forgiven sinner can be.[2] The next great awakening will result in the reprioritizing of issues of concern to Christians. Their supreme concern will be the glory and holiness of God, and how they can live for that glory and share in that holiness. Since all genuine revivals are manifestations of the glory of God in the present, which expose sin and create a craving for holiness, Christians will become again gripped by such questions as:

- How does God manifest his presence in the world today?
- What are the implications of Christ's past death and future return for the world in the present?
- What is the role of the Holy Spirit in the individual and in the world?
- Is the normal experience of the people of God a cyclical one: sin, judgement, repentance, restoration?

These questions focus on the manifest presence of God. That is what Christians are hungry for today. Typical unrevived churches struggle to see the relevance of Christianity to the present age. The next great firestorm of the Lord will vaporize that struggle. The sense of irrelevance will disappear into the unseen ether. The implications of the eternal gospel for the present will be seen with such clarity that the church's mission of proclamation and reclamation will be led and organized according to a strategy stunning in its brilliance. And it will be conducted with an energy untiring in its vigour. The feet of

---

[2] A.A. Bonar, *Memoir and Remains of Robert Murray McCheyne*, p. 159. See also Phil. 3:10–14.

Jesus, the hero, will walk again among the satanic mills. He who is called 'Faithful and True' will ride forth again to make war on the armies of Satan and release many of his prisoners in anticipation of that great day when he will destroy Satan entirely and release all his prisoners. We shall have another glorious victory as a prelude to his eternal victory.

A number of my students had experienced hurt in the fellowship of the church, and their longing was for a revival that would create Christian fellowships where the ethos and ethics of the kingdom prevailed. They wanted to see the healing of relationships with God and each other, involving forgiveness, openness and honesty. One said that he longed for a revival that would be a deep experience of the Holy Spirit within congregations, 'giving a new freedom – a catalyst, to help people open up to God'. Another said that he hoped the next great awakening would not be 'a militant crusade with leaders who will tell us authoritatively how to do things right'. He hoped for a revival that would surround Christians with 'the patient resources of healing'.

4. A revived leadership

This sentiment was provoked by a discussion on leadership to which a number of the students contributed. Many Christians obviously feel that the quality of leadership in the church today is not what it should be and they believe that in the next great awakening this is one of the first things the Lord will put right. The next great awakening, one student suggested, will raise up the leadership which the church needs: scripturally sharp, pastorally sensitive, morally courageous, spiritually alive. The flock will not be left without shepherds.

I found it significant that a number of students preferred the word 'mentor' to that of 'leader'. One spoke of 'the desperate need in the church today for mentors, to come alongside us and lead us to experience God in a way which they have already experienced him'. He applied this specifically to the experience of being filled with the Spirit, which many in the class considered essential to effective Christian servant leadership. He reminded the class that Billy Graham, who had received a lot of attention in our course, would probably never have been heard of were it not for that experience which he received under the guidance of a mentor. Billy was involved in a rather ordinary evangelistic crusade in Britain when a Welshman, Stephen Olford, came alongside Billy and told him that he needed to be filled with the Spirit and stayed with him until he had been so filled.[3]

Another student, referring to the problems which revivals nearly always bring to awakened congregations, said that mentoring, or having 'wise guides', is so very important in dealing with fanaticism. 'There is a great need for teachers of the faith who teach that gifts and blessing are for now, but eradication of sin is not for now.' This student was himself involved in a very interesting campaign to awaken Episcopalians in America to the need to pray and work for revival. He agreed that 'what the church needs is teachers who have themselves had the experience of revival and who have learned how to walk with God, and who can nurture people'.

5. A revived confidence in God's word

Although I think most of my students were evangelical Christians, a number expressed surprise at the emphasis in the lectures on the importance of studying and preaching the word of God. At the end they felt encouraged to apply themselves with greater faithfulness to the study and proclamation of the pure word of God, unmixed and uncorrupted by human concepts. Without resolving the issue, we often looked at the issue of whether preaching produced revival, or revival revived preaching. No doubt, both are true. We have seen revivals where great preaching seems to follow rather than precede revival, but there can, by definition, be no genuine revival without hearing the word of God. It is that word that exposes the deceits of Satan, the lies of sin and the emptiness of the world, which pierces the soul, refines all our thoughts, defines reality and shows us what God wants us to be and do – both now and in eternity.

Humanly speaking, it is very unlikely that we shall see another great awakening unless preachers recover an indomitable conviction about the sufficiency and efficiency of Scripture alone. But should the Lord in his sovereign mercy, as he has done in the past, send the

---

[3] Martin, *Prophet*, p. 98.

next great awakening to a church whose preachers have not yet reached that conviction, they will reach it pronto when the revival comes. There will be no wishy-washy thinking that because we have the Spirit now, we do not need the word. Nor will any be tempted to imagine that, because of the great outpouring of the Spirit, we need to be alert to the contemporary specific guidance of the Spirit to supplement the ancient, general words of Scripture. The very words of Scripture will not be felt to be ancient and general, but the Spirit will awaken us to see and accept these words for what they are. They are alive. They are themselves so contemporary and specific that they discern our present deepest thoughts and intentions (Heb. 4:12). 'God's words, creating and saving words every one, hit us where we live.'[4] Precisely because Jesus is the hero of all genuine revivals, the word will never be discounted, for Jesus is the Word of God. 'He is clothed in a robe dipped in blood, and his name is called The Word of God' (Rev. 19:13, NRSV).

6. A revived involvement of Christians with the community and nation

Another who attended the course at Regent College, and who currently works with university students, expressed his longing that the next great awakening would mean that secular students would hear the gospel gladly again. He recalled witnessing an extraordinary evangelistic mission at the University of British Columbia in the 1960s when thousands of students gathered to hear the gospel preached. He longed for the day when students would again hunger for the only bread that satisfies. He suggested that the surest demonstration and proof of the extent to which our modern world is secularized is that it does not cross the mind of the average university student that the Bible might have the answers. As if to prove the point, a rock festival was held on the campus of the university on the very night that I gave a public lecture at Regent on preaching for revival. The cars that brought the thousands who attended the festival lined the roads for miles around the campus. At the conclusion of my lecture, one student immediately moved to the microphone and

---

[4] Eugene Peterson, *Answering God: The Psalms as Tools for Prayer*, p. 25.

with tears asked that we might pray that those concert-goers might hear and respond to the gospel. The next great awakening will give Christians a revived heart for the evangelization of the world. It will hearten Christians to work for and expect a great expansion in the numbers of people who profess Christ.

It will also result in a great strengthening of the influence of Jesus in the world. Revival, as we have seen, might come first to the church – but it is not primarily for the church. It is primarily for the community, for those outside the church. In the next great awakening, the eyes of those who cannot see that the answer is Jesus will be opened, and the hearts of those crushed by the tyranny of Satan's rule will be healed.

The culture that has seeped into the soul of the church as well as into the souls of the unsaved will be confronted. The cancer of our culture will be seen for what it really is: the materialism which makes us want more when we already have more than is good for us; the activism which makes us do more when we are already doing more than is good for us; the secularism which makes us deny more than is good for us; the egotism which makes us want more self-satisfaction than is good for us.

The history of revivals has taught us that revivals not only challenge the culture and reduce, even in the unsaved, the appetite for sinful practices. But revivals also energize Christians for massive and effective efforts to reform and renovate local communities and societies. The next great awakening will see Christians sacrificially serving the poor even though they know that, because the poor will always be with us in a fallen world, the task seems impossible. They will persevere in the apparently hopeless task of bringing peace to a world that they know by its very nature will continue to have wars. And the underprivileged themselves, the poor and the hungry, the underclass and the underdogs, the marginalized and the relegated, the unnoticed, the unseen and the ignored, will be empowered to help themselves and will achieve the dignity of political power. Those who are no people will know that they are God's people (1 Pet. 2:10). Others, who knew what it was like to be God's people once, and who have looked on in dismay and despair at the decline of a great and noble people as their leaders have resolved that their nation should live without God (Rom. 1:28–31), will rejoice to witness the regeneration of national character. The next great awakening will strengthen people to withstand great adversity or it will be the means by which a people avert national disaster.

If there are any grounds for believing that the next great awakening will indeed lead to revival in the six areas identified in this conclusion, might it not be wise to work towards them now? If you long to see the glorification of God through the justification and sanctification of a myriad of individuals, the forging of Christian fellowships where believers can become more open to God and more like Christ, and the reform and regeneration of our society and culture, then why not determine to:

- Understand, teach and preach the gospel.
- Allow your heart to be filled with the love of the Trinity.
- Train yourself in the disciplines which enable you to experience the manifest presence of God.
- Pray for the raising up of experienced mentors in the church who are filled with the Spirit and know how they came to be filled – so that they can nurture Christians in this experience.
- Fortify your mind and heart with the word of God and seek to teach it purely and obey it fully.
- Engage deliberately with those outside of Christ, seeking both to share the gospel with them and to reclaim the culture and the nation for Christ.

Bibliography

Ambassador: Official Journal of the Bible College of Victoria (December 1993).

Arndell, R. Seton, 'The Revival among the Kyaka Enga People of Papua New Guinea', *South Pacific Journal of Mission Studies* 2.1 (Nov. 1991), pp. 9–13.

Ball, Leslie James, 'Queensland Baptists in the Nineteenth Century: The Historical Development of a Denominational Identity' (PhD, University of Queensland, 1994).

Balmer, Randall, 'Eschewing the "Routine of Religion": Eighteenth-Century Pietism and the Revival Tradition in America', in Edith L. Blumhofer and Randall Balmer, *Modern Christian Revivals* (Urbana: University of Illinois Press, 1993).

Barnett, Paul, *Apocalypse Now and Then* (Sydney: Anglican Information Office, 1989).

— *The Second Epistle to the Corinthians* (Grand Rapids, MI: Eerdmans, 1997).

Barrett, David B., 'The Twentieth-Century Pentecostal/Charismatic Renewal in the Holy Spirit, with its Goal of World Evangelization', *International Bulletin of Missionary Research* 12.3 (July 1988), pp. 119–29.

Bebbington, David, 'Revival and Enlightenment in Eighteenth-Century England', in Edith L. Blumhofer and Randall Balmer, *Modern Christian Revivals* (Urbana: University of Illinois Press, 1993).

Beech, Greg, 'The Outpouring of the Holy Spirit at Randwick Baptist Church, 6 November 1994' (typescript, 10 January 1995).

Beougher, Timothy K., and Lyle W. Dorsett (eds.), *Accounts of a*

Campus Revival: Wheaton College 1995 (Wheaton, IL: Harold Shaw Publishers, 1995).

Bernard of Clairvaux, 'Sermon 43', in *On the Song of Songs*, IV (trans. Kilian Walsh; Kalamazoo, MI: Cistercian Publications, 1976).

— 'Sermon 67', in *The Works of Bernard of Clairvaux*, III (trans. Kilian Walsh; Kalamazoo, MI: Cistercian Publications 40, 1980).

Beverley, James A., *Holy Laughter and the Toronto Blessing* (Grand Rapids, MI: Zondervan, 1995).

Bingham, Geoffrey, *The Day of the Spirit* (Blackwood: New Creation Publications, 1985).

Blackburn, Peter J., 'The National Fellowship for Revival', *Interchange* 40 (1986), pp. 5–12.

Blacket, John, *Fire in the Outback* (Sutherland: Albatross, 1997).

— ' "I Will Renew the Land": Island on Fire' (unpublished MS of history of the Aboriginal Revival, 18 May 1993).

— ' "Rainbow or the Serpent?" Observing the Arnhem Land Aboriginal Revival, 1979 and Now', in Mark Hutchinson and Stuart Piggin (eds.), *Reviving Australia* (Sydney: Centre for the Study of Australian Christianity, 1994), pp. 291–301.

Blacklock, Merv, et al., 'Minjung in Australia', *South Pacific Journal of Mission Studies* 1.1 (July 1989), pp. 8f.

Blair, William Newton, and Bruce F. Hunt, *The Korean Pentecost and the Sufferings which Followed* (Edinburgh: Banner of Truth Trust, 1977).

Blumhofer, Edith L., and Randall Balmer, *Modern Christian Revivals* (Urbana: University of Illinois Press, 1993).

Bollen, J.D., *Religion in Australian Society* (Sydney: Leigh College, 1973).

Bonar, A.A., *Memoir and Remains of Robert Murray McCheyne* (Edinburgh: Banner of Truth Trust, 1844, 1966).

Bos, Robert, 'The Dreaming and Social Change in Arnhem Land', in T. Swain and D.B. Rose, *Aboriginal Australians and Christian Missions* (Adelaide: The Australian Association for the Study of Religions, 1988), pp. 422–37.

Boyd, Jeanette, 'The Arnhem Land Revival of 1979: An Australian Aboriginal Religious Movement' (unpublished paper, October 1986).

Brewer, Vernon, 'Prayer: The Keystone of Revival', *Fundamentalist Journal* 3.11 (December 1984), p. 27.

Bruce, F.F., *This is That: The New Testament Development of some Old Testament Themes* (Exeter: Paternoster Press, 1968).

Bryant, David, *Concerts of Prayer* (Ventura, CA: Regal Books, 1988).

Bunyan, John, *Grace Abounding to the Chief of Sinners* (Oxford: Clarendon Press, 1962).

Burns, William C., *Revival Sermons* (Edinburgh: Banner of Truth Trust, 1869, 1980).

Butler, Jon, 'Enthusiasm Described and Decried: The Great Awakening as Interpretative Fiction', *Journal of American History* 69 (1982), pp. 305–25.

— *Awash in a Sea of Faith, Christianizing the American People* (Cambridge, MA: Harvard University Press, 1990).

Cairns, E.E., *An Endless Line of Splendor* (Wheaton, IL: Tyndale House Publishers, 1986).

Carson, D.A., 'The Purpose of Signs and Wonders in the New Testament', in Michael Scott Horton (ed.), *Power Religion* (Homebush: Anzea, 1992), pp. 89–118.

Carwardine, Richard, 'The Second Great Awakening in Comparative Perspective: Revivals and Culture in the United States and Britain', in Edith L. Blumhofer and Randall Balmer, *Modern Christian Revivals* (Urbana: University of Illinois Press, 1993).

— 'The Welsh Evangelical Community and "Finney's Revival" ', *Journal of Ecclesiastical History* 29.4 (1978), pp. 463–80.

— *Trans-Atlantic Revivalism* (Westport, CT: Greenwood Press, 1978).

Cassidy, Michael, *The Prophetic Word in the Crisis Context* (Olivier Beguin Memorial Lecture; The Bible Society in Australia, 1986).

Chant, Barry, 'The "Toronto Blessing": Priestly or Prophetic?' (unpublished typescript, 1995).

Chevreau, Guy, *Catch the Fire* (London: Marshall Pickering, 1994).

Cho, Paul Y., *Prayer: Key to Revival* (Dallas, TX: Word Publishing, 1984).

Christian Advocate and Wesleyan Record (Sydney: 21 December 1858).

Christian Pleader (10 September 1959).

Church, J.E., *Quest for the Highest: An Autobiographical Account of the East African Revival* (Exeter: Paternoster, 1981).

Coleman, Robert E., *Dry Bones Can Live Again: A Study Manual on Revival in the Local Church* (Old Tappan, NJ: Fleming H. Revell, 1969).

Colson, C., 'The Secularization of America', *Discipleship Journal* 83 (1987), p. 43.

Colwell, James, *The Illustrated History of Methodism* (Sydney: William Brooks, 1904).

Conzelmann, Hans, *Acts of the Apostles* (Minneapolis: Fortress Press, 1987).

Cook, Thomas, *Days of God's Right Hand: Our Mission Tour in Australasia and Ceylon* (London: Charles H. Kelly, 1896).

Craston, Colin, (ed.), *Open to the Spirit: Anglicans and the Spirit of Renewal* (Sydney: Anglican Information Office, 1987).

Crawford, Michael J., 'The Invention of the American Revival: The Beginnings of Anglo-American Religious Revivalism, 1690–1750' (PhD thesis, Boston University, 1978).

— *Seasons of Grace: Colonial New England's Revival Tradition in its British Context* (New York: Oxford University Press, 1991).

Crossman, Eileen, *Mountain Rain* (London: Overseas Missionary Fellowship, 1982).

Currie, Robert, Gilbert, Alan, and Horsley, Lee, *Churches and Churchgoers: Patterns of Church Growth in the British Isles since 1700* (Oxford: Clarendon Press, 1977).

Cusack, Carole M., 'An Examination of the Process of Conversion among the Germanic Peoples in Late Antiquity and the Early Middle Ages' (PhD thesis, University of Sydney, 1995).

Davies, R.E., *I Will Pour out my Spirit: A History and Theology of Revivals and Spiritual Awakenings* (Tunbridge Wells: Monarch, 1992).

Deane, Arthur Davidson, 'The Contribution of the New Evangelical Movements of the Late Nineteenth Century to Evangelical Enterprise in Australia, 1870–1920' (MA thesis, University of Sydney, 1983).

DeArteaga, William, *Quenching the Spirit: Discover the REAL Spirit behind the Charismatic Controversy* (Orlando, FL: Creation House, 1992, 1996).

Deere, Jack, *Surprised by the Power of the Spirit* (Grand Rapids, MI: Zondervan, 1993).

Delumeau, J., *Catholicism between Luther and Voltaire* (Paris: Nouvelle Clio, 1971, 1977).

Dieter, Melvin Easterday, *The Holiness Revival of the Nineteenth Century* (Metuchen, NJ: Scarecrow Press, 1980).

Dixon, Patrick, *Signs of Revival* (Eastbourne: Kingsway Publications, 1994).

Drayton, Dean, *Five Generations: Evangelism in South Australia* (Adelaide: South Australian Synod, Uniting Church in Australia, 1980).

Drummond, Lewis, *The Awakening that Must Come* (Nashville, TN: Broadman Press, 1978).

Duewel, Wesley, *Revival Fire* (Grand Rapids, MI: Zondervan, 1995).

Duffy, E., 'The English Secular Clergy and the Counter-Reformation', *Journal of Ecclesiastical History* 24 (1983), pp. 214–30.

Duffy, Eamon, 'Wesley and the Counter-Reformation', in Jane Garnett and Colin Matthew (eds.), *Revival and Religion since 1700, Essays for John Walsh* (London: Hambledon Press, 1993).

Dumbrell, Bill, 'Should Christians be Praying for a Spiritual Awakening and the Spread of the Gospel?', *The Cry for Spiritual Awakening* 4 (March 1992), pp. 6–9.

Dyer, Alan F., *God was their Rock* (Sheffield: Pioneer Publishers, 1974).

Dyer, Helen S., *Revival in India* (London: Morgan & Scott, 1907).

Edwards, Brian H., *Revival! A People Saturated with God* (Darlington: Evangelical Press, Wales, 1990).

Edwards, Jonathan, *A History of the Work of Redemption* (ed. John F. Wilson in *The Works of Jonathan Edwards*, IX; New Haven: Yale University Press, 1989).

— *Apocalyptic Writings* (ed. Stephen J. Stein in *The Works of Jonathan Edwards*, V; New Haven: Yale University Press, 1977).

— *Ethical Writings* (ed. Paul Ramsey in *The Works of Jonathan Edwards*, VIII; New Haven: Yale University Press, 1989).

— *Freedom of the Will* (ed. Paul Ramsey in *The Works of Jonathan Edwards*, I; New Haven: Yale University Press, 1957).

— *Letters and Personal Writings* (ed. George S. Claghorn in *The Works of Jonathan Edwards*, XVI; New Haven: Yale University Press, 1998).

— *Original Sin* (ed. Clyde A. Holbrook in *The Works of Jonathan Edwards*, III; New Haven: Yale University Press, 1970).

— *Religious Affections* (ed. John E. Smith in *The Works of Jonathan Edwards*, II; New Haven: Yale University Press, 1959).

— *Scientific and Philosophical Writings* (ed. Wallace E. Anderson in *The Works of Jonathan Edwards*, VI; New Haven: Yale University Press, 1980).

— *Sermons and Discourses 1720–1723* (ed. Wilson H. Kimnack in *The Works of Jonathan Edwards*, XX, New Haven: Yale University Press, 1992).

— *The Great Awakening* (ed. C.C. Goen in *The Works of Jonathan Edwards*, IV; New Haven: Yale University Press, 1972).

— *The Life of David Brainerd* (ed. Norman Pettit in *The Works of Jonathan Edwards*, VII; New Haven: Yale University Press, 1985).

— *The Works of Jonathan Edwards* (2 vols.; Edinburgh: Banner of Truth Trust, 1834, 1974).

Ellsworth, Roger, *Come Down Lord!* (Edinburgh: Banner of Truth Trust, 1988).

Erb, P.C., *Pietists: Selected Writings* (London: SPCK, 1983).

Evans, Eifion, *Daniel Rowland and the Great Evangelical Awakening in Wales* (Edinburgh: Banner of Truth Trust, 1985).

— *Revival Comes to Wales: The Story of the 1859 Revival in Wales* (Bryntirion: Evangelical Press of Wales, 3rd edn, 1986).

— *Revivals: Their Rise, Progress, and Achievements* (Bryntirion: Evangelical Press of Wales, 1960, 3rd edn, 1986).

— *The Welsh Revival of 1904* (Bryntirion: Evangelical Press of Wales, 3rd edn, 1987).

— *Two Welsh Revivalists* (Bryntirion: Evangelical Press of Wales, 1985).

Evans, Robert, 'Collecting for Revival: Library Resources Relating to the Study of Revival', in Mark Hutchinson and Stuart Piggin (eds.), *Reviving Australia* (Sydney: Centre for the Study of Australian Christianity, 1994), pp. 58–74.

— and Roy McKenzie, *Evangelical Revivals in New Zealand* (New Zealand: ColCom Press, 1999).

Facius, Johannes, International Co-ordinator, International Fellowship of Intercessors, Report on 'The Toronto Blessing' (typescript).

Faggotter, Trevor, 'Revival Fire at Wudinna', *Renewal Journal* 4 (1994), pp. 43–52.

Fairbairn, Patrick et al., *Revival in Practice* (Strathpine North: Covenanter Press, 1840, 1978).

Fee, Gordon D., *God's Empowering Presence: The Holy Spirit in the Letters of Paul* (Peabody, MA: Hendrickson Publishers, 1997).

Finke, Roger, and Rodney Stark, *The Churching of America, 1776–1990* (New Brunswick: Rutgers University Press, 1992).

Finney, Charles G., *An Autobiography* (Old Tappan, NJ: Fleming H. Revell, 1876, 1908).

— *The Memoirs of Charles G. Finney* (ed. Garth M. Rosell and Richard A.G. Dupuis; Grand Rapids, MI: Zondervan, 1989).

Fletcher, Lionel B., *Mighty Moments* (London: The Religious Tract Society, n.d.).

Foord, Dudley, *Restoring Spiritual Health to your Church* (Kingsford: St Matthias Press, 1991).

Garraghan, Gilbert J., *The Jesuits of the Middle United States* (Chicago: Loyola Press, 1984), vol. 2.

Geil, W.E., *Ocean and Isle* (Melbourne: William T. Pater, 1902).

Whitefield, George, *George Whitefield's Journals* (Edinburgh: Banner of Truth Trust, 1960).

Gesswain, Armin, 'Spiritual Awakening: Our Nation's Greatest Need', *The Australian Evangelical* 113 (1993), pp. 5, 6.

Gibson, William, *The Year of Grace: A History of the Ulster Revival of 1859* (Edinburgh: Oliphant, 1909).

Gill, Stewart, ' "Revival Days at Mt Margaret": The UAM and the 1982 Revival', in Mark Hutchinson and Stuart Piggin (eds.), *Reviving Australia* (Sydney: Centre for the Study of Australian Christianity, 1994), pp. 275–90.

Gilley, Sheridan, 'Catholic Revival in the Eighteenth Century', in Keith Robbins (ed.), *Protestant Evangelicalism: Britain, Ireland, Germany and America, Essays in Honour of W.R. Ward* (Oxford: Basil Blackwell, 1990), pp. 99–108.

Gillies, John, *Historical Collections of Accounts of Revivals* (Edinburgh: Banner of Truth Trust, 1754, rev. 1845, 1981).

Gilling, Bryan D., 'Revival as Renewal: J. Wilbur Chapman in New Zealand, 1912–1913', *American Presbyterians* 70.2 (Summer 1992), pp. 81–92.

Godet, Frédéric, *Commentary on St Paul's Epistle to the Romans*, I (Edinburgh: T & T Clark, 1880).

Goforth, Jonathan, *By My Spirit* (Minneapolis: Bethany Fellowsip, 1964).

Goppelt, L., *Typos: The Typological Interpretation of the Old Testament in the New* (Grand Rapids, MI: Eerdmans, 1982).

Gordon-McCutchan, R.C., 'Great Awakenings', *Sociological Analysis* 44 (1983), pp. 83–95.

— 'The Irony of Evangelical History', *Journal for the Scientific Study of Religion* 20 (1981), pp. 309–26.

Gore, Charles, *St Paul's Epistle to the Romans*, I (London: John Murray, 1899).

Graham, Billy, 'What's the Next Step?' *Christian Life* (June 1956), p. 22.

— *The Holy Spirit* (London: Collins, 1979).

Griffiths, Alison, *Fire in the Islands: The Acts of the Holy Spirit in the Solomons* (Wheaton, IL: Harold Shaw Publishers, 1977).

Grubb, Norman P., *Continuous Revival* (Washington, DC: Christian Literature Crusade, 1971).

Guinness, Michele, *The Guinness Legend* (London: Hodder & Stoughton, 1989).

Haenchen, Ernst, *The Acts of the Apostles* (Philadelphia: Westminster Press, 1971).

Hambrick-Stowe, Charles, *The Practice of Piety: Puritan Devotional Disciplines in Seventeenth-Century New England* (Chapel Hill: University of North Carolina Press, 1982).

Hamilton, M., *The Charismatic Movement* (Grand Rapids, MI: Eerdmans, 1975).

Harris, John, *One Blood: 200 Years of Aboriginal Encounter with Christianity: A Story of Hope* (Sutherland: Albatross, 1990).

Hart, Max, *A Story of Fire: Aboriginal Christianity* (Blackwood: New Creation Publications, 1988).

Hempton, David, *Methodism and Politics in British Society, 1750–1850* (London: Hutchinson, rev edn 1987).

Hill, Myrtle, 'Ulster Awakened: The '59 Revival Reconsidered', *Journal of Ecclesiastical History* 41.3 (1990), pp. 443–62.

Hilliard, David, *Popular Revivalism in South Australia* (South Australia: Uniting Church Historical Society, 1982).

Hindson, Edward, *Glory in the Church* (New York: Thomas Nelson, 1975).

Hughes, Selwyn, 'Heaven-Sent Revival', *Every Day with Jesus* (2 May 1989).

Hutchinson, Mark and Stuart Piggin (eds.), *Reviving Australia* (Sydney: Centre for the Study of Australian Christianity, 1994).

Jackson, Hugh, *Churches and People in Australia and New Zealand, 1860–1930* (Wellington: Allen & Unwin, 1987).

Johnstone, Patrick, *Operation World* (Australia: OM Publishing, 1993).

Kaiser, Walter C., *Quest for Renewal: Personal Revival in the Old Testament* (Chicago: Moody Press, 1986).

Käsemann, Ernst, *Commentary on Romans* (London: SCM Press, 1980).

Kemp, Winnie, *Joseph W. Kemp* (London: Marshall, Morgan & Scott, 1936).

Kent, John, 'Have we been there before? A Historian Looks at the Toronto Blessing', in Stanley E. Porter and Philip J. Richter (eds.), *The Toronto Blessing – Or is it?* (London: Darton, Longman & Todd, 1995).

Knox, R.A., *Enthusiasm* (Oxford: Clarendon Press, 1950).

Koch, Kurt E., *Revival Fires in Canada* (Grand Rapids, MI: Kregel Publications, 1973).

Lamb, Margaret Yarwood, *Going it Alone: Mary Andrews – Missionary to China* (Sydney: Aquila Press, 1995).

Lambert, Tony, *The Resurrection of the Chinese Church* (London: Hodder & Stoughton, 1991).

Lane, A.N.S., 'Bernard of Clairvaux: A Forerunner of John Calvin?', in John R. Sommerfeldt (ed.), *Bernardus Magister, Papers Presented at the Nonacentenary of the Birth of Saint Bernard of Clairvaux* (Cistercian Studies Series 135; Spencer, MA: Cistercian Publications, 1992).

Lang, Amy Schrager, 'A Flood of Errors', in Nathan O. Hatch and Harry S. Stout (eds.), *Jonathan Edwards and the American Experience* (New York: Oxford University Press, 1988).

Laqueur, Thomas W., *Religion and Respectability: Sunday Schools and Working-Class Culture, 1780–1850* (New Haven: Yale University Press, 1976).

Lawrence, Carl, *Against All Odds: The Church in China* (Basingstoke: Marshall Morgan & Scott, 1986).

Lawson, James G., *Deeper Experiences of Famous Christians* (Anderson, IN: Warner Press, 1911).

Leclercq, Jean, 'The Intentions of the Founders of the Cistercian Order', in M. Basil Pennington (ed.), *The Cistercian Spirit: A Symposium: In Memory of Thomas Merton* (Cistercian Studies Series 3; Washington, DC: Cistercian Publications, 1973).

Lewis, H. Elvet, 'With Christ among the Miners', in Richard Owen Roberts (ed.), *Glory Filled the Land: A Trilogy on the Welsh Revival of 1904–1905* (Wheaton, IL: International Awakening Press, 1989).

Lewis, John, *The Weekly History* (London: 1741–47).

Lillyman, John, 'Taylor of Down Under: The Life Story of an Australian Evangelist' (MA thesis, Wheaton, IL, 1994).

Lindsay, Ian, *Fire in the Spinifex* (Lawson: Mission Publications of Australia, 1986).

Lloyd-Jones, D.M., *Authority* (Leicester: Inter-Varsity Press, 1958).

— *Growing in the Spirit* (Eastbourne: Kingsway Publications, 1989).

— *Joy Unspeakable* (Eastbourne: Kingsway Publications, 1984).

— *Preaching and Preachers* (London: Hodder & Stoughton, 1971).

— *Revival* (Basingstoke: Marshall Pickering, 1986).

— *The Doctor Himself and the Human Condition* (London: Christian Medical Fellowship, 1982).

— *The Love of God: Studies in 1 John* (Wheaton, IL: Crossway Books, 1994).

— *The Puritans: Their Origins and Successors* (Edinburgh: Banner of Truth Trust, 1987).

Lovelace, Richard F., *Dynamics of Spiritual Life* (Downers Grove, IL: InterVarsity Press, 1979).

Luker, David, 'Revivalism in Theory and Practice: The Case of Cornish Methodism', *Journal of Ecclesiastical History* 37.4 (1986), pp. 603–19.

Lyall, Leslie T., 'Historical Prelude', in Marie Monsen, *The Awakening: Revival in China, a Work of the Holy Spirit* (London: China Inland Mission, 1961).

— (ed.), *The Clouds His Chariot: The Story of 1937* (London: CIM, 1937).

Macfarlan, D., *The Revivals of the Eighteenth Century . . . with Three Sermons by the Rev. George Whitefield* (Glasgow: Free Presbyterian Publications, 1988).

Mackenzie, Edgar C., 'British Devotional Literature on the Rise of German Pietism' (PhD thesis, University of St Andrews, 1984).

MacNeil, Hannah, *John MacNeil: A Memoir* (London: Marshall Brothers, 1897).

MacNutt, Francis, *Healing* (Notre Dame, IN: Ave Maria, 1974).

Martin, William, *A Prophet with Honor: The Billy Graham Story* (New York: William Morrow & Co., 1991).

McCulloch, William, *The Glasgow Weekly History* (Glasgow: 1741, 1742).

McGrath, Alister, *A Cloud of Witnesses: Ten Great Christian Thinkers* (Leicester: Inter-Varsity Press, 1990).

McLoughlin, William G., *Revivals, Awakenings, and Reform: An Essay on Religion and Social Change in America, 1607–1977* (Chicago: University of Chicago Press, 1978).

Middlekauff, Robert, *The Mathers: Three Generations of Puritan Intellectuals, 1596–1728* (New York: Oxford University Press, 1971).

Mikhaiel, Nader, 'Slaying in the Spirit: Is it Biblical?', *New Day* (March 1995), pp. 17–20.

— *Slaying in the Spirit: The Telling Wonder* (Earlwood, NSW [published by the author], 1992, 2nd edn, 1995).

Moran, Gerald F., 'Christian Revivalism and Culture in Early America: Puritan New England as a Case Study', in Edith L. Blumhofer and Randall Balmer, *Modern Christian Revivals* (Urbana: University of Illinois Press, 1993).

Morgan, Derec Llwyd, *The Great Awakening in Wales* (London: Epworth Press, 1988).

Morgan, G.J., *Cataracts of Revival* (London: Marshall, Morgan & Scott, London, n.d.).

Morris, Colin, *The Papal Monarchy: The Western Church from 1050 to 1250* (Oxford: Clarendon Press, 1989).

Moule, H.C.G., 'Introduction' to Alexander Smellie, *Evan Henry Hopkins, A Memoir* (London [1920], 2nd edn, 1921).

— *Charles Simeon* (London: Methuen, 1892).

Mukherjee, S.K., et al., *Source Book of Australian Criminal and Social Statistics, 1900–1980* (Canberra: Australian Institute of Criminology, Canberra, 1981).

Murray, Andrew, *With Christ in the School of Prayer* (Pittsburgh, PA: Whitaker House, 1981).

Murray, Iain H., 'Lessons from Australia's Evangelical Heritage' (Address to the Revival Fellowship of the Uniting Church, 1988).

— *Australian Christian Life from 1788* (Edinburgh: Banner of Truth Trust, 1987).

— *David Martyn Lloyd-Jones: The First Forty Years, 1899–1939* (Edinburgh: Banner of Truth Trust, 1982).

— *David Martin Lloyd-Jones: The Fight of Faith* (Edinburgh: Banner of Truth Trust, 1990).

— *Jonathan Edwards: A New Biography* (Edinburgh: Banner of Truth Trust, 1987).

— *Revival and Revivalism: The Making and Marring of American Evangelicalism, 1750–1858* (Edinburgh: Banner of Truth Trust, 1994).

— *The Puritan Hope* (London: Banner of Truth Trust, 1971).

Murray, Jocelyn, *Proclaim the Good News, A Short History of the Church Missionary Society* (London: Hodder & Stoughton, 1985).

New Day 145 (March 1995), devoted to 'The Toronto Blessing: An Evaluation'.

Nicholson, W.P., 'Hindrances to Revival', *The Alliance News* (n.d.), pp. 3–6.

Nolan, Jay P., *Catholic Revivalism: The American Experience 1830–1900* (Notre Dame, IN: University of Notre Dame Press, 1978).

'No Laughing Matter', *Briefing* 152 (Sydney: 7 March 1995).

Noll, Mark A., 'Revival, Enlightenment, Civic Humanism, and the Development of Dogma: Scotland and America, 1735–1843', *Tyndale Bulletin* 40 (1989), pp. 49–76.

— Bebbington, David, and Rawlyck, George A., *Evangelicalism: Comparative Studies of Popular Protestantism in North America, the British Isles, and Beyond, 1700–1990* (New York: Oxford University Press, 1994).

Norling, Allan, *Jesus: The Baptiser with the Holy Spirit* (Beecroft, Australia, 1994).

Nuttall, Geoffrey, 'Howell Harris and the "Grand Table": A Note on Religion and Politics, 1744–50', *Journal of Ecclesiastical History* 39.4 (1988), pp. 531–544.

O'Farrell, Patrick James, *The Catholic Church and Community in Australia: A History* (Melbourne: Nelson, rev. 1992).

Orr, J. Edwin, *All Your Need: 10,000 Miles of Miracle through Australia and New Zealand* (London: Marshall, Morgan & Scott, 1936).

— 'Evangelical Revival in Australia in the Mid-nineteenth Century' (Lecture, Pasadena, 1968).

— *Evangelical Awakenings in the South Seas* (Minneapolis: Bethany Fellowship, 1976).

— *My All, His All* (Wheaton, IL: International Awakening Press, 1989).

— *The Eager Feet: Evangelical Awakenings, 1790–1830* (Chicago: Moody Press, 1975).

— *The Event of the Century: The 1857–1858 Awakening* (Wheaton, IL: International Awakening Press, 1989).

— 'The Role of Prayer in Spiritual Awakening' (unpublished lecture; Fellowship for Revival, NSW, 1987).

Osborn, H.H., *Fire in the Hills: The Revival which Spread from Rwanda* (Crowborough: Highland Books, 1991).

Outler, Albert C., *The Works of John Wesley*, I (Nashville: Abingdon Press, 1984).

Packer, J.I., *Keep in Step with the Spirit* (Leicester: Inter-Varsity Press, 1994).

— *Among God's Giants: The Puritan Vision of the Christian Life* (Eastbourne: Kingsway Publications, 1991).

— *God in our Midst: Seeking and Receiving Ongoing Revival* (Reading: Word Publishing, 1987).

Paik, L. George, *The History of Protestant Missions in Korea, 1832–1910* (Seoul: Yonsei University Press, 1980).

Paisley, Ian R.K., *The 'Fifty-Nine' Revival* (Belfast: Nelson and Knox, 1958).

Palamountain, W.J., *A.R. Edgar: A Methodist Greatheart. The Life Story of Alexander Robert Edgar, who Founded the Central Mission, Melbourne* (Melbourne: Spectator Publishing Co., 1933).

Peters, George W., *Indonesia Revival: Focus on Timor* (Grand Rapids, MI: Zondervan, 1973).

Peterson, Eugene, *Answering God: The Psalms as Tools for Prayer* (San Francisco: Harper San Francisco, 1991).

Pfisterer, K. D., *The Prism of Scripture: Studies on History and Historicity in the Works of Jonathan Edwards* (Frankfurt-on-Main: Peter Lang, 1975).

Phillips, Thomas, *The Welsh Revival* (Edinburgh: Banner of Truth Trust, 1989).

Phillips, Walter, 'Gipsy Smith in Australia in 1926', in Mark Hutchinson and Stuart Piggin (eds.), *Reviving Australia* (Sydney: Centre for the Study of Australian Christianity, 1994), pp. 185–201.

Piggin, Stuart, 'A Marxist Looks at Methodism: A Critique of E.P. Thompson's Assessment of the Role of Methodism in an Age of Revolution', in J.S. Udy and E.G. Clancy (ed.), *Dig or Die* (Sydney: World Methodist Historical Society, 1981), pp. 290–305.

— 'Billy Graham in Australia, 1959 – Was it Revival?', *Lucas: An Evangelical History Review* 6 (Oct. 1989), pp. 2–33.

— 'Halévy Revisited: The Origins of the Wesleyan Methodist Missionary Society: An Examination of Semmel's Thesis', *The Journal of Imperial and Commonwealth History* 9.1 (October 1980), pp. 17–37.

— 'Religion and Disaster: Popular Religious Attitudes to Disaster and Death with Special Reference to the Mt Kembla and Appin Coal Mine Disasters', *Journal of Australian Studies* 8 (June 1981), pp. 54–63.

— and Henry Lee, *The Mount Kembla Disaster* (Melbourne: Oxford University Press, 1992).

— *Evangelical Christianity in Australia: Spirit, Word and World* (Melbourne: Oxford University Press, 1996).

— *Faith of Steel* (Wollongong: University of Wollongong, 1984).

— *The Fruitful Figtree, A History of All Saints Anglican Church Figtree, 1888–1983* (Figtree: All Saints Parish Council, 1983).

Porter, Stanley E., and Philip J. Richter (eds.), *The Toronto Blessing — Or is it?* (London: Darton, Longman & Todd, 1995).

Pratney, Winkie, *Revival* (Pittsburgh, PA: Whitaker House, 1983).

Pratt, Douglas, ' "Rescue the Perishing": Comparative Perspectives on Evangelism and Revivalism' (Auckland: College Communications, 1989).

Prince, Thomas, *The Christian History* (Boston: 1743–45).

Ravenhill, Leonard, *Why Revival Tarries* (Bromley, Kent: Send the Light Trust, 1972).

Rawlyk, George A., *Wrapped up in God: A Study of Several Canadian Revivals and Revivalists* (Burlington, Ontario: Welch Publishing Co., 1988).

— 'Writing about Canadian Religious Revivals', in Edith L. Blumhofer and Randall Balmer, *Modern Christian Revivals* (Urbana, IL: University of Illinois Press, 1993).

— and Mark Noll, *Amazing Grace: Evangelicalism in Australia, Britain, Canada, and the United States* (Grand Rapids, MI: Baker, 1993).

Reed, Colin, 'Australia and the East Africa Revival', in Mark Hutchinson and Geoff Treloar (eds.), *This Gospel shall be Preached: Essays on the Australian Contribution to World Mission* (Sydney: CSAC, 1998), pp. 164–79.

Restoration in the Church: Reports of Revivals, 1625–1839, 1839 (Belfast: Ambassador Productions, 1989).

Renewal Journal (Strathpine, Queensland).

Riss, Richard M., *A Survey of Twentieth-Century Revival Movements in North America* (Peabody, MA: Hendrickson, 1988).

Robe, James, *Faithful Narrative of the Extraordinary Work of the Spirit of God at Kilsyth, Edinburgh, Glasgow, and London* (Glasgow: William Duncan, 1742, 1790, 1840).

— *The Christian Monthly History* (Edinburgh: 1743–46).

Roberts, Dave, *The 'Toronto' Blessing* (Eastbourne: Kingsway Publications, 1994).

Roberts, Emyr, *Revival and its Fruits* (Bryntirion: Evangelical Press of Wales, 1981).

Roberts, Richard Owen, *Backsliding* (Wheaton, IL: International Awakening Press, 1982).

— *Lord, I Agree* (Wheaton, IL: International Awakening Press, 1990).

— *Revival!* (Wheaton, IL: Richard Owen Roberts, 1991).

— *Revival Literature: An Annotated Bibliography, Richard Owen Roberts* (Wheaton, IL: Richard Owen Roberts, 1987).

— *The Solemn Assembly* (Wheaton, IL: International Awakening Press, 1989).

Roberts, Richard Owen, (ed.), *Glory Filled the Land: A Trilogy on the Welsh Revival of 1904–1905* (Wheaton, IL: International Awakening Press, 1989).

Roberts, R. Philip, *Continuity and Change: London Calvinistic Baptists and the Evangelical Revival 1760–1820* (Wheaton, IL: Richard Owen Roberts, 1989).

Rowell, Geoffrey, *The Vision Glorious: Themes and Personalities of the Catholic Revival in Anglicanism* (Oxford: Oxford University Press, 1983).

Ryken, Leland, *Worldly Saints: The Puritans as they Really Were*, (Grand Rapids, MI: Academie Books, 1986).

Sargent, Tony, *The Sacred Anointing: The Preaching of Dr Martyn Lloyd-Jones* (London: Hodder & Stoughton, 1994).

Scotland, Nigel, *Charismatics and the Next Millennium: Do they have a Future?* (London: Hodder & Stoughton, 1995).

Sharp, John, 'Juvenile Holiness: Catholic Revivalism in Victorian Britain', *Journal of Ecclesiastical History* 35.2 (1984), pp. 220–38.

— *Reapers of the Harvest: The Redemptorists in England and Ireland, 1843–1898* (Dublin: Veritas Publications, 1989).

Slosser, Bob, *Miracle in Darien* (Plainfield, NJ: Logos International, 1979).

Smellie, Alexander, *Evan Henry Hopkins, A Memoir* (London: Marshall Brothers, 1920, 2nd edn 1921).

Smith, Eddie, 'Prayer Plus', *Evangelical Action* (Dec.–Jan. 1990–91), p. 9.

Smith, M.A., 'Were there Revivals before 1000 A.D.?', *The Christianity and History Newsletter* 6 (July 1990), pp. 7–18.

Social Issues Update 3.2 (October 1993), the occasional newsletter of the Social Issues Committee, Anglican Diocese of Sydney.

Spicer, Tobias, *Christian Advocate and Journal* (New York: 4 November 1846).

Sprague, W.B., *Lectures on Revival* (London: Banner of Truth Trust, 1832, 1958).

Stacey, Geoff, ' "Revival" in the Old Testament?', in Mark Hutchinson and Stuart Piggin, *Reviving Australia* (Sydney: Centre for the Study of Australian Christianity, 1994), pp. 34–57.

Stanley Smith, A.C., *Road to Revival: The Story of the Ruanda Mission* (London: CMS, c. 1946).

Stibbe, Mark, *Times of Refreshing: A Practical Theology of Revival for Today* (London: Marshall Pickering, 1995).

Stock, Eugene, *My Recollections* (London: Nisbet, 1909).

Stout, H., *The Divine Dramatist: George Whitefield, and the Rise of Modern Evangelicalism* (Grand Rapids, MI: Eerdmans, 1992).

Strachan, George, *Revival – Its Blessings and Battles: An Account of Experiences in the Solomon Islands* (Laurieton: South Sea Evangelical Mission, rev. edn, 1989).

Sweet, William Warren, *Revivalism in America* (Gloucester, MA: Peter Smith, 1965).

Taylor, W., *William Taylor of California, Bishop of Africa* (London: Hodder & Stoughton, 1897).

— *Story of my Life* (New York: Hunt & Eaton, 1895).

The Revival of Religion: Addresses by Scottish Evangelical Leaders delivered in Glasgow in 1840 (Edinburgh: Banner of Truth Trust, 1984).

Thompson, Augustine, *Revival Preachers and Politics in Thirteenth-Century Italy: The Great Devotion of 1233* (Oxford: Clarendon Press, 1992).

Thornbury, J.F., *God Sent Revival: The Story of Asahel Nettleton and the Second Great Awakening* (Welwyn: Evangelical Press, 1977).

Timms, D., 'Developing a Biblical Approach to the Phenomenon' (Toronto Blessing Seminar, Churches of Christ Theological College, Carlingford, 1 April 1995).

Torrey, R.A., *How to Promote and Conduct a Successful Revival* (Chicago: Fleming H. Revell, 1901).

— *Revival Addresses* (Chicago: Fleming H. Revell, 1903).

— *The Power of Prayer and the Prayer of Power* (Grand Rapids, MI: Zondervan, 1924, 1971).

Tracy, Joseph, *The Great Awakening* (Edinburgh: Banner of Truth Trust, 1842, 1976).

Turner, J.G., *The Pioneer Missionary: Life of the Rev. Nathaniel Turner* (London: Wesleyan Conference Office, 1872).

Tyler, Bennet, and Bonar, Andrew A., *Nettleton and his Labours* (Edinburgh: Banner of Truth Trust, 1854, 1975).

— *New England Revivals: As they Existed at the Close of the Eighteenth and the Beginning of the Nineteenth Centuries* (Wheaton, IL: Richard Owen Roberts, 1846, 1980).

Valenze, Deborah M., *Prophetic Sons and Daughters: Female Preaching and Popular Religion in Industrial England* (Princeton, NJ: Princeton University Press, 1985).

Varley, H., Jr, *Henry Varley's Life Story* (London: A. Holness, 1916).

Vinden, G., 'Miss Anna Christensen in Western Szechwan', *Through Fire, The Story of 1938* (London: China Inland Mission, 1939).

Walker, A., *Breakthrough: Rediscovering the Holy Spirit* (Nashville: Abingdon Press, 1969).

Wallis, Arthur, *China Miracle* (Eastbourne: Kingsway Publications, 1985).

Ward, W.R., ' "An Awakened Christianity", The Austrian Protestants and their Neighbours in the Eighteenth Century', *Journal of Ecclesiastical History* 40.1 (1989), pp. 53–73.

— 'Mysticism and Revival: The Case of Gerhard Tersteegen', in Jane Garnett and Colin Matthew (eds.), *Revival and Religion since 1700, Essays for John Walsh* (London: Hambledon Press, 1993).

— *Religion and Society in England, 1790–1850* (London: Batsford, 1972).

— *The Protestant Evangelical Awakening* (Cambridge: Cambridge University Press, 1992).

Warren, W., 'The Genesis of the Australian Revival', *The Missionary Review of the World* 26 (March 1903), p. 201.

Watsford, John, *Glorious Gospel Triumphs* (London: Charles H. Kelly, 1900).

Webber, F.R., *A History of Preaching in Britain and America* (Milwaukee, WI: Northwestern Publishing House, 1955), vol. II.

Welbourne, F.B., *East African Christian* (London: Oxford University Press, 1965).

Wesleyan Magazine (1858), p. 468, letter of the Revd Isaac Harding, 15 February.

Westerkemp, Marilyn J., *Triumph of the Laity: Scots-Irish Piety and the Great Awakening, 1625–1760* (New York: Oxford University Press, 1988).

Wheaton Record (Wheaton, IL: 24 March 1995).

Whitefield, G., 'The Duty of a Gospel Minister', in D. Macfarlan, *The Revivals of the Eighteenth Century . . . with Three Sermons by the Rev. George Whitefield* (Glasgow: Free Presbyterian Publications, 1988).

— 'The Method of Grace', in D. Macfarlan, *The Revivals of the Eighteenth Century . . . with Three Sermons by the Rev. George Whitefield* (Glasgow: Free Presbyterian Publications, 1988).

Whittaker, Colin, *Korea Miracle* (Eastbourne: Kingsway Publications, 1988).

Williams, Ron, *Nuggets from the Goldfields* (Gosnells, Centre Press, October 1984), pp. 16–18.

Williamson, H.G.M., *Israel in the Book of Chronicles* (Cambridge: Cambridge University Press, 1977).

Wilson, J.F., 'Perspectives on the Historiography of Religious Awakenings', *Sociological Analysis* 44 (1983), pp. 117–20.

Wright, Don, *Mantle of Christ: A History of the Central Methodist Mission* (St Lucia: University of Queensland Press, 1984).

Author Index

Scripture Index

Old Testament

Genesis
6 144
7 144
32:22–30 183

Exodus
32–36 30

Numbers
11:29 34

Deuteronomy
28:23 173
28:47 24
31:17 33
31:18 33

Judges
2:10–19 30
2:18 31
3:9 31
3:10 31
3:15 31
6:6 31
6:7 31
6:34 31
10:10 31
11:29 31
13:25 31
14:6 31
14:19 31
15:14 31

1 Samuel
7 30

10:10 34
12:23 163

2 Samuel
4–7 30
6 14
6:7 14
6:8 14
6:9 14

1 Kings
16–18 30

2 Chronicles
7:1–3 163
7:13 177
7:14 7, 23, 30, 171,
        176–7, 203
15–17 30

Ezra
9:9 33

Psalms
2:12 24
4:6 184
4:7 184
15 106
24 52
24:3–5 187
27:8 184
29:2 195
30:7 184
44:9 33
45:4 197
66:18 187
84:1 20

84:11 107
85:6 18, 179
96:9 20
104: 4, 9, 21, 202
139:7–12 185
139:23 185
139:24 185
144:1 107

Proverbs
11:30 159

Song of Songs
5:10 16
5:16 16
6:4 172

Isaiah
32:15 13
50:4 157
57:15 177
60:3 24
61:1 34
62:7 187
63 27, 33
63:10 33
63:11 33
63:15 33
64 33
64:1 179
64:7 187

Jeremiah
6:14 152
31:33 37
48:10 22

Subject Index